Encountering Jesus

True Stories from the Middle East and Beyond

Brian Becker a/k/a Abu William

Encountering Jesus
Copyright © 2016 by Brian Becker

Published by Brian Becker
Printed by CreateSpace, An Amazon.com Company

ISBN-13: 978-1516812363
ISBN-10: 1516812360

All profits from the sales of this book will be used to help people in physical or spiritual need and regardless of what they believe.

Please contact the author at brianbecker3@icloud.com to let him know your thoughts and feedback. Thank you.

All rights reserved. No portion of this book may be reproduced, stored in a retrieval system, or transmitted in any form or by any means—electronic, mechanical, photocopy, recording, scanning or other—except for brief quotations in critical reviews or articles, without the prior written permission of the publisher.

All Scripture quotations, unless otherwise indicated, are taken from the *Holy Bible*, New Living Translation. Copyright © 1996, 2004, 2007, 2013 by Tyndale House Foundation. Used by permission of Tyndale House Publishers, Inc., Carol Stream, Illinois 60188. All rights reserved.

Scripture quotations marked (NIV) are taken from the Holy Bible, New International Version®, NIV®. Copyright © 1973, 1978, 1984, 2011 by Biblica, Inc.™ Used by permission of Zondervan. All rights reserved worldwide. www.zondervan.com The "NIV" and "New International Version" are trademarks registered in the United States Patent and Trademark Office by Biblica, Inc.™

Scripture quotations marked (ESV) are from The Holy Bible, English Standard Version® (ESV®), copyright © 2001 by Crossway, a publishing ministry of Good News Publishers. Used by permission. All rights reserved.

Italics in quotations reflect the author's added emphasis.

Excerpts from *The Hiding Place* by Corrie ten Boom with Elizabeth and John Sherrill, 35th Anniversary Edition. Copyright © 1971 and 1984 by Corrie ten Boom and Elizabeth and John Sherrill. Copyright © 2006 by Elizabeth and John Sherrill. All rights reserved.

Extracts from *The Heavenly Man: the remarkable true story of Chinese Christian Brother Yun* by Brother Yun with Paul Hattaway. Copyright © Brother Yun and Paul Hattaway 2002. Used with permission of Lion Hudson plc.

Excerpts from *God's Smuggler* by Brother Andrew with John and Elizabeth Sherrill. Copyright © 1967, 2001 by Brother Andrew and John and Elizabeth Sherrill. Open Doors International. All rights reserved.

Sections of this book entitled "*JOURNAL ENTRY*…" are exact quotes from the author's personal journal made in close time proximity to the events described in them.

Sections of this book entitled "*EMAILS TO*…" or "*EMAILS FROM*…" are exact quotes from emails sent from and received by the author on the dates indicated.

Cover photo of the Mediterranean port city of Jaffa, Israel (May 2012).

There is no greater love than to lay down one's life for one's *friends*.
--Jesus

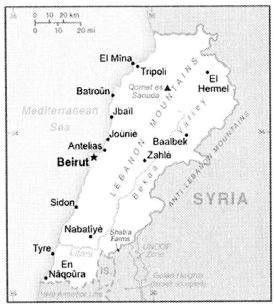

Map of Lebanon

Contents

Dedication ·9
Thank you ·9
The Middle East Cries Out ·10
Lebanon Info ·13
Preface ·15
Quotes ·16
Introduction: Close Friends ·19
Prologue: Pray, Take Risks and Go ·22
    Story: Go ·28
1   Lunch With Jesus ·34
    Story: Sitting on a Rock in the Woods ·35
    Story: Drinking from the Same Well that Jesus Drank from · · · · · · · · · · · ·37
2   Jesus the Human Was Born and Walked Among Us · · · · · · · · · · · · · · · · · · ·40
    Story: Visiting the Place in Bethlehem Where Jesus was Born · · · · · · · · · · ·41
3   Text Message from Jesus ·45
    Story: Our Daughter's Unexpected "Friend" ·46
4   My Friend Jesus? ·48
    Story: Standing Up for My Friend ·50
5   Wow Jesus, You're Really Here! ·54
    Story: Driving One Morning with Jesus ·58
    Story: Jesus Reveals Himself to a Muslim ·59
6   Jesus Loves in Ways That Are Hard to Understand ·62
    Story: Witnessing the Death of Jesus ·63
    Story: Visit to Refugee Camps near Syrian Border: Jesus Cares · · · · · · · · ·65
    Story: Praying for Terrorists in Istanbul: Jesus Loves His Enemies · · · · · ·68
7   Laughing With Jesus ·72
    Story: Driving Towards the War Zone: Still Finding Laughter · · · · · · · · · · ·73
8   Tears On a Dusty Face ·78
    Story: Crying with Jesus in Jerusalem ·79
    Story: Crying with a Pastor from Africa ·82
    Story: Children Born and Dying in Camp Baserma: Jesus Weeps · · · · · · · ·84

CONTENTS

Story: Visit to a Yazidi Refugee Camp: Jesus's Heart Breaks ········ 86
9   Would I Hang Out With Jesus? ·· 91
Story: Visit to a New Refugee Camp: Shia Muslims ····················· 93
Story: The Ski Resort Overlooking the Refugee Camps ··········· 96
10 Playing Tag With Jesus ·· 99
Story: Playing Tag with Our Son ··· 100
Story: Game with the Little Refugee Girls ································ 101
11 Hammering Nails With Jesus ·· 105
Story: Visiting Jesus's Childhood Town ·· 107
Story: Standing where Jesus was Nailed to the Cross ·········· 109
Story: Building a Pinewood Derby Car with Our Son ··········· 111
12 Jesus My Brother? ·· 113
Story: My Brother Who Lives in the West Bank ······················ 115
13 Jesus the Miracle Man ··· 117
Story: Jesus Makes Seeing Eyes Blind ·· 123
14 Thank You Jesus For the Gifts! ··· 129
Story: Dying in a Shanty in Nairobi ·· 133
Story: The Gift of the Holy Spirit ··· 137
Story: Gifts with My Friend...Who Happens to be Muslim ········ 140
15 Hanging Out at the Shopping Center With Jesus ·················· 145
Story: Beggars in the Parking Lot ·· 146
Story: Taking a Homeless Man Shopping ·································· 147
16 Hanging Out at the Homeless Shelter With Jesus ················· 150
Story: Living in a Shanty...in America ··· 151
Story: Little Boy at the Homeless Shelter ·································· 158
Story: Lego Pieces at the Homeless Shelter ····························· 160
Story: Showing Respect and Kindness to a Prostitute ········· 161
Story: A Little Homeless Girl Says Grace ···································· 162
17 Becoming Friends With Jesus: Go On a Trip Together ········· 167
Information about Lebanon ··· 168
Story: Unknown Plans in Lebanon: Jesus Leads the Way ········ 171
Story: Trip to Erbil: The Journey to Beirut Begins ··················· 174
Story: Feeling Alone in Iraq: Jesus the Faithful Friend ········· 176
Story: Encouragement in Iraq: Jesus Wakes Me Up ············· 179

CONTENTS

Story: Driving to the Iraq Airport at Night: Jesus Watches ········· 184
Story: Digging into God's Word: Jesus Leads the Way ············ 186
Story: Flight to Beirut: Jesus Leads Through Kindness ············ 192
Story: Passport Control in Beirut: Jesus Whispers ················ 196
Story: Hezbollah's Turf: Jesus Drives with Us ···················· 198
Story: Hi From Beirut! Arrival with Jesus ························ 202

18 Eating Pizza With Jesus ··· 205
Story: Enjoying Sweets with New Friends in Beirut ·············· 206
Story: Teapot on the Kitchen Counter··························· 208

19 Having a Glass of Wine With Jesus ······························ 211
Story: Glass of Wine at the Hotel in Beirut····················· 212

20 Hugging Jesus ··· 214
Story: Return to Camp Baserma: My Friend the Refugee ········· 215

21 Jesus Had Compassion for the Crowds of People ·············· 218
Story: Veiled Face in Istanbul: Compassion of Jesus ·············· 219
Story: Life in the Middle East Beyond the Headlines·············· 220
Story: Sights in Beirut: Jesus Loves Everyone ·················· 223
Story: Traffic Beirut Style: Jesus Loves Us All ·················· 225

22 Going Through Tough Times With Jesus ······················· 227
Story: A Refugee Child Washes Up on Turkey's Shore ············ 229
Story: Visit to Refugees in Hezbollah/UN Area ·················· 231
Story: The Pastor and His Wife Spend War-Time with Jesus········ 234

23 Jesus, I Need Some Quiet Time ································ 238
Story: Peace and Quiet at the Sea of Galilee ··················· 239
Story: Quiet Time under an Olive Tree in Jerusalem ·············· 242
Story: Relaxing with Jesus on the Mountainside of Lebanon ········ 244

24 Jesus, You're Bleeding ·· 247
Story: Via Dolorosa in Jerusalem ······························· 249

25 I'm Tired, Jesus·· 251
Story: Refreshed by Jesus Somewhere in Lebanon ··············· 252

26 Jesus, Please Catch Me ·· 254
Story: Alone in Istanbul: Jesus is Always with Us ················ 255
Story: The Gate to Iraq: "Feeling" Alone without Jesus············ 256
Story: Encouragement from Jesus ······························ 258

CONTENTS

27	Jesus, Let's Go For a Walk	261
	Story: Going for a Walk with a New Friend in Israel	262
	Story: Walking Where Jesus Walked	264
	Story: Walking on the Streets of Beirut: Jesus Walks With Us	266
28	Jesus, Let's Go for a Swim	269
	Story: Visiting the Site Where Jesus Was Baptized	270
	Story: Swimming Laps at the Pool with Jesus	273
29	Jesus, I Like Children Too!	276
	Story: Laughing with Refugee Children in Iraq	277
	Story: Gifts for Surprised Refugee Children in Iraq	279
30	Campfire With Jesus	281
	Story: Kabobs Cooking over Hot Coals in Iraq	282
	Story: Gifts of Food and Drinks in the West Bank	284
31	Jesus the Medal of Honor Winner	287
	Story: Mothers Abandoning Babies in Nairobi	288
32	Jesus the Boss	292
	Story: Worshipping God at the Office	293
33	Going to Church in Iraq With Jesus	297
	Story: Info about Northern Iraq	298
	Story: Soran: City of Refugees	299
	Story: Worship Service in Iraq: No Church Building	301
34	Jesus the Prince of Peace	304
	Story: Day of Contrasts in Iraq	305
	Story: Hungry for Peace in Beirut: Jesus is the Only Source	307
35	Friendship With the World Instead of With Jesus	310
Epilogue		313
A	Resources	316
B	Ways to Help Refugees	317
C	Photo of drowned boy sparks outcry	319
D	Drowned boy's father speaks of heartbreak	325
E	Lebanon pivotal to Iran's reach across Middle East	328
F	Luke 15:11-32 in Arabic	334

Dedication

This book is dedicated to my family. Y'all are an *amazing* gift and a great source of love and laughter. Also to the millions of refugees who are suffering so greatly, especially the *refugee children*. And to my close friend Ahmad in Saudi Arabia...we have shared much laughter and wonderful cups of tea together. And to my special Syrian refugee friend Lokman in Iraq...a father, husband, teacher and survivor. He's a great *inspiration* to me, and I miss him dearly.

And to Jesus...my brutally faithful *friend*.

Thank you

Thank you to my family for all of your encouragement, prayers, love and friendship. Y'all are amazing. Thank you again mom and dad for taking me to Israel in 2012...that was a life-changing experience. Thank you dad for helping me with the pictures for the first book, *Vacation in Iraq*, and now for this one. Thank you Josh for all of your editing help with both books. You've been a great guide into the worlds of editing and publishing. Thank you, Bill, for your friendship and for all of the times we have shared challenges, encouraged each other, cried together and laughed so hard that we cried. A close friend is a *great gift*. Thank you Ahmad, my dear friend in Saudi Arabia, for inviting me to join you for tea that second day of our new friendship, and for all of the great meals, laughs, tears and hugs we have shared in the United States. Thank you to *you*, the reader, for taking the time to read this book.

Thank you God for sending me to the Middle East four times now. I never imagined the adventures and friendships that You had planned for me. And Jesus, I never expected to get to know You in places like Iraq, Lebanon, Turkey, Jordan, Israel and the West Bank. In refugee camps. At border crossings and security checkpoints. In the lonely moments along these journeys.

Jesus, You are full of surprises. And I'm so thankful for Your *friendship*.

---

[1] Arabic for "*sadiqi*," which means friend.

The Middle East Cries Out

AS I WRITE this, the Middle East continues its war spiral. Millions of refugees have fled Syria. Many have died along the perilous journey to safety...the journey to *anything* better than war. ISIS battles Hezbollah. Hezbollah battles Al-Qaeda. Russia battles Syrian rebels. The U.S. drops bombs. Russia drops bombs. The Syrian government drops bombs. Suicide bombers kill hundreds of people in Paris, Tunisia, Yemen, Saudi Arabia and Beirut. Terrorists blow up a Russian civilian airliner over the Sanai Peninsula. The war machine cranks on. Terrorists are killed. Civilians are killed. Christians are killed. Muslims are killed. Children are traumatized. And people *go and serve* at great risk to themselves. People who can leave...but *don't*. They stay because they care. Yet so many of us live our lives doing *little or nothing* to help. I was like that. So I was shocked to end up over there for vacation. Vacation in dangerous places again and again. And you know what? The strangest thing happened. Words like *refugee* became *personal* to me. And now my struggle is not with trying to stay *out* of that mess. My struggle is with wanting to be over *in* that mess. Because it all became *personal* to me. It's no longer just headlines. I now have friends who are refugees. Friends who are living in camps in Iraq right now. And I struggle with what I should do with the precious life that God has given me as an area of the world...as precious millions...*cry out for help*. And I struggle with whether I know Jesus...*really* know Him. God knew I was struggling with knowing Jesus, so He sent me to the Middle East for vacation. And both my life and my relationship with Jesus have changed forever.

Please Lord, bless each person who reads this book May the Middle East...may the refugees...may Jesus...become personal to each and every one of them. Amen

[2]

---

[2] Hebrew for "*merea*," which means friend.

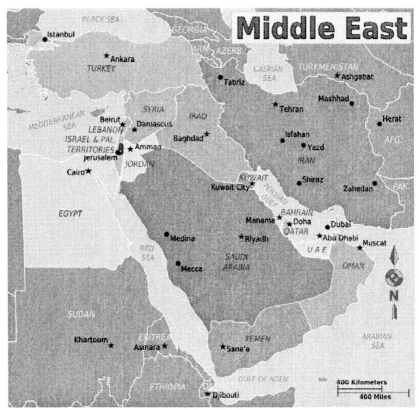
Map of the Middle East

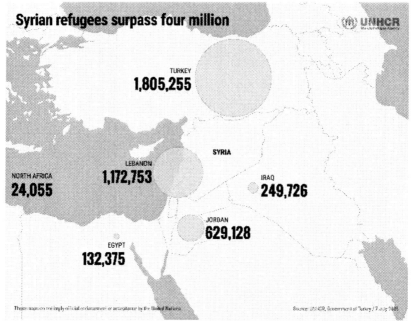

Map of registered Syrian refugee numbers as of July 2015
(source: United Nations High Commissioner for Refugees, otherwise
known as the UN Refugee Agency, http://www.unhcr.org/)

Lebanon Info

AS OF JULY 2014, Lebanon had a population of approximately 5.8 million people, of which 3.1 million are Muslims and approximately 1.55 million are refugees. It's a relatively small country. And it hosts the largest number of refugees in the world in relation to its population: 27%. That is a *massive* percentage. It would be like the United States hosting about 85 million refugees. Currently, the United States is home to about 263 *thousand* non-Palestinian refugees (.08 percent, as in .0008). Granted, the United States provides an extensive amount of aid for refugees around the world, most of whom are living in developing countries.

As of July 2014, Lebanon hosted about 1.1 million Syrian refugees and an additional 450,000 Palestinian refugees. There are no official UNHCR refugee camps in Lebanon. As of January 2015, the number of Syrian refugees living in Lebanon had increased to 1,166,000.[3]

On November 12, 2015, twin suicide bombings struck a Hezbollah suburb in Beirut...an area I was driven through in June 2015 on my way from the Beirut airport just after landing in Lebanon.[4] The bombings killed 43 people and wounded more than 200 others. ISIS claimed responsibility for the bombings as retaliation against the Shia Muslim Hezbollah militant group for supporting the Syrian government in its war against ISIS and other Sunni Muslim rebel and militant groups.

The people living in Lebanon are primarily Muslims (54 percent). About 40 percent are Christians and approximately 5 percent are Druze.[5] God calls us to bless them *all*.

---

[3] An additional 1,622,000 Syrian refugees were living in Turkey as of December 2014.
[4] http://www.heraldstandard.com/news/world/middle-east/lebanon-mourns-victims-of-deadly-suicide-bombings/article_cd205e75-bbc9-5e64-adf7-bb795e995ffa.html
[5] The Druze faith incorporates elements of multiple religions and philosophies. The Druze believe in reincarnation.

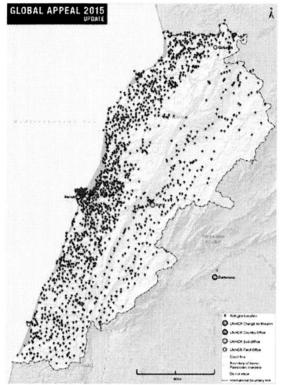

Dots representing locations of refugees in Lebanon (November 2015) (map by the UN Refugee Agency)

Preface

THIS BOOK IS the story of how I got to know Jesus better through travels to the Middle East. I have met many amazing and inspiring people along the way. I have gone to places I never dreamed I would go to...places I never *wanted* to go to. Slums. Refugee camps. Military zones. Mosques. Dark roads in places like Iraq and the West Bank. Vacation in places like Iraq and Beirut. Apartments and damaged buildings with war scars on them where refugees try to survive. Schools for refugee children. Churches with no crosses or even walls for that matter. Checkpoints and questionings. Detainment. Picnics and even a ski resort of all things in Iraq. Deserts, mountains and police stations. Backyards, kitchens and alleys. Coffee shops and cemeteries. Places where Jesus walked. Places where terrorists walked. Places where refugees fled. Places where snipers shot at Christians. Places where I made *wonderful* friends...and heard *heartbreaking* stories. Places where I cried and laughed. Places where, much to my surprise, I got to know Jesus more personally...not just as my Lord and my Savior...but as *my Friend*.

صـــديقي

Driving through Hezbollah's suburb in Beirut (June 2015)

Encountering Jesus

Quotes

Then he said to Thomas, "Put your finger here, and look at my hands. Put your hand into the wound in my side. Don't be faithless any longer. Believe!" "My Lord and my God!" Thomas exclaimed. Then Jesus told him, "You believe because you have seen me. Blessed are those who believe without seeing me."
Jesus in John 20:27-29

Jesus is a reality…He lives…He is victor. I knew it from experience.
Corrie ten Boom

Security is mostly a superstition. It does not exist in nature…Life is either a daring adventure or nothing.
Helen Keller

Only those who will risk going too far can possibly find out how far one can go.
T.S. Eliot

We are not alone on our journey. The God of love…sent us His only Son to be with us at all times and in all places, so that we may never have to feel lost.
Henri J. M. Nouwen

God puts each fresh morning, each new chance of life, into our hands as a gift to see what we will do with it.
Author unknown

To live without risk is to risk not living.
Brennan Manning

One morning during prayer I was overcome by the Lord's presence. He spoke to me like a friend.
Brother Yun

ENCOUNTERING JESUS

I am with you and will watch over you *wherever you go.*
                                                God in Genesis 28:15

Go...
                                                Jesus in Matthew 28:19

מֵרֵעַ

Syrian refugee girl (Northern Iraq) (June 2015)

Introduction: Close Friends

I have called you *friends*. (Jesus in John 15:15b NIV)

I REMEMBER BEING at the office one day. I was talking with a very close friend of mine about what a gift it is to have close friends…the type of friends that you can call any time, day or night, and you *know* they will be there for you. I told him that I am finding that as you go through life, that type of friend is few and far between. Oftentimes you can count them on the fingers of one or maybe two of your hands. Sometimes you have five friends like that…sometimes seven…sometimes three. They are rare and cherished. As we talked, I pictured my friends that I consider to be so very close and trusting…as I counted them on my fingers…one…two…three… And then my great friend at work and I moved on to another topic of conversation. Just as quickly as the conversation had started, it was over.

Who do *you* count on *your* fingers as that type of friend? The type of friend you can call day or night. And you *know* they will *be there for you. No matter what.* Maybe a friend you've known since childhood. Maybe someone you met later in life with whom you became instant friends. You know what that's like…that immediate connection with someone. The types of friends that you can go five years without seeing and then, when you finally see each other again or talk on the phone, it's as if you didn't miss out on a minute of that friendship. Those are special and rare friendships. So…who do you count on your fingers? I encourage you to stop reading right now…think about that for a few minutes…and then read on.

So…who's on your list? Who did you count on your fingers as those very special friends? I bet you *smiled* as you thought about them. I bet it brought back *special memories* with those friends just to think about them. I bet it made you *feel good* to think about them.

Well, back to the story of that day in that office. I was counting fingers as I thought about those very special friends in my life. I counted them and thought about them. It was fun to do. And later that same day it dawned on me that *I had not included Jesus* as one of those fingers on my list…one of those very close friends. In fact, Jesus had not even *crossed my mind* as being one of them. And it hit me why: because *He wasn't one of them.* And I was so sad about that. It *never even crossed my mind* to include Him. The Guy who gave His life for me. The Guy who is always there for me. The Guy who loves me no matter what. The Guy who wants the best for me...and for my family. The Guy who *gave His life* not just for me but for my whole family. He *hadn't even been considered* for the top 10 friends list. *He had never even crossed my mind.*

Jesus is oftentimes an afterthought, isn't He? Kind of like that faithful friend that is always only a phone call away...always ready to drop what they are doing and help us out...who we take for granted. I take Jesus for granted. He'll always be there...so no need to focus on that friendship, right? It's a guaranteed friendship. I can't do anything to cause Jesus to stop being my friend. To stop Him from caring about me. So I take Him for granted. What a *lousy friend* I have been to Him. I think what I could count on my fingers about Jesus is how many times I have asked Him what I can do *for Him*. Not many fingers to count on that one. How sad.

God knew I needed to get to know Jesus better. He knew that I needed to work on our friendship. In fact, I asked Jesus one day in 2013 while sitting on a large rock in a dense forest during a camping trip...as the wind blew through the trees...to *appear* to me...to make Himself *known to me*. I wanted to *see Him*. So what did He do in response? Tell me to spend more time in a Bible study? Tell me to join some committees at church? Tell me to say, "Amen!" and "Praise God!" more often? Tell me to give more to the church and to people in need? Nope. He decided in His *unlimited* and *unimaginable* wisdom and grace to send me first to refugee camps in the West Bank in 2013, and then to refugee camps in Iraq and Jordan in 2014, and then to refugee camps in Beirut in 2015 by way of Iraq refugee camps again. To spend some quality time with Him...with Jesus...somehow by going and spending time with refugees in war-torn areas of the world...in order to get to know Jesus better. And He told me while I was there to *pray for terrorists*, including the terrorists who killed my friend's brother in Baghdad in 2013. So that's what I did...I went and prayed and loved and cried. And you know what? Much to my surprise, *I did get to know Jesus better.* Remember that Bible verse about God's ways not being our ways? (Isaiah 55:8). He sure wasn't kidding with that one. Go to refugee camps in the West Bank, Iraq, Jordan and Beirut to get to know Him better. Go to war-torn countries. Take *risks*. And pray for terrorists while you're there. Who would have thought? I sure didn't.

This book is about the journey to Beirut in 2015 by way of Iraq, as well as about parts of the prior journeys I have taken to the Middle East and Africa.[6] These trips have had a deep impact on my *relationship* with Jesus...with

---

[6] The first book was *Vacation in Iraq: My Journey from America to the Muslim World*, self-published in April 2015 through CreateSpace. All profits are used to help people in physical and spiritual need regardless of what they believe.

Introduction: Close Friends

Muslims...with refugees...with Christians...with friends, family and day-to-day enemies...and even with terrorists. And I've gotten to develop a *friendship* with Jesus along the way. I hope that the journeys in this book will help you with *your* friendship with Jesus too. So please join me...and Jesus...on my vacation to Beirut.

صــديقي

Syrian refugee family in Lebanon (June 2015)

Prologue: Pray, Take Risks and Go

Go and make disciples of *all* the nations. (Jesus in Matthew 28:19)

*W*E ARE WIRED to *avoid risk*. Our instinct is to survive…to not die, to not get injured. Yet there is our Creator saying, "Go" *everywhere*…to war zones, refugee camps, "closed" countries, homeless shelters, prisons…on and on the risky list goes. Our humanness screams, "No!" to going to risky places. Yet there is Jesus whispering…nudging…drawing us to *"Go."*

In struggling with Jesus's tugging on me to go to Israel and the West Bank in 2012, then in 2013, and then to Iraq and Jordan in 2014, and finally to Iraq and Lebanon in 2015…I got to an unexpected and surprising point where I agreed with God in my soul that *I'd rather die following Jesus than live running away from Him.* It was not easy getting to that point…it was messy and painful and gut wrenching. But there I was. So I went. I went to the Middle East…again and again and again. I had to confront fears and anxieties; and I hungered to know if God was really with me…was really telling me to go to places like that…to refugee camps, to checkpoints, to vulnerability that I had never experienced in my life. I'm part of a great and loving family, I'm a lawyer with a good job, we attend a bomb-free church, we have a nice life…so I found myself *struggling* with why God would tell me to *risk* and go to places like that…for *vacation* of all things.

I found along the way that God's desire is very much for us to trust Him and to encounter Jesus…not only His Son Jesus but the human Jesus too…to not be afraid, and to listen to the voice of Jesus the Shepherd as He loves us and tells us very clearly…to *"go"*:

> *Trust* in the Lord with all your heart, and do not lean on your own understanding. In all your ways submit to [*acknowledge*] Him, and He will make your paths straight. (Proverbs 3:5-6 NIV)

> Look! I stand at the door and knock. If you *hear* my voice and *open* the door, I will come in, and we will share a meal together as friends. (Revelation 3:20)

Prologue: Pray, Take Risks and Go

But Jesus spoke to them at once. *"Don't be afraid,"* he said. "Take *courage*. I am here!" (Matthew 14:27)

My sheep *listen* to my voice; I know them, and they *follow* me. (John 10:27 NIV)

On judgment day many will say to me, "Lord! Lord! We prophesied in your name and cast out demons in your name and performed many miracles in your name." But I will reply, "I never *knew you*. Get away from me, you who break God's laws." (Matthew 7:22-23)

Pray in the Spirit at all times and on every occasion. Stay alert and be *persistent* in your prayers for all believers everywhere. (Ephesians 6:18)

Go... (Matthew 28:19a)

And along the way I have read in many books about other followers of Jesus being tugged to go and how they responded. As Brennan Manning put it in *The Signature of Jesus*:

> The Spirit sets us free from our self-imposed limits and moves us out into unchartered waters. Our secure, well-regulated, and largely risk-free lives are *blown apart*. (p.184)[7]

As Canon Andrew White, the Vicar of Baghdad puts it: "Don't take care. *Take risks!*"

Brother Andrew in *God's Smuggler* explained it this way as God tugged him to go to a missionary school in England while people close to him encouraged him *not* to go...not to take *so much risk*:

> Every *reasonable* sign seemed to point away from the school in Glasgow. And yet, unmistakable inside me, sublimely indifferent to every human and logical objection, was a little voice that seemed to say "Go." It was the voice...that *never made sense at a logical level*. (p.60)

Mary Slessor, a petite slim girl from Scotland, was tugged by Jesus in the 1800's to go to Calabar, Africa...a jungle area of Africa where ruthless cannibalistic tribes ruled. She was tugged to go and share about Jesus and to help

---

[7] *The Signature of Jesus* by Brennan Manning, © 1988, 1992, 1996 by Brennan Manning, Multnomah Books, a division of Random House. All rights reserved.

the tormented and suffering people there. And so she went…against the *reasonable* advice of many…and God did *extraordinary* things through her that changed many of the cannibal's lives *for eternity*:

> "I am going to an unknown tribe up country," Mary wrote a friend. "A fierce, cruel people, and everyone tells me they will kill me. But I do not fear any hurt"…[Mary] was the only ray of Christian light in [that] dense darkness…God had given her an opportunity to reach the fierce cannibals [of Calabar], and she was willing to die in the attempt to bring the Gospel to them. (*Mary Slessor*, pp.54, 107)[8]

And she asked her friends to pray that the *Holy Spirit* would lead her:

> Pray that I will make no false moves, but that the Spirit will say, "Go here" and "go there." (p.138)

And that's what the Holy Spirit did. So she went.

Corrie ten Boom's family, at great personal risk, hid Jews in their home in Holland from the occupying German soldiers during World War II. They were eventually caught and sent to concentration camps. Her father and other family members died after being arrested, some of them dying in the concentration camps…the *death camps*, including Corrie's sister Betsie. After the war and Corrie's miraculous survival in the death camps, Jesus called her to share about God's love and forgiveness in over 60 countries throughout the world. She tirelessly traveled the world sharing such a wonderful message until shortly before her death in 1983. At one point, she was growing weary from all of the travelling and struggled with whether she should call it a day and head back to Holland to relax. As she searched God's Word, she was convicted that God had prepared her for such a duty and was calling her to continue sharing such a healing word in such a hurting world. She explained in *Tramp for the Lord*:

> I sat for a long time—thinking. It is not our task to give God instructions. We are to simply report for duty. (p.140)[9]

---

[8] *Mary Slessor* by Basil Miller, © 1974 by Basil Miller. Baker Publishing Group. All rights reserved.
[9] *Tramp for the Lord* by Corrie ten Boom, © 1974 by Corrie ten Boom and Jamie Buckingham. Used by permission of CLC Publications. May not be further reproduced. All rights reserved.

Prologue: Pray, Take Risks and Go

So that is what Corrie did. She went. And thousands of people's lives around the globe were impacted by God through her.

Brother Yun was born in 1958 in communist China. He suffered greatly for following Jesus there. He was arrested, imprisoned and beaten multiple times for sharing God's Word and, as a result, separated from his family for years at a time. And he experienced God's miracles in many ways. As he describes in *The Heavenly Man*, he is a firm believer that, when God calls you to go…you *go*:

> I have learned that when the Lord tells us to do something there is no time for discussion or rationale, regardless of the situation we face. When we are sure God has told us to act, as I was on this occasion [escaping a prison], blind obedience is called for. Not to obey God implies that we are wiser than him, and that we know better how to run our lives than he does. (p.255)

As I struggled with God's call for me to go to the Middle East, I kept reading about these people who kept being told by Jesus to go…to go to places that did not make sense…to go and *risk so much*. And, you know what? Over and over…at great risk…*they went*. Brennan Manning went. And Canon Andrew White went. And Brother Andrew went. And Mary Slessor went. And Corrie ten Boom went. And Brother Yun went. And God has done amazing things through them and through so many others over the centuries in Communist countries, in the Middle East, in the United States, in Africa, in cities, in jungles, and in so many other places throughout the world. They were told to *"Go."* So *they went*.

Looking back at what God has done through people like these who heard his voice to go, who *risked so much*, and went…it is sad to imagine them choosing the "safe" path and not going. How it must break God's heart to give His Son's life for us…to see us called to go…yet we run the other way…away from God's wonderful plan for our lives. How much is *wasted*. As John Piper put it in *Risk is Right*:

> But what happens when the people of God do not escape from the beguiling enchantment of security? What happens if they try to live their lives in the *mirage of safety*? The answer is wasted lives…Oh, how much is wasted when we do not risk for the cause of God! (pp.34-35)[10]

Amy Carmichael was called by God in the late 1800's to leave Ireland to go serve Him in India. God did so much to bless suffering and abused children

---

[10] *Risk is Right: Better to Lose Your Life Than to Waste It* by John Piper, © 2013 by Desiring God Foundation. Crossway. All rights reserved.

there through her. She no doubt struggled with fear about going to such a far off land. She also struggled with ill health and was turned down by a missions group when she applied to go and serve in India due to her poor health. But she did not give up and went any ways…because God told her to. In dealing with fear and anxiety about going to such a far off land, she explained:

> Fear can hamstring the soul…Faith does not ask why, does not even wonder why. Faith accepts. (pp.60, 286)

Brother Andrew summed it up so well in *God's Call*, the sequel to *God's Smuggler*. He was visiting a church in communist Poland, where persecution of Christians was so severe. Brother Andrew took great risks to be there. And, as the local pastor introduced him, God revealed something "extremely significant" to Brother Andrew about the importance of going to *risky* places…to *dangerous* places:

> Much to my surprise, I found myself standing before a crowded church—alive, vibrant, and full of young people. As the pastor introduced me, he said, "Andrew, *your being here* means more than ten of the best sermons." Well, that was okay with me, since I'm not much of a preacher anyway. But as I thought about the pastor's words, I realized he had said something extremely significant. Not that preaching was unimportant, but that my *presence* was much more important. I simply needed to be there! When I speak of presence, I mean that *we consciously steer our lives into danger areas.* We go there *in person.* Not to start a church or heal the sick or sponsor a big campaign, but simply to *bring the presence of Christ into that situation.* Jesus said, "Blessed are the peacemakers." Peacemakers can make peace only where there is war. The people around us may not yet know that we are Christians, but at this stage all they need to see is *our presence.* Think of it: If Jesus lives in me, and I go to a trouble spot in the world, then Jesus is there, too. And once we are there, we see *opportunities we would never hear about by staying behind*, because the opportunities didn't exist then. They come into being only *the moment we get there.* (pp.138-39)[11]

So, as I sorted through what God wanted me to do…and as I confronted my fears, anxieties and outright terror about going to the Middle East of all places…a place of war and terror that I was seeing in the headlines every day…God was graciously teaching me to trust Him, to get to know Jesus as a

---

[11] *God's Call* by Brother Andrew with Verne Becker, © 1996, 2002 by Brother Andrew. Open Doors International. All rights reserved.

Prologue: Pray, Take Risks and Go

friend, to not be afraid, to follow Him...to *go*. And little did I know, this call to *go*...this call to *risk*...was the way I was going to get to know Jesus as *my friend*...which was about the last thing I expected to happen.

As Amy Carmichael put it in *Gold Cord*:

> But "Faith is not intelligent understanding; faith is a deliberate commitment to a Person where you see no way," if, deep in your heart, you know that He is directing your goings. "A foreign land draws us nearer God. He is the only one whom we know [t]here. We go to Him as to one we know; all else is strange"...but He is enough. (p.287, quoting missionary Robert Murray McCheyne as he described being in the unknown world of Genoa)
>
> It was in gentle, generous, patient ways like this that we learned *not to fear* any strange land. Even if He is the only one whom we know there, *He is enough*. (p.289)[12]

Please Lord, help us each believe that You are enough.

מֵרֵעַ

Street sign, night of arrival in Erbil, Iraq (June 2015)

---

[12] *Gold Cord* by Amy Carmichael, © 1991 by The Dohnavur Fellowship. Used by permission of CLC Publications. All rights reserved.

ENCOUNTERING JESUS

Map of Iraq

Story: Go

And then he told them, *"Go* into *all* the world and preach the Good News to *everyone."* (Mark 16:15)

I FIRST VISITED the Middle East in 2012 with my parents as part of a Holy Land tour group trip made up of people who attend the church that they attend. I was afraid to go...but I went.[13] It was an *amazing* experience. I found myself jogging one morning in Jericho (which is in the West Bank) before the day's tour activities began...and ended up unexpectedly jogging into a refugee camp named Camp Aqabat Jabr. I had never been in a refugee camp before. I didn't even know there was one in Jericho. I even more unexpectedly found myself drinking grape juice with several *Palestinian police officers* at an outpost in the camp...one of whom was holding a machine gun. We loved visiting with

---

[13] So many Americans are afraid to go to Israel and the West Bank...the Holy Land. Even on a tour group trip where so much emphasis is placed on safety by the tour group operators. That saddens my heart because it is an *experience of a lifetime* to walk where Jesus walked. I can relate...I was afraid as well. But there is Jesus telling us to *"go."*

Prologue: Pray, Take Risks and Go

each other. And I had tea with three *Palestinian soldiers* that were manning the military checkpoint on the main road through Jericho. Wow was that trip an experience of a lifetime. I returned to the US and God whispered to me to learn Arabic and learn about Islam through a Christian program, so that's what I did.

I returned to the Middle East in 2013. I went back to Israel and the West Bank. This time, instead of a tour group, I spent the trip with two former Muslims who are now Christians. I returned to help the Palestinian refugees in Camp Aqabat Jabr. So that's what we did. It was another amazing experience spending time with the refugees, hearing their stories, becoming friends, helping instill hope.

In 2014, I returned again to the Middle East, this time to Iraq and then on to Jordan and finished in Israel. A close Muslim friend of mine from Iraq had a brother who graduated from a University in the US and returned to Baghdad to get married. Four days after he got married, he found himself in the Baghdad market buying food in the *wrong place* at the *wrong time*. A series of car bombs went off that day; he was one of the innocent bystanders who got killed…because he went grocery shopping. I mourned with my friend in his apartment in the US while I *hated* those far-away terrorists. And then God told me…to my shock…to pray for, forgive, love and *bless* those terrorists…the people I *hated*…just like Jesus commands. And that sent me on a difficult struggle…*pray* for the people who *killed* my friend's brother? *Love* them? *Forgive* them? *Bless* them? I searched God's Word, confronted fear, and heard God's voice clearly to *go*. So God sent me to Iraq to pray for and forgive the terrorists, and to also visit a refugee camp in Iraq to help the refugees, many of whom are Muslims. And also to encourage the church that is suffering so greatly there. I went on to Jordan and helped refugees with a local program, and then I crossed the border into Israel by bridge over the Jordan River, where I was detained and questioned for several hours. This was one place where Jesus showed up in a mighty way during the detainment. That story and many others from those trips are detailed in the first book, *Vacation in Iraq*.

God once again told me to return to Iraq in 2015 and to go on from there to Lebanon. Like with Iraq the previous year, I had never been to Lebanon. I had never imagined going to Beirut for vacation or anything else. The goals of the trip were once again to help the refugees, encourage the church, and pray for the terrorists. So once again, I took risk…and I went.

Here's an excerpt from the email I sent to friends shortly before departing once again for Iraq. I hope it encourages you as you seek out where God is calling *you* to *go*:

"Hi y'all, I hope you are doing great! Please feel free to forward this email.

"I head to N. Iraq on June 19 and then to Lebanon on June 24, returning on June 28. I am excited to serve the refugees, encourage the church, and pray for the terrorists. I believe God wants me to go and do all of this like He did last year. Your prayers would again be a special blessing. It's a strange experience to fly 6,475 miles to get closer to ISIS, who is in N. Iraq 6,525 miles away from [the state we live in]. I'm so thankful that God radically changed my life through Jesus, and that no one is beyond God's grace.

"I am so excited to spend time with the refugees, and always humbled to spend time with members of the church who are living and serving in these areas full time. The refugees have suffered terribly and it is such a gift to get to spend time with them and hopefully encourage them. I want to let them know that we care about them and have not forgotten them, and more importantly that Jesus loves them and cares deeply for them, and that He offers the one true hope.

"Lebanon is 1/3rd the size of Maryland and has almost 2 million refugees from Palestine and Syria living in numerous camps and around the country. Almost 20% of the entire population of Lebanon are refugees, making it the country with the highest per capita population of refugees in the world. The church is caring for refugees there and being a light to that area of the world. There is a particular checkpoint I hopefully will be going through near the Syrian border in Lebanon. Please pray about that and for the local church near the Syrian border where I will be visiting, as well as the churches and refugees near Beirut and Tyre. Hezbollah is the predominant militant/terrorist group in Lebanon and they are aligned with Syria's leader and against ISIS. Please pray for all of them. They are just people and I am not afraid of them, only because I know the King of kings and the Lord of lords, and because I am sealed for eternity through Jesus and because Jesus *promises* that He will *never leave me or forsake me*. What a great promise that we are never alone.

"Imagine things being so bad in Syria that it is safer to risk your life fleeing to Iraq than to stay in Syria. I met refugees last year who did exactly that. Many precious families have had to do that, as well as flee Mosul in N. Iraq when ISIS took it over in June 2014. That city (the 2nd largest in Iraq) is 50 miles from Erbil, which is where I fly in and out of and where many of the families in Mosul fled to last summer. I hope to spend time with some

Prologue: Pray, Take Risks and Go

of them. I also hope to return to the refugee camp I was at last year near the Iranian and Turkish borders as I now have some special friends there who are refugees. I hope I get to see them and give them copies of the book Vacation in Iraq that includes pictures of them and some of their stories. I hope that encourages them...that they will know that people are reading about them and seeing their faces...that they have not been forgotten.

"My heart breaks for the terrorists...that they could be so lost, may God save them. May God pour out His blessings on the refugees who have been through so much terror, war, pain and loss. May God encourage His church to keep the faith and to finish the race. And may God stir in our hearts to prompt us to *take risks* and do something to help the people of the world who are suffering so greatly.

"Please pray for everyone in Iraq and Lebanon as well as in Syria and all other conflict areas in the world. The church is there and alive and being used in a mighty way by God.

...

"I'm scheduled to depart at 6:30pm ET on June 19 and arrive in Iraq on June 20 at 6pm ET (1am Iraq time on June 21). I travel from Iraq to Lebanon a good part of June 24 (through Turkey), and travel from Lebanon (through Turkey) [back to the US] all of June 28. God did amazing things at the security checks/checkpoints last year, as well as with the refugees and with strangers on the streets, as well as with the church. Please pray about all of that.

"Please also pray for my family.

"Thank you for your friendship and prayers, and for being part of this journey. Knowing you is a great gift. Be encouraged to take the risky path of love because love never fails. And be encouraged to go wherever God calls you to go. Because He's worth it.

"Blessings in Christ,
Brian a/k/a Abu William"

God has been amazingly *gracious* to allow me to take these journeys and make so many friends in so many *unexpected* places. It's a privilege to share the journeys with you in this book. As David said in Psalms:

I will not die; instead, I will live to *tell* what the LORD has done. (Psalm 118:17)

So, please join me now on my vacation in Beirut as well as in other countries in the Middle East, as well as in Africa and America, where I have gotten to know Jesus as my *friend* in some wonderful and surprising ways. My hope and prayer is that you will grow in *your personal friendship* with Jesus as you join me…and Jesus…on this journey.

New Iraqi Shia Muslim refugee friend at camp in Iraq (June 2015)

Prologue: Pray, Take Risks and Go

New Muslim refugee friend at camp in Lebanon (June 2015)

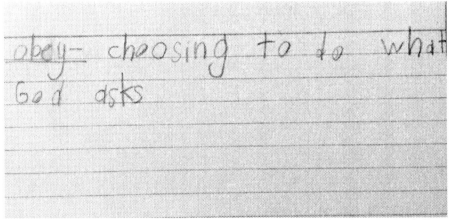

Notecard our son wrote in school ("<u>obey-</u> choosing to do what God asks") (America) (approximately 2012)

1   Lunch With Jesus

> Later, Levi invited Jesus and his disciples to his home as dinner guests, along with many tax collectors and *other disreputable sinners*. (There were many people of this kind among Jesus' followers.) (Mark 2:15)

*W*HAT WOULD YOU think if you saw a friend at work or somewhere else…or even a stranger…and he told you, "I had lunch with Jesus last Tuesday!" What jumps into your mind first? Crazy? Strange? Bizarre? Awesome? Jesus *promises* that where two or more are gathered, He is with them. And He promises He is always with us. And He means it.

We often refer to Jesus, and rightly so, as our "Lord and Savior"…but that can be *somewhat impersonal,* regardless of whether we have grown up under a Lordship like a monarchy. How often do you consider Jesus a *personal friend?* How often do you consider that Jesus was also a *human* and walked among us here on Earth…that He ate food, built things out of wood, got thirsty, enjoyed friendships, cried, laughed,[14] died…and then rose.

So, how do you become friends with someone who died in the Middle East 1,982 years ago…yet who is alive and well today at this very moment as you read this? This book is intended to help with exactly that. That *friendship.*

---

[14] The Bible does not expressly state that Jesus "laughed," but I find it hard to believe that He didn't laugh. After all, he enjoyed being around children and spending time having a meal with His friends. I like to picture Him laughing…enjoying a fun conversation around the table with friends or enjoying a laugh with children.

Lunch With Jesus

Delicacies of Middle East for sale in city market
(Erbil, Iraq) (June 2015)

Story: Sitting on a Rock in the Woods

Moses said, "Then show me your glorious *presence*." (Exodus 33:18)

OUR SON AND I enjoy great adventures together in Scouting.[15] During one of the campouts in a beautifully forested area with rolling hills and large rocks, I went for a hike "by myself" as our son was not able to attend that campout.[16] I love hiking on a path through a forest. I love the sounds of the forest. Wind, birds, silence. The rustling of the leaves. The crunch of the trail beneath your feet. There was a popular hike at that camp that followed a creek and took you to a large rock formation. Along the way, there was a smaller rock about the size of a small car next to the path. As the wind blew through the tops of the trees and I found myself there…just me and the forest…I stopped at that first large rock. I climbed up on it, sat down and took in a big breath of the fresh forest air and let it out.

---

[15] www.scouting.org
[16] As followers of Jesus, we are never truly by ourselves since Jesus tells us that "I am with you always" (Matthew 28:20b NIV).

And I began to think about Jesus. It was the year 2013. I had been to Israel and the West Bank on the Holy Land tour group trip the year before. What an amazing experience that had been looking out over Jerusalem for the first time, walking through the back roads of refugee Camp Aqabat Jabr in Jericho, getting baptized in the Jordan River. I had returned to the Middle East…again to Israel and the West Bank…earlier in 2013 to serve the refugees in Jericho and to encourage Christians serving in that area. And here I was so far from the Middle East sitting on a rock in a beautiful forest taking in the fresh air, quiet and peace. Some of the lyrics of a song come to mind as I think back to that moment on that rock in the woods:

Open the eyes of my heart, Lord. Open the eyes of my heart. I want to *see You.* I want to *see You.*[17]

So there I was sitting on that rock. For possibly the first time in my life, I asked Jesus to *please reveal Himself to me*. To please *appear to me* right then in that forest. I wanted *so badly* to *see Him*. I asked over and over, "Please show Yourself to me Jesus…I want to see You." Not just casually asking or kind of hoping. I very much *wanted* to see Jesus right then and there in that forest. And then I waited. I sat there…on a rock…waiting. Hoping. Wanting. But He didn't show Himself to me. At least not on my timing (immediately) and not in my way (to see His face…to see Him…right there in that forest). I was sitting on a "a rock" not realizing that Jesus was truly going to show Himself to me…that my prayer had been heard and answered…but not right there…not right then. Instead, unbeknownst to me that day, Jesus was indeed going to reveal Himself to me, not there but instead in a far-away land…a war-torn land…called "Iraq" (pronounced in Arabic, "*ee-rock*"). Yes, God had heard me and had answered my prayer…but in a way I could never have imagined and in a place I had never considered going to…a place I very much *didn't* want to go to.

מֵרֵעַ

---

[17] *Open The Eyes Of My Heart* by Michael W. Smith.

Lunch With Jesus

The forest where I asked Jesus to reveal Himself to me (America) (October 2013)

Story: Drinking from the Same Well that Jesus Drank from

> Eventually he came to the Samaritan village of Sychar, near the field that Jacob gave to his son Joseph. Jacob's well was there; and Jesus, tired from the long walk, *sat wearily beside the well* about noontime. Soon a Samaritan woman came to draw water, and Jesus said to her, "Please give me a drink." (John 4:5-7)

*J*ESUS WAS WEARY and thirsty. Think about that for a moment. He was so human that He was tired from walking…and he wanted a drink on a hot desert day. I so often focus on Jesus as sitting in Heaven or I spend time looking at a rendition of him in a stain glass window at church…but rarely have I focused on Him being tired…weary…thirsty. I find that focusing on Him from a human perspective helps me grow in my personal friendship with Him…better appreciate that He walked here on this earth. He was *really* here. Visiting places where He walked and drank water and rested is a powerful way to connect more personally with Him. And I got to do just that in the West Bank.

Journal Entry, West Bank, May 17, 2012:

"We stopped in Nablus at Jacob's Well. The guide explained that this is without a doubt Jacob's Well given its location and how deep it is. The Church on this site built over the well was constructed on a prior church's foundation in 1998 with approval of Yasser Arafat.[18] The Greek Orthodox are in charge of it. Justin the priest at the church had the church built and he personally painted many of the works of art on the walls and ceilings in it. It is beautiful inside with colorful and very large paintings throughout it. We were allowed to take pictures in it but not below at Jacob's Well. A stone stairway on each side of the altar has about a dozen steps that lead down to a stone room about the size of a bedroom in which Jacob's Well is contained in the center of it. The well has a rope and crank and is 130 feet deep! The story of Jesus and the Samaritan woman at this well was read...what a powerful and special moment as we stood around the exact well where the words being read were spoken originally by Jesus and the Samaritan woman!

"The ladies were allowed to take turns cranking the bucket up, and only the ladies since Jesus asked the Samaritan woman to get him a drink of water from the well. The guide explained that back in Jesus' day people going from town to town would carry a bucket and rope to use at wells. However, Jesus' and the disciples' rope was probably too short for such a deep well as this, so Jesus had an opportunity to ask her to pull one up for him. It was noon [when Jesus was at the well] and would have been very hot like it was today [as we visited] the well. After the bucket was drawn up, we were allowed to drink some of the water. I did and took another drink, it was delicious and I felt as though I had just been baptized from the inside out. What an experience! It was one of the moments I have felt most close to God. An amazing moment in time for me. I was humbled by the presence of the Lord and how compassionate and full of love Jesus was to the Samaritan woman. Wow! I knelt and prayed by the well. Justin sold water from the well as a fundraiser for the church. He was an older man with a long grey beard, a Greek Orthodox priest."

---

[18] Former Chairman of the Palestinian Liberation Organization (PLO).

Lunch With Jesus

Jesus walked here on this planet. He was so human that He got thirsty. And He drank at a well you can visit today. He was really here living among us.

Children in the West Bank near the location of Jacob's well (Israel) (May 2012)

2   Jesus the Human Was Born and Walked Among Us

We proclaim to you the one who existed from the beginning, whom we have heard and seen. *We saw him with our own eyes and touched him with our own hands.* He is the Word of life. (1 John 1)

THINK ABOUT THAT for a moment…the living God who spoke the Universe into existence…who created you…who placed the stars in the sky…who put the Earth in just the right place for us to live on it…became human and lived among humans, ate with humans, laughed with humans, and died with humans. Wow:

So *the Word became human* and made his home among us. He was full of unfailing love and faithfulness. And we have seen his glory, the glory of the Father's one and only Son. (John 1:14)

And He didn't just become human, He also set aside His deity. In fact, he made himself *nothing*…he became a *servant*. Wow again:

In your relationships with one another, have the same mindset as Christ Jesus: Who, being in very nature God, did not consider equality with God something to be used to his own advantage; rather, *he made himself nothing* by taking the very nature of a servant, *being made in human likeness*. And *being found in appearance as a man*, he humbled himself by becoming obedient to death—even death on a cross! (Philippians 2:5-8)

And since we are humans, He became a human. So we could relate to God…to Jesus…on a *personal* level. That's amazing. And He was born to die so that those of us who were dying could live:

Because God's children are human beings--made of flesh and blood--*the Son also became flesh and blood*. For only as a human being could he die, and only by dying could he break the power of the devil, who had the power of death. (Hebrews 2:14)

Jesus the Human Was Born and Walked Among Us

He was on this planet walking around, making friends, getting his feet dirty, wiping the sweat from his brow, drinking a cool cup of water on a hot Judean Desert kind of day. Right here on this planet. Wow.

מֵרֵעַ

View of Israel from Mount Nebo in Jordan, from where Moses was allowed by God to view the Promised Land (March 2014)

Story: Visiting the Place in Bethlehem Where Jesus was Born

This is how the birth of Jesus the Messiah came about: His mother Mary was pledged to be married to Joseph, but before they came together, *she was found to be pregnant* through the Holy Spirit. Because Joseph her husband was faithful to the law, and yet did not want to expose her to public disgrace, he had in mind to divorce her quietly. But after he had considered this, an angel of the Lord appeared to him in a dream and said, "Joseph son of David, do not be afraid to take Mary home as your wife, because what is conceived in her is from the Holy Spirit. She will *give birth to a son*, and you are to give him the name Jesus, because he will save his people from their sins." All this took place to fulfill what the Lord had said through the prophet: *"The virgin will conceive and give birth to a son, and they will call him Immanuel"* (which means "God with us"). When Joseph woke up, *he did what the angel of the Lord had commanded* him and took Mary home as his wife. But he did not consummate their marriage until she gave birth to a son. And he gave him the name *Jesus.* (Matthew 1:18-24)

*V*ISITING THE BIRTHPLACE of Jesus...the place that so many people around the globe hear about at Christmas time each year. The manger scenes sit in our homes and churches each Christmas reminding of that most glorious *arrival* of our Savior...as a *baby*. To sit where Jesus was born...to connect across time to that most amazing moment in history...is personal and unforgettable. My parents were incredibly kind and gracious to take me there.

Map of the West Bank, Gaza and part of Israel as well as the wall/fence being built by Israel around the West Bank and Gaza

Jesus the Human Was Born and Walked Among Us

JOURNAL ENTRY, West Bank, May 14, 2012:

"After another great meal of Middle Eastern food, we headed to the Church of the Nativity. We arrived in Bethlehem and there was a large church steeple and mosque tower near the Bethlehem town square. Across the square from them is the site of where Mary gave birth to Jesus. There was no room in the inn when they arrived, so they took up shelter in a cave equipped with a manger/feeding trough built into the wall of the cave. The Church of the Nativity is a church that was built on top of the site of Jesus' birth and is one of the most ancient Christian churches. It is under the care of the Greek Orthodox and a part of it is under the care of the Armenians and the Catholics built a church that is connected to it. It was a powerful and humbling experience to walk into the sanctuary.

"To get to the birthplace of Jesus, if you are facing the very ornate Greek sanctuary, you enter down into the ground/cave below the altar area to the right of it through a small doorway you have to hunch down to go through. Many pilgrims are here and we waited for a group of Russians to go in before we did. There were lots of candles burning and amazing works of art on the walls. This was the only church that was not destroyed during I think the Persian invasion. It was not destroyed because there was a mosaic on one of the walls of the Magi (three wise men), who were from Persia so the Persians did not want to destroy the church when they saw that work of art. You step down into the cave and there is a Greek altar with a silver star on the ground below it marking the actual spot where Jesus was born. It states in Greek on the star that, 'Here the Word was made Flesh.' You can kneel down under the altar (about the size of a fireplace at home) and touch the star and kiss it. Nearby a Greek priest keeps watch over the spot. Across from the small room/cave is the location of the stone manger/trough where Jesus was laid as a newborn baby. I felt so blessed and humbled to be in this most holiest of places in the world.

"We exited the cave on the left side of the church sanctuary and emerged back to the ground level. We walked over to another sanctuary in that building and yet another small one built by the Crusaders ('recently' per the guide since it was only the 12th century!). We sat in that small sanctuary together as a group (about the size of a bedroom at home) and sang Amazing Grace as our voices echoed off the stone walls. It was another powerful moment."

The birthplace of Immanuel. *God with us.* Jesus was born. And you can get on a plane tonight and be at that most amazing place tomorrow. *That's* up close and personal.

صـــــديقي

Location in cave where Jesus was believed to have been born (Jerusalem, Israel) (May 2012)

3   Text Message from Jesus

> On judgment day many will say to me, "Lord! Lord! We prophesied in your name and cast out demons in your name and performed many miracles in your name." But I will reply, "I never *knew you*. Get away from me, you who break God's laws." (Matthew 7:22-23)

ONE DAY, I thought about what it would be like to receive a text message *from Jesus*: "Hi Brian, how are you doing? Hope you're having a great day! BFF, Jesus."[19] How would I react? How would *you* react? I confess, it would be strange, especially before I went on trips to the Middle East for the last four years. Because four years ago, I don't think I knew Jesus very much at all…let alone as a *close friend*. So it would have been uncomfortable…strange…to receive such a *personal* message from someone *I didn't know very well.*[20]

מֵרֵעַ

---

[19] Our daughter has taught me that "BFF" means "Best Friends Forever." Jesus has taught me that it can also refer to Him being a "Brutally Faithful Friend."
[20] Kyle Idleman in *Not a Fan* tells a great story of what it would be like to be sitting at a local coffee shop and have Jesus walk over, sit down across from you, and say to you, "It's time we define this relationship" (p.23).

Encountering Jesus

Mountain Dew...Middle Eastern style
(Northern Iraq) (June 2015)

Story: Our Daughter's Unexpected "Friend"

A friend loves at *all* times. (Proverbs 17:17a NIV)

OUR DAUGHTER WENT ice skating with a close friend of hers at a local ice skating rink. While sitting at the rink putting on her ice skates, a girl she *did not know* sat down next to her and told her very energetically, "I'm your newest friend!" Our daughter felt awkward and uncomfortable...because she didn't know the girl *at all*. I think most of us would react the same way.

I wonder how we would react if *Jesus* sat down next to us and energetically hugged us and told us that He loves being our friend...our *close friend*...our *best friend*. It's hard to be a friend...especially a close friend...and certainly a best friend...when you don't know someone much at all. So, how awkward (or not) would it be for you if Jesus walked over, sat down, and said, "It's great to see you friend!"

My hope and prayer is that you will get to *know* Jesus better through this book and the stories in it.

My first new *friend* in the West Bank, a local Arab Palestinian Christian priest; he asked me to tell the church in America that the Arab Christians are suffering greatly in the West Bank (May 2012)

4   My Friend Jesus?

> I no longer call you servants, because a servant does not know his master's business. Instead, I have called you *friends*, for everything that I learned from my Father I have made known to you. (John 15:15)

I ADMIT THAT, at first, even just imagining God or Jesus as my *friend* almost seemed to be a bit too *informal*…even *sacrilegious*. After all, we're talking about the God who created the Universe…who created you and me…the One who is worshipped in the church we attend and throughout the world. Getting friendly with Him seemed *awkward* to me…kind of unreligious in a way…almost *disrespectful*. Interestingly, it also made me feel more *vulnerable* just thinking about being friends with Him. After all, to be a close friend, that takes vulnerability and trust. Part of me preferred to worship Him *from a distance*…to *learn about* Him from a distance. That felt safer…less risky…than *actually being friends* with Jesus.

I went searching in the Bible for verses about God and Jesus having friends…and there it was…over and over…God and Jesus referring to people as their *friends*. Here's some of God's Word that I found:

> And the scripture was fulfilled that says, "Abraham believed God, and it was credited to him as righteousness," and he was called *God's friend*. (James 2:23)

> There is no greater love than to lay down one's life for one's *friends*. (Jesus in John 15:13)

> You are my *friends* if you do what I command. (Jesus in John 15:14 NIV)

> The Son of Man has come eating and drinking, and you say, "Look at him! A glutton and a drunkard, a *friend* of tax collectors and sinners!" (Jesus in Luke 7:34 ESV)

> Dear *friends*, don't be afraid of those who want to kill your body; they cannot do any more to you after that. (Jesus in Luke 12:4)

My Friend Jesus?

Then he said, "*Our friend* Lazarus has fallen asleep, but now I will go and wake him up." (Jesus in John 11:11)

The Greek word translated to "friend" in each of the above verses is *philos*, which connotes a *dear* friend, someone you are *fond of*, a *trusted confidant*, someone with whom you have a *close bond of personal affection*.[21]

So, the question for me...for you...is whether I consider Jesus a *dear friend*, someone I am *fond of*, a *trusted confidant*, someone with whom I have a *close bond of personal affection*? And, if not, whether I want to have a friendship like that with Jesus? And, if I do, what do I need to do to gain a friendship like that with Him? Regardless of where you are in this kind of a personal, intimate friendship with Jesus, my hope and prayer is that what you read in this book will help you gain a closer level of friendship with Him. A real, up-close-and-personal friendship.

My dear *friend* Lokman (pronounced "Loke-mahn") with refugee children (Northern Iraq) (June 2015)

---

[21] *Strong's Greek Concordance* is a great reference tool, as is Bible Hub (http://biblehub.com/greek/philos_5384.htm). Also check out e-Sword (www.e-sword.net) for help looking at the Hebrew and Greek original Bible text and meaning.

ENCOUNTERING JESUS

Story: Standing Up for My Friend

He said to them, "But who do you say that I am?" Simon Peter replied, "You are the Christ, the *Son of the living God.*" (Matthew 16:15-16 ESV)

OUR FAMILY LOVES to spend time in the mountains of the Western United States. We were there in the summer of 2015 staying in a small town in the mountains after I had returned from Iraq and Beirut. There are churches there, as is usually the case in communities throughout the US. We were there on a Sunday, so my dad, my son and I went to the service at one of those churches. There was a visiting pastor, and his message was about, "Who is Jesus?" The pastor told the people gathered that morning that he has been a pastor for 18 years. He shared that, if someone asked him who Jesus is, he could point people to other people who he thinks would have an answer. He said he would point to people like Mother Teresa as someone who might be able to answer that question. And to people who go to dangerous places in the world to serve others…places that he would not be willing to go to. And he could point to friends of his who adopted a child. And then, much to my surprise and sadness, he said, "As your visiting pastor, I don't have an answer for you as to who Jesus is." I was shocked…dumbfounded…angry…and sad. Here was a pastor of 18 years telling us that he *did not know who Jesus is.* While I admired his honesty, my heart broke.

Unfortunately, I believe there are many people who go to church…who do "Christian kinds of things"…yet who do not *know* who Jesus is. They know *about Him*, but they don't *know Him.* I can say that because I went to church for *many* years before I actually got to know Jesus personally. So I know what that's like. I was previously going through the motions, doing the "nice church thing" and otherwise living my life like I wanted to live it. It was about *me*, not Jesus. And it certainly wasn't about having a *friendship* with Him.

And more importantly, I can say this about the church because Jesus says it:

> On judgment day many [most] will say to me, "Lord! Lord! We prophesied in your name and cast out demons in your name and performed many miracles in your name." But I will reply, "*I never knew you.* Get away from me, you who break God's laws." (Matthew 7:22-23)

These will be people…*many* people…including people who even did miracles in the name of Jesus…*miracles!* Yet they didn't know Jesus. Jesus is warning

My Friend Jesus?

us...in essence asking us...*do we really know Him*, or do we just *know things about Him?*

I enjoy the book, *not a fan* by Kyle Idleman.[22] He's got a great sense of humor...and he's good at cutting straight to the heart of the issue about whether you know Jesus...or, as he puts it, whether you're a *follower* of Jesus or just a *fan*. Here's some of that heart-piercing message about whether we know Jesus...an issue that Jesus discusses in Matthew 7 as being a *critical* one:

> [Fans of Jesus are] saying—I believe in Jesus, I'm a big fan, but don't ask me to follow. I don't mind coming to church on the weekends. I'll pray before meals. I'll even slap a Jesus fish on my bumper. But I don't want Jesus to *interfere* with my life. (p.36)

> Fans have a tendency to confuse their knowledge for intimacy. They don't recognize the difference between knowing *about* Jesus and truly knowing Jesus...The problem isn't knowledge. The problem is that *you can have knowledge without having intimacy.* (p.44)

> That's what it comes down to in Matthew 7. That's the dividing line that Jesus identified. In verse 23 he says to the fans, "I never knew you." So it comes down to a personal relationship with Jesus where you know him and are known by him...Jesus identifies his true followers based upon an *intimate relationship.* (p.107)

So, back at the church in the mountains, as my heart broke trying to comprehend what I had just heard, God nudged me to go up to the front of the church. To go stand up for *my friend Jesus*. That was the end of the pastor's message, and the offering was beginning to be taken and a final song sung before the service was over. I have learned through the Middle East trips that, when God nudges you to do something, you need to do it no matter how *foolish* or *terrifying* it seems. So, while the offering plate was being passed and as the congregation began singing the final song, I went up to the front of the church where the visiting pastor and the church's pastor were sitting. I knelt down next to the visiting pastor and told him that I believed that the Lord was asking me to give a short testimony about going and helping refugees in the Middle East, and that I had just done that the month before. I assured him that it would not last longer than one minute. He wasn't sure what to do. He turned looking somewhat surprised to the church pastor and explained the situation and what I

---

[22] Taken from *Not a Fan* by Kyle Idleman, Copyright © 2011 by Kyle Idleman, Used by permission of Thomas Nelson. www.thomasnelson.com.

was asking. They both somewhat hesitatingly agreed and he stressed that it should not be more than one minute. I assured him it would not be. And there we sat up at the front of that church in the mountains…the three of us…waiting for the song to finish.

The song finished. The visiting pastor walked up to the podium and explained to the people that a visitor wanted to share a short testimony. So it was time to share.

I walked up to the podium and looked out at everyone gathered there. I was getting ready to stand up for *my friend*. I shared that God tells me to go to places like Iraq and Beirut to help the refugees…so I go. And that during all the journeys through so many checkpoints and refugee camps, Jesus has proved Himself a *faithful friend*. He has *always* been there for me. I told them I appreciated the pastor asking the question that morning of who Jesus is. And that I admired his honesty about that. I then looked at everyone…I looked *at their eyes*…and I said, "Here's my answer as to who Jesus is: He's the Christ, the Son of the Living God…and He's also *my friend*." And that was it. I stepped back from the podium, thanked the pastors, and returned to my seat. And the service ended.

I know Jesus doesn't need me…doesn't need anyone…to stand up for Him. But I must tell you, it felt great to be standing up for a friend…not a thing or a religion or a belief…but *a friend*. That's what friends do. And so that's what I did. Jesus has always been there for me. It felt great to be there for Him.

מֵרֵעַ

"Beautiful Jesus, beautiful Savior
Nothing is greater, brilliant creator
Friend of mine"

Song lyrics from *Beautiful Jesus* by
Kristian Stanfill and Edmond Martin Cash

My Friend Jesus?

Sunrise at the Sea of Galilee where Jesus spent much of His time with His *friends* (Tiberias, Israel) (May 2012)

5   Wow Jesus, You're Really Here!

> Look! I stand at the door and knock. If you hear my voice and open the door, *I will come in*, and we will share a meal together as *friends*. (Revelation 3:20)

WHAT WOULD IT be like if Jesus was sitting in a chair in my office? How would I work, talk, think and act differently? I know it would be different…my *life* would be *different*. I can see how wearing a pin that says, "WWJD" ("What Would Jesus Do?") could be helpful…at least at first. How about a pin that says, "WWIDIJWHWMAD" ("What Would I Do If Jesus Was Here *With Me* All Day?"). That sure would be different…imagine that…Jesus *actually being with us* all day long.

But for so long…for so many years…as I tried to live my new "Christian life," Jesus was more of an afterthought to me, if a thought at all. Sure, I attended church and sang worship songs and read my Bible and some daily devotional messages that get emailed to me on my iphone. But I could hardly say that I had a real, daily, "He's right here with me" type of relationship with Him. I'll say it again. I did a lot of the things that you do as a Christian…and I enjoyed them very much…but it didn't seem like He was *actually with me* in my office, in my car, at meals. It was more like He had lived His life here on this planet and gone back Home, and now I was here living my life. We weren't here living our lives *together*. At least, it seemed that way to me. After all, I figured, He was back Home with God standing at God's right hand (Luke 22:69).

I guess you could say our *relationship* didn't seem like *a real one*…a real "I'm here with you…right here by your side…up close and personal" kind of relationship. At best, it felt more like *a long-distance relationship*, if you could call it a relationship at all.

Since asking Jesus into my heart and receiving God's amazing grace in my car back in 2004, I have enjoyed reading biographies of people…just normal everyday people…who God has used in amazing ways. And as I struggled with God's call for me to go to Iraq "by myself," I read many biographies and I was greatly encouraged by them…by the people in them…by what seemed to be the intimate, personal, *real* "He's right here with me" kind of relationships that they had with Jesus. And at some level, not always consciously, I found myself struggling with why my relationship with Jesus seemed to be more of *a long distance one.*

Before going to Iraq the first time, I was reading the biography of a woman named Gladys Aylward who became a missionary to China.[23] Two paragraphs struck me about her *personal friendship* with Jesus:

> Gladys spoke to Jesus in everyday language, as someone who was always there beside her—a companion. Now she found herself apologizing to Him for being so silly, with her grand ideas, and she imagined Him *smiling at her* with the understanding of a *close friend.* (p.12)

> She didn't think of her dear Jesus as someone remote. Sometimes she would kneel in quiet prayer, but that didn't mean she couldn't pray and talk to Him the rest of the time. He was *always there beside her* for her to talk to as she went about her daily tasks. Jesus didn't just listen to you when you were on your knees with your eyes closed. That would make praying into some kind of telephone call. (p.68)

Now that sounds like a *real, personal,* "He's-right-here-with-me" kind of relationship with Jesus.

Isobel Kuhn was also a missionary to China. In *Isobel Kuhn,*[24] she explained:

> "Lord, help me!" she cried silently, trying to steady herself. She *felt a hand on her shoulder,* and strength flowed through her body so that the nausea and faintness disappeared. For a moment she was in heaven, in communion with her Lord; then the commonplace closed in around her again. She was elated for days. Only once more in her entire life, during early years in China, did she have such an experience. "He is not far away—He is *here with me* in my everyday life' was the lesson she learned." (p.48)

And I read about African missionary Mary Slessor. And, once again, I was struck with how *real* and *personal* her relationship was with God and Jesus:

> God was a living presence to Mary Slessor, and Christ was almost *visibly near.* "When I am out there in the [jungle], I have often no other one to

---

[23] *Gladys Aylward* by Catherine Swift, © 1984, 1989 by Catherine Swift. Harper Collins UK. All rights reserved.
[24] *Isobel Kuhn* by Lois Hoadley Dick, © 1987 by Lois Hoadley Dick. Baker Publishing Group. All rights reserved.

speak to, and so I just talk to Him," she said in speaking of her conversation with God. (pp.138-39)

Amy Carmichael was the same way. She was convinced of how real and close to her Jesus was...as real as the presence of Jesus was to Peter:

Peter did not think it a strange thing to walk on the sea, nor did his heavenly Master say one word about its being unusual to expect to be able to do so. He, the Lord of heaven and earth, *was there*; the unnatural thing was not to do it, to sink. (p.288)

And then there was Corrie ten Boom in the concentration camps experiencing Jesus in an up-close-and-personal kind of way:

"Dear Jesus," I whispered as the [prison cell] door slammed and [the guard's] footsteps died away, "how foolish of me to have called for human help when You are here." (*The Hiding Place*, p.170)

Corrie described her sister Betsie's intimate and up close relationship with Jesus, which was evident in the notorious Ravensbruck women's extermination camp where they were both trying to survive, and where Betsie died:

I hated the dismal place [Ravensbruck sick ward] full of sick and suffering women, but we had to go back, again and again, for Betsie's condition was growing worse. She was not repelled by the room as I was. To her it was simply a setting in which to talk about Jesus...Betsie spoke to those around her about *His nearness* and His yearning to come into their lives. (*The Hiding Place*, p.216)

After Corrie miraculously survived Ravensbruck and the German army was defeated, Corrie travelled around the world sharing about God's love and forgiveness. In *Tramp for the Lord*, the sequel to *The Hiding Place*, Corrie explains how real the presence of Jesus was to her after she returned back to her hometown in Holland...her parents having died during the war:

Now Father was dead. Only my Heavenly Father remained...How thankful I was for my Heavenly Father's *strong hand around mine*...The old [house our family lived at in Holland where we hid Jews], the old hiding place, was no longer mine. Ravensbruck had taught me much I needed to learn. My hiding place was now in Jesus alone..."Thank You, Jesus, that I

Wow Jesus, You're Really Here!

am alive," I said. In my heart I *heard Him reply*, "Lo, I am with you always, even unto the end of the world." (pp.30, 31)

And, towards the end of her life, she described her closeness with Jesus during times of fear:

In all these years that I have been a "tramp for the Lord," I have often been afraid. But in those moments I have always reached up and touched the hem of Jesus' garment. He has never failed to wrap me *close to Him*. (pp.94-95)

I read in book after book about a *real, up-close-and-personal* kind of relationship with Jesus that I just didn't seem to have. And a *hunger* for that kind of relationship with Him continued to rise up within me.

Muslim *friend* in Jerusalem at his coffee shop (Israel) (April 2013)

ENCOUNTERING JESUS

Story: Driving One Morning with Jesus

> As they talked and discussed these things, Jesus himself suddenly came and began *walking with them*. (Luke 24:15)

I AM PART of a small group of guys who meet once a month for breakfast to talk about God's dreams that He has for our lives. Not our dreams...but *God's dreams*.[25] We've been meeting each month for over three years. We've eaten together, cried together, prayed together, laughed together, and learned a lot about God's dreams for our lives.

One early morning while driving to meet with the group, I began to pray in the car while I drove (don't worry mom, I kept my eyes opened ☺). I started to ask Jesus for some things. And right away, I stopped praying and instead pretended that Jesus was *sitting next to me* in the Jeep. I so often pray *to* Him. I wondered what it would be like for Him to just be sitting *next to me* instead. To be sitting *with* the Man I so often pray *to*. I thought, "What would I say to Him?" And I confess, it was awkward...*very* awkward. It wasn't awkward pretending that He was there. It was awkward because of how uncomfortable I felt that would be if He was really there. I thought, "Wow, I don't know what I would say to Him." If He was going to spend the entire day with me, I wondered what we would talk about. What would my prayers be like? I ended up getting comfortable with the thought of Him being right there in the seat next to me, and finally figured out what I would ask Him: "Jesus, what would you like to do today?" And I thanked Him for what He has done in my life.

I want Jesus to be *that real* to me.

---

[25] www.dreambuildersnetwork.com

Driving by a mosque with protective barriers in Southern Lebanon (June 2015)

Story: Jesus Reveals Himself to a Muslim

This was the third time Jesus had *appeared* to his disciples since he had been raised from the dead. (John 21:14)

THE PASTOR WHO was hosting me in Lebanon shared a story with me about a man who attends a church there in Beirut. The man is a Syrian and was not a Christian when he was in Syria...presumably he was a Muslim. He was kidnapped in Syria by ISIS and held captive for 10 days. The pastor explained that, during those 10 days, the man was brainwashed as ISIS prepared him for how he was going to be killed. I cannot imagine the terror of those 10 days. Practicing with terrorists how they are going to kill you. The Syrian hostage *begged* God to please *reveal* Himself to him. And, unbeknownst to him, God was going to answer his prayer.

On the day he was to be killed, he was taken to a rooftop in Syria. But, before ISIS could kill him, God miraculously rescued him as his captor slept. He escaped and now attends the church. The pastor says that, while he preaches, that man is in the congregation *taking in every word*. Praise God for how He revealed Himself to that man!

Hearing a story like that encourages me in my faith that God's Word truly is the Word of God:

> The LORD has *heard my cry* for mercy; the LORD accepts my prayer. (Psalm 6:9 NIV)

God appeared. And a man's life was changed for eternity.

מֵרֵעַ

The church in Lebanon where the Syrian refugee Christian attends (June 2015)

Arabic Bible at that same church in Lebanon
(June 2015)

6 Jesus Loves in Ways That Are Hard to Understand

Jesus said, "Father, forgive them, for they *don't know what they are doing.*" (Luke 23:34a)

FORGIVE THE PEOPLE who are *torturing* and *killing* you? Why? Because God forgave you. And because they don't know what they are doing. That's a level of forgiveness that is hard to comprehend...*impossible* to understand. But that is the level of forgiveness that Jesus showed on the Cross and the level of forgiveness that He expects from those who choose to follow Him. Those who choose to follow Him all the way to the Cross.

Jewish soldier and children praying at the Wailing Wall
(Jerusalem, Israel) (April 2013)

Jesus Loves in Ways That Are Hard to Understand

Story: Witnessing the Death of Jesus

For God calls you to do good, even if it means suffering, just as *Christ suffered for you*. He is your example, and you must follow in his steps. (1 Peter 2:21)

*I*MAGINE BEING ONE of the people witnessing the day's events leading up to the crucifixion of Jesus. It's Roman-occupied Jerusalem, the year 33 A.D. He has been arrested, beaten, tortured, spit on and slapped. He is bloody and dying. A crown of razor-sharp thorns has been shoved onto His head. His clothes have been taken from Him. And there you are having watched Him drag His cross through the streets of Jerusalem…through the crowds of onlookers…until He could drag it no more. You saw when Simon of Cyrene was pulled from the crowd and ordered by the brutal Roman soldiers to carry it for Jesus. Watching a bloody mess of a man struggle through the streets on the way to His *execution*.

You follow along with the crowd as you walk beyond the city walls. On the crowd goes following the soldiers, Jesus and Simon as the bloody Man heads to His execution. You wonder how a man can endure what Jesus is enduring. He is a *bloody mess of a man*. Your heart breaks but you are so thankful it is not you going through such horrific suffering and humiliation. You can't imagine that level of suffering and pain. Jesus somehow arrives at the place where He and two criminals are to be crucified. Where they will be nailed to wood and hung up on display to die.

The soldiers are rolling dice to see who gets the garments that they stripped off Jesus. They are nice garments…they don't want to rip them apart in order to divide them up. The wind is blowing and the blood is flowing out of the bruised and battered Jesus. He is dying. He is *taunted* by the crowd…and even by one of the criminals being crucified next to Him. He is being *mocked*…some *king* He turned out to be…some *messiah* He turned out to be. Humiliated and hanging on a tree to die a disgraceful death.

Right when you think He must be dead…that no human could possibly endure any more…someone asks you surprisingly, "Did you hear what he just said?!" You're in shock at the scene and numb from all you have watched…numb from all the blood you have smelled…shaken by the sound of the long steel nails being driven…*pounded*…through flesh into the wood as the clink of the hammer on the nails echoes throughout Jerusalem. Your initial thought is that your friend must be referring to one of the soldiers or high priests. Of course you heard the soldiers gambling for Jesus's clothes. Of course you heard the criminal on one side of Jesus sarcastically yelling at Him to save

Himself if He's the so-called messiah. In the numbness of the moment, you shakily respond, "What *who* said?" He responds somewhat bitterly and surprised, "What *Jesus* said!" You're shocked that Jesus could say *anything* at that point, and ask, "I…I…didn't hear…what did he say?" Your friend grabs your shoulder and stares you straight in the eyes, not smiling, and slowly answers, "He said, 'Father, *forgive* them, for they don't know what they are doing." Your mouth instinctively gapes open. You are speechless. You are numb. You don't know what to say to that. You just don't know how to react. You don't understand that…that kind of forgiveness.

So, as the breeze blows and as the dying die and as the blood begins to dry, you slowly walk away not able to fathom what has happened. A man has been *slaughtered* but did nothing wrong. Two criminals on each side of Him also were killed. The three of them hung there on those wooden crosses. Life seems to have stopped for you…to have paused. But, there is a part of you…a part deep down inside of you…*in your heart*…that somehow senses that *God* spoke that day…that only God could have spoken those words…those dying man's words. And as you slowly walk away, you realize that you will never be the same again.

Jesus Loves in Ways That Are Hard to Understand

The "place of the skull" (Golgotha) where Jesus is believed to have been crucified outside of the Jerusalem city walls (May 2012)

Story: Visit to Refugee Camps near Syrian Border: Jesus Cares

Then Peter came to him and asked, "Lord, how often should I forgive someone who sins against me? Seven times?" "No, not seven times," Jesus replied, "but *seventy times seven!*" (Matthew 18:21-22)

JESUS CALLS US to not just forgive our enemies one time…but over and over *and over*. Refugees oftentimes have many enemies, including people who wanted to kill them or at least take their homes, land, cars, children and ways of life. They sometimes are also disliked by people in the countries where they have fled to. Refugees deal with a lot of *conflict*…a lot of *hurt*…and

Encountering Jesus

sometimes a lot of *betrayal*. There is much pain and many people to forgive. Jesus is clear that we must forgive over and over *and over*.

Journal entry, Beirut, June 26, 2015:

"Today was one of those days where you can't believe that God is so gracious as to allow you to be there. I met up with two wonderful Lebanese Pastors and the 13 year old son of one of them, and we drove East to within 5 or so miles of the Syrian border to a town named Zahle. The war is just beyond there at the Syrian border between the Lebanese military and Hezbollah, on one side, and ISIS on the other. We had to pass through a military checkpoint...it was like a scene from a war movie to watch the military vehicles full of soldiers and machine guns heading towards Beirut while we drove towards the war.

"It was wonderful to spend time with the Syrian refugees, especially the children and the Christians who are committed to helping them with food, education and healing. The children loved meeting an American who speaks some Arabic...they loved calling me 'Abu William' and giggled and laughed. It was such a privilege to be there with them.

"We sat inside some of the [refugee] tents visiting with the families. One Syrian refugee mother served us tea. What an amazing act of kindness by her. I look at those children and want so badly to bring them to a better place. I am so humbled to get to be there with them.

"God blessed us with an amazing day, thank y'all so much for your prayers."

מֵרֵעַ

Jesus Loves in Ways That Are Hard to Understand

Refugee children with their bikes
(Zahle, Lebanon) (June 2015)

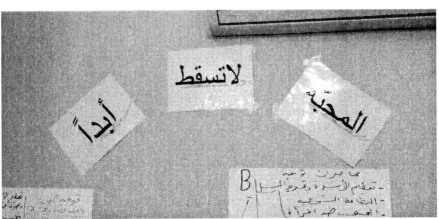

Signs in Arabic at refugee school classroom reading, "Love never fails"
(Zahle, Lebanon) (June 2015)

Story: Praying for Terrorists in Istanbul: Jesus Loves His Enemies

> But I tell you, *love your enemies* and pray for those who persecute you. (Matthew 5:44 NIV)

*P*RAY FOR THOSE who *persecute you?* That's another very difficult command. But there is Jesus telling us exactly that. When I first began praying for terrorists, I learned very quickly that it was just as much about the condition of *my own heart* as it was about the condition of the terrorist's heart. The hatred I had for terrorists…for the people who are the terrorists…was replaced with love and compassion for them. I continue to hate what is done through them…the evil that is done through them…but I love the person who "does not know what they are doing."[26]

As Brother Andrew put it so well: "The Christian's only method of destroying his enemies is to 'love' them into being his friends."

Journal Entry, Beirut, June 26, 2015:

"Hi y'all, the flight to Istanbul takes off at 11:45pm tonight. As you know, one of the purposes of the trip is to pray for the salvation of terrorists, that they would turn from their evil ways and receive Christ and radically follow Him and be a powerful witness of God's grace. I am going to be in Istanbul for three layovers on this trip. The times for the layovers (in ET) are below. It's amazing how God set up this trip as Istanbul is one of the main airports used by jihadists to get in and out of Syria. People will fly to Istanbul and then go by ground to the Syrian border where smugglers take them into Syria. Same when they leave Syria, they will oftentimes get out of Syria using smugglers and go by land to Istanbul and fly out of Istanbul. I'll be there praying for them and ask you to please join me at the Eastern Times below as best you can (some of the layovers are in the middle of the night ET). Prayer is a powerful way that God works…the prayers of a righteous person availath much…and praise God that God's grace is sufficient for every person no matter what they have done.

---

[26] Romans 12:9, Luke 6:35, Luke 23:34.

Jesus Loves in Ways That Are Hard to Understand

"Layovers in Istanbul:
June 20: 9:25am to 1:15pm
June 24: 11:45pm to 3:40am
June 28: 12:15am to 4:25am

"Please do not forward this email.

"Thank you so much for your friendship. I'm praying for you and your families.

"You're a blessing. Blessings, Brian"

JOURNAL ENTRY, BEIRUT, JUNE 26, 2015:

"I arrived in Istanbul and am so privileged to be praying that terrorists would turn from their evil ways. Some of them travel via Istanbul airport to join IS/ISIL by land from here into Syria using smugglers to get in and out of Syria. What a privilege to pray for them during this layover that will last until 1:15pm today ET. Prayer is an awesome privilege. Thank you for your prayers from the other side of the ocean!"

Map of Turkey (© maps.com)

Flying over the mountains of Turkey after departing Istanbul for Beirut (June 2015)

Jesus Loves in Ways That Are Hard to Understand

Driving in Erbil, Iraq; terrorists detonated a car bomb outside the US Consulate in Erbil in April 2015 (June 2015)

7   Laughing With Jesus

When the Lord brought back his exiles to Jerusalem, it was like a dream! We were *filled with laughter*, and we *sang for joy*. And the other nations said, "What amazing things the Lord has done for them." Yes, the Lord has done amazing things for us! What joy! (Psalm 126:1-3)

*L*AUGHTER IS A *wonderful gift*. How fun it is to laugh with friends…to laugh with Jesus. It's a sad day when we stop laughing. I love that the Bible talks about people laughing…singing with joy…*rejoicing*. I can picture Jesus laughing with his friends as they share a meal together. Peter remembers the time he walked on water and then started sinking. I can picture him jokingly saying, "I think I'm a better fisherman than a water-walker!" And he shakes his head slowly as he lets out a belly of a laugh. And I can see Jesus and the others around the table joining in with him. I like picturing Jesus laughing. Laughing with children. Laughing with friends. Laughing with me.

How refreshing to know that *God laughs too*:

But the one who rules in heaven *laughs*. (Psalm 2:4a)

Abraham's wife, Sarah, laughed…and attributed that to God:

Abraham was a hundred years old when his son Isaac was born to him. Sarah said, "God has brought me *laughter*, and everyone who hears about this will *laugh with me*." And she added, "Who would have said to Abraham that Sarah would nurse children? Yet I have borne him a son in his old age." (Genesis 21:5-7)

I enjoy picturing God laughing. I enjoy picturing Sarah and Abraham laughing together. They were no doubt so thankful for their son Isaac that they smiled and laughed. I'm smiling a big smile right now as I type this and as I picture Jesus and his friends laughing…as I picture Sarah and Abraham laughing…as I picture God laughing.

While in Lebanon, I visited a group of wonderful people who are helping Syrian refugees very close to the war. And even there, to my surprise, I found laughter.

Laughing With Jesus

صــديقي

Laughing with three new Palestinian friends in Camp Aqabat Jabr (Jericho, West Bank) (April 2013)

Story: Driving Towards the War Zone: Still Finding Laughter

A *cheerful heart* is good medicine, but a broken spirit saps a person's strength. (Proverbs 17:22)

I DIDN'T EXPECT to be laughing with a new friend so close to the war. Laughter is a great gift. And I enjoyed my new friend and the laughter that we shared together so close to the Syrian border…in a town named Zahle, located in the Bekka Valley of Lebanon.

מֵרֵעַ

New friends at refugee camp in Lebanon...amazing people who choose to be there to serve the refugees so close to the war (Zahle, Lebanon) (June 2015) (faces blurred for privacy reasons)

<u>Journal Entry, Beirut, June 25, 2015:</u>

"Military checkpoints on road to Bekka Valley where Zahle is located, many military vehicles driving from Syrian border back to Beirut, like being in a war movie. Bekka Valley is a very fertile land, many crops. I can see why other countries would like to take over Lebanon, it's beautiful with lots of food grown here. Beirut is a massive city right on the Mediterranean Sea. The temperatures here this time of year and the breeze off the sea are wonderful. Lows in the 70's and highs in the 80's. We drove back over the mountain on way back to Beirut yesterday through fog as mist rolled over the mountain from the Mediterranean Sea. Soldiers at checkpoints on the mountain had camouflaged winter coats on.

"ISIS sneaking in from Syria by way of the large mountain range that is the border between Syria and Lebanon. They shave their beards in order to blend in and try to make it past the checkpoints. Driving East from Beirut in the Mediterranean Sea, there is a high mountain range that you drive over (I am guessing 3,000 to 5,000 feet high) and then down into the massive and fertile Bekka Valley. The next massive mountain range is the border with Syria.

"We were in Zahle today about a 10 minute drive to Syria and where a battle recently occurred between the Lebanese military and ISIS.

"Met Pastor Kadin[27] who is in charge of a church in Zahle that is reaching out to the refugees, his wife runs a school for children from the refugee camps, school is located right next to some of the camps. Ate apricots (*'mishmish'* in Arabic) right off of a tree...delicious! Pastor Kadin asked me if I knew what [his real Arabic name] means in Arabic. I told him that I did, that it means generous. He responded in an animated voice as he pointed up in the air, "I am generous *by name only*!", and then he laughed and I joined in with him. I immediately liked him...a new friend who can still joke while he lives so close to the war.

"Landowners rent the land to the refugees as these are not official UN camps. There is a 'lord' in each camp that runs the camp and gets a share of anything received by the refugees in the camp. The 'lord' usually has the nicest tent (one 'lord' yesterday actually had kitchen cabinets built in the tent), and you can't visit one of these unofficial refugee camps without the 'lord's' permission. We took a man with us to the camp near the Syrian border as he teaches the refugees in that camp and so has a good relationship with the 'lord.' It was so nice of them to take me into these camps to see the children and laugh with them. That camp was about a five minute drive from the Syrian border.

"I met a former Muslim at the school for refugee children who they lovingly refer to as the 'Sunni evangelical'...we laughed about that. He's a nice man with a kind smile. He helps at the school. His daughter is 10 years old and is so cute. I smiled with her too. I think she enjoyed having a visitor from such a faraway land.

"Hezbollah does not do suicide bombings or attacks against civilians. A caravan of black cars sped by us on the highway today, people got out of their way, I was told that was Hezbollah as the cars were all unmarked and driving fast in a caravan.

"I made a comment at lunch regarding the Turkish coffee I was drinking and how it reminded me of the coffee in the Old City of Jerusalem. They

---

[27] Name changed for privacy reasons. *Kadin* is an Arabic name and means "friend" and "companion."

got very serious and said I should not mention that in public, I guess because I could be expelled from Lebanon and it may be dangerous for them. A stark reminder of how serious that issue is here."

Syrian refugee children signing a song (Zahle, Lebanon) (June 2015)

Smiling with Pastor Kadin and some of the refugee children (Zahle, Lebanon) (June 2015) (face blurred for privacy reasons)

Dirt-floor classroom in a tent run by inspiring people who have chosen to *go and be close* to the Syrian war to serve the refugee children (Zahle, Lebanon) (June 2015)

8 Tears On a Dusty Face

> When Mary reached the place where Jesus was and saw him, she fell at his feet and said, "Lord, if you had been here, my brother would not have died." When Jesus saw her weeping, and the Jews who had come along with her also weeping, he was *deeply moved* in spirit and troubled. "Where have you laid him?" he asked. "Come and see, Lord," they replied. *Jesus wept.* (John 11:32-35)

THE SHORTEST VERSE in the entire Bible: "Jesus wept." If there were two words that sum up the humanness of Jesus, it was these two. *Jesus*...the Son of God...the Messiah...God with us...*wept*. The Greek word translated to "wept" is *dakruo*, which signifies shedding tears and weeping silently with tears. Jesus wept silently as tears streamed down his cheeks. Down his *dusty face*. I've spent enough time in Israel and the West Bank to appreciate how hot and dry it gets in that Middle Eastern desert region. I can picture His tears running down His face...slowly catching some of the desert dust as they fall. His heart clearly hurt for them as he watched Mary weep at His feet and as he watched their friends weeping at the loss of a friend. Jesus knows what the perfection of Heaven is like...where there is no more crying...no more death...no more sorrow or pain (Revelation 21:4). And here He was at that moment in that dusty desert town having agreed to leave Heaven...leave the tranquility of being there with God...and being reminded of and experiencing the pain that is the fallen and broken world on earth.

Shepherd with sheep along dry, dusty desert road approaching the Israeli border (Jordan) (March 2014)

Story: Crying with Jesus in Jerusalem

He will wipe every tear from their eyes, and there will be *no more* death or sorrow or *crying* or pain. (Revelation 21:4a)

CLOSE FRIENDS WILL spend time crying together. Life has its painful moments and close friends are there for each other. I cried with my friend Jesus in Jerusalem. It was an intimate moment with Him. Jesus is such a loving and faithful friend. And He *feels our pain* like a good friend would.

JOURNAL ENTRY, ISRAEL, MAY 19, 2012:

"We first visited the Mount of Olives that overlooks the Eastern wall of Jerusalem across the Kidron Valley. This was a special place of prayer for Jesus and He and the disciples would have passed through here often as they typically entered Jerusalem through the Eastern wall. Jesus wept over Jerusalem from here, the only other time He wept that we know of was when Lazarus died. Past the gold Dome of the Rock to the right of it is the Church of the Holy Sepulchre over the rock where Jesus was crucified. It is a high point in the area and was located outside the original walls of Jerusalem, it was easily seen from all over this area as He was publicly displayed on the Cross. To the left at the corner of the wall is where Jesus was tempted by the Devil to jump from there, the wall was much higher at that time. The gate of the sheep is to the right along the Eastern wall, which is a gate through which Jesus entered and exited many times since He traveled to and from the east often.

"As we began walking down a narrow stone-walled, paved road into the city, we walked past the Russian Orthodox Church of Mary Magdalene, the only known church built in her honor. It has shiny gold towers shaped like the ones you see in pictures of Moscow. I could picture Jesus walking into Jerusalem. We entered into the Garden of Gethsemane further down to the left and walked around 2,000 year old olive trees that sat behind low fencing. They were large and wrinkled from age, twisting up towards the sky. Gethsemane means olive press and Jesus was being pressed and sweat great drops of blood. Someone was selling pieces of olive branches for $1 as we entered, I recalled Jesus being so upset at the merchants at the Temple. I was not mad but sad. It was very special to picture Jesus praying in this Garden with great agony knowing Judas and the Roman soldiers would be there that night to arrest Him, and the disciples falling asleep there.

"We entered the church built there. It is intentionally dark inside to remind visitors about Jesus praying here in the garden at night. A priest was leading a service in what sounded like Italian. Behind him and on the sides were massive mosaics in great color. The stain glass on the ceiling about 100 feet above us was in the shape of a cross...beautiful! I took some pictures and walked over to the rock in the left back corner of the church where I think it is believed Jesus prayed at. I knelt, prayed and kissed the rock with both of my hands open against the cool-to-the-touch stone. Many people were here from India praying at the stone as well. I then went over to the wall-length bench, knelt and prayed. I apologized to Jesus for Him suffering and I sensed Him respond, 'do not weep for me, weep for your sons and daughters.' To my left, two women were weeping and crying in Chinese...I began to cry for the first time of the trip, I cried for my wretchedness, the smell of the Dead Sea mud still on me, and the priest still conducting the service in Italian. It was an overwhelming moment. I wept with Jesus and felt a shift in my spirit from focusing on my own pain to focusing on Christ's, against which my pain barely registers.

"I wiped the tears and walked over to the other side of the church in the soft darkness, knelt by the bench over there, and took in the suffering of Jesus, absorbing Him. The people attending the service joined the priest singing in Italian, the dark mosaic overhead. I could have stayed there for a long time. Rick[28] came over, tapped on my shoulder, and said it was time to go and that he was sorry to interrupt. Later, he said it looked like I was in a trance and as I looked up to him, it was the look of someone being woken up. *Please Lord, wake up my spirit. Amen.* This was a 'wow moment' for me during this trip and a very intimate and special time with my Lord."

מֵרֵעַ

Inside the church at the Garden of Gethsemane (Jerusalem, Israel) (May 2012)

---

[28] A dear friend with whom I also walked the Via Dolorosa one morning in Jerusalem. An intimate experience with Jesus that we both cherish.

Story: Crying with a Pastor from Africa

The LORD will be your everlasting light, and your days of sorrow *will end*. (Isaiah 60:20b NIV)

AFTER I RECEIVED Jesus into my heart in February 2004...received unconditional forgiveness...received a new heart, life and destiny...I found myself in the slums of Nairobi, Kenya only four months later. That trip was an amazing opportunity to visit different ministries and programs in and around Nairobi. We spent time at orphanages, schools, hospitals, churches, villages of the Maasai tribe, and a ministry right in the heart of the massive Mathare Valley slum called Fountain of Life. Fountain of Life at that time was run by Pastor James Mbai ("muh-bye") and his wife who is affectionately referred to by many people as "Mama Florence." Their program includes a school for children in desperate need who have come out of the slum...out of the streets...and into the loving arms of James and Mama Florence and the wonderful staff and volunteers at that program. There are many children there and it is a wonderful opportunity for the children to experience the love of Jesus and God's kindness and goodness. It was a short visit with them but I became instant friends with James and Mama Florence...like we had known each other our whole lives. We exchanged contact information and the group I was with headed off to the next place to visit.

Unbeknownst to me at the time, Fountain of Life was in great need of resources as there were so many children at the program. Precious children. God apparently led Pastor Mbai to sell their van and buy a ticket to America several months after our visit. He travelled to the city where we were living and where I had been sharing with friends about Fountain of Life, and called me. He was at the airport and wanted to see if he could connect with me. I was surprised to hear from him! A friend of mine and I drove to the airport and, sure enough, there he was...the Pastor from Africa! Our children at the time were one and three years old. And there I was asking my wife if a Pastor I met in Africa could stay with us. She graciously approved and it ended up being an amazing time with him and so many friends in that area. Just amazing. I have fond memories of Pastor Mbai playing the guitar in our living room while our kids jumped and danced around and sometimes sat on his lap. Children *loved* Pastor Mbai in Nairobi and in America.

The life expectancy in Africa is lower than America...no surprise about that. Pastor Mbai passed away and went Home to be with Jesus two years later. I

Tears On a Dusty Face

returned to Nairobi with a group of friends to help host a medical clinic in the slums with Fountain of Life...it was a powerful experience for everyone there. During the trip, we visited the grave of Pastor Mbai. It's a moment I hope to always remember...standing there by my friend's grave in the peaceful countryside of Kenya...my friend whom God used to impact me in many ways.

While Pastor Mbai was visiting us in the US, I was driving him in my car as we headed back to our house. Pastor Mbai and I had shed many tears together during that visit. My heart had been broken...shattered...in the slums of Nairobi at the abject poverty and hopelessness that I had experienced there. As we drove across a bridge over a lake, Pastor Mbai said to me, "When we cry, God is ministering to us." I'm so thankful that God shared those words with me through Pastor Mbai. I think of that moment and those words often...as tears drop down my face. I am reminded that God is ministering to me...that I am not alone in my pain...that God is a loving Daddy.

Pastor Mbai preaching at the Fountain of Life
(Nairobi, Kenya) (July 2004)

Encountering Jesus

Map of Kenya, including Machakos, where Pastor Mbai was buried in 2006

Story: Children Born and Dying in Camp Baserma: Jesus Weeps

He will swallow up death forever! The Sovereign LORD will *wipe away all tears*. (Isaiah 25:8a-b)

SOMETHING ELSE I didn't realize about having friends who are refugees is that, when you see them and then a year goes by before you see them again, a lot can happen...enough tragedy to last a *lifetime*. I found that out after returning to see my friends at the camp in Northern Iraq.

Journal Entry, Iraq, June 21, 2015:

"Muhammad teaches too [with my refugee friend Lokman] and also taught at the new high school for free for six months (they now get a paycheck). He was single when I met him last year and was blessed to escape Syria with his life. He has since married and they had a cute little baby boy a couple of months ago. Another baby born as a refugee.

"On the sadder side, the tent next to the tent he and his wife and baby lived in caught on fire and a 1 year old and a 3 year old died in that fire in this camp...how much can a family take, first fleeing for their lives and then living in a tent, and then two children die in a fire.

"Muhammad's wife as a new mother was so strongly affected by what happened that they now live in two cinder block rooms, which others in tents are converting to...a sign that the refugees believe they will be here for a long time. Muhammad and Lokman hope to go back to their homelands in Syria in 10 years."

My Syrian refugee friend Muhammad; He's a kind man (Northern Iraq) (June 2015)

ENCOUNTERING JESUS

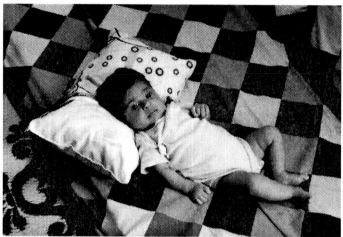

Muhammad's son...born in a refugee camp
(Northern Iraq) (June 2015)

Story: Visit to a Yazidi Refugee Camp: Jesus's Heart Breaks

Their life will be like a watered garden, and all their *sorrows will be gone*. (Jeremiah 31:12c)

IT'S QUITE A contrast between small neighborhood style refugee camps, like the one made up of 16 families that I visited in Iraq, and a typical large UN camp that can have anywhere from 3,000 to 130,000 refugees.[29] Both are needed, the UN camps for urgent immediate needs, and the neighborhood style camps for long term needs as people settle in to a new way of life that could last for a decade or longer. Trauma counseling is needed regardless of the size of the camp.

During the visit to Iraq in 2015, I was fortunate to visit a small Yazidi refugee camp. The Yazidi people have suffered greatly at the hands of ISIS.[30] It was a privilege to spend time with them.

---

[29] Camp Zaatari is a UN refugee camp in Northern Jordan near the Syrian border. It is a heavily militarized area in the dry Jordanian desert. I visited there in 2014 and, at that time, the camp had approximately 130,000 refugees living in it. Camp Zaatari is now known as the fourth largest *city* in Jordan.

[30] http://time.com/3091932/yazidi-iraq-isis-obama/

Tears On a Dusty Face

Journal Entry, Iraq, June 22, 2015:

"We picked up a Muslim dentist this morning who is fasting for Ramadan but who graciously is volunteering to help at a dental clinic at a refugee camp today. Exciting day for the refugees as dental care is in big demand.

"Nawfal[31] was previously in a town in Iraq where ISIS was and heard the drone strikes that killed an ISIS leader. He is now in Soran.

"After picking Nawfal up, Tim warned us that the stories of what the families at the refugee camp today have gone through are very harrowing. I didn't know what that was going to sound like.

"Tim prayed as he drove us and Nawfal the Muslim dentist along the dry dusty desert road in Iraq to the refugee camp. Christians and a Muslim going to help refugees together. I love that.

"It turned out the refugee camp is for Yazidis who fled ISIS from a village near Mosul, Iraq (Mosul is 50 miles west of Erbil). 15 of their girls/women were taken by ISIS. I found myself inside a UN tent at the camp and in walked a man who is living at the camp. My friend told me that two of the girls who were taken were his daughters. One of his daughters was taken by ISIS to Falluja, Iraq and one to Raqqa, Syria, where ISIS has its headquarters. Suddenly headlines and articles I have been reading for months about the horrific persecution of the Yazidi people by ISIS became personal. I was sitting in a UN tent in a refugee camp consisting of persecuted Yazidis who fled for their lives. Thousands of the Yazidis were slaughtered by ISIS in an attempt to exterminate them as a people group/tribe. The Yazidis are an unusual mix of Zoroastrianism, Christianity and Islam, and stay to themselves. They don't particularly get along well with anyone, including the Arabs and Kurds. And here was a Muslim dentist going with Christians to serve them. Nawfal is a great guy.

"So I sat there in shock that I was looking at a man who had two daughters (in their early 20's) kidnapped by a terrorist group. Thanks be to God that the father recently found out that his daughters were released by ISIS and are now apparently in a refugee camp in Dohuk, Iraq about two hours [west] of here. They are hopefully receiving counseling for what they

---

[31] Name changed for privacy reasons. *Nawfal* is an Arabic name and means "generous."

have been through. This was wonderful news but bitter sweet for these 15 Yazidi families as 13 of their women are still being held hostage by ISIS. Once again like yesterday, it's hard to imagine how someone can endure this much suffering.

"When the Yazidis fled ISIS about four months after I was in Iraq [in March 2014], some of their families made it to Soran. What a gift today was to spend time with them. The children are so cute. We taught them some English by teaching them the 'head, shoulders, knees and toes' song, they liked that and were giggling. They served us hot tea and cold water, which was very kind of them.

"The camp they live at was built recently next to a large abandoned futbol stadium that was built by Saddam Hussein. The stadium is very run down and now has cows and donkeys on the field chewing on the weeds.

"The children have no access to school right now. The 15 year old boy I spent much of the morning with is learning English on an App on a phone he got. He's a sharp kid with aspirations of being a doctor. I sit there looking at him wondering what his life could be like if he was just given the resources to go to school and university. His future is not bright right now and he was so interested to hear about America and enjoyed introducing me to his family around camp. He's been through a lot for a 15 year old. I can't imagine as a parent telling a child that some of his relatives have been kidnapped and we must flee immediately or we will be killed. Maybe he asks where are we going. Somewhere...I guess that would be the answer. What must go through a child's mind as a family flees for their lives."

Upon returning to the United States, an opportunity presented itself for some of us to pay for a Kurdish man to go to all three of the refugee camps and teach English to the children twice a week. He is a gifted English teacher who teaches at a private college in a town in Iraq. With school closed for the summer, it was such a blessing that he would be able to teach the kids until school opens in September! The 15-year old boy's family was so excited that he will now be getting English lessons. Praise God!

מֵרֵעַ

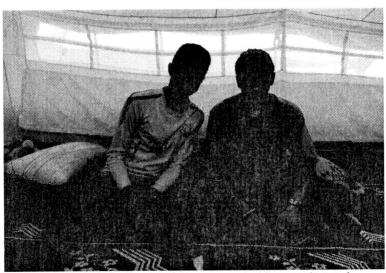

My new Yazidi Muslim friend; a teenager with a passion to learn English (Northern Iraq) (June 2015)

Yazidi refugee children; cherished by God
(Northern Iraq) (June 2015)

Tim teaching the refugee children a song (Northern Iraq) (June 2015)

9   Would I Hang Out With Jesus?

> He was despised and rejected—a man of sorrows, acquainted with deepest grief. *We turned our backs on him* and looked the other way. He was despised, and *we did not care*. (Isaiah 53:3)

CONCEIVED OUT OF wedlock. Born in a *stable*. The former *refugee*.[32] Raised in the dusty rural town of Nazareth. Did people whisper behind His back about Him? Would I have been *friends* with Him? We are associated with the people we associate with. Would I want to be associated with Him? What if it could cost me my job or many of my friends? Would I be comfortable sitting next to Jesus in church or going to a restaurant with Him? How about working alongside Him?

Jesus was *despised, rejected, ridiculed and laughed at*:

> They said, "Isn't this Jesus, the son of Joseph? We know his father and mother. How can he say, 'I came down from heaven'?" (John 6:42)

> "Nazareth!" exclaimed Nathanael. "Can *anything* good come from Nazareth?" (John 1:46a NIV)

> Then they began to *spit* in Jesus' face and beat him with their fists. And some slapped him. (Matthew 26:67)

> In the same way the chief priests, the teachers of the law and the elders *mocked* him. "He saved others," they said, "but he can't save himself! He's the king of Israel! Let him come down now from the cross, and we will believe in him." (Matthew 27:41-42 NIV)

> While he [Jesus] was still speaking to her [a woman who had just been healed by touching the garment of Jesus], a messenger arrived from the home of Jairus, the leader of the synagogue. He told him, "Your daughter

---

[32] As soon as Joseph, Mary and the infant Jesus crossed the border into Egypt (Matthew 2:13-14), they became refugees. My Lord and Savior was a *refugee*. Take a minute to let that sink in if you have not thought about that before: *Jesus was a refugee*.

is dead. There's no use troubling the Teacher now."...When they arrived at the house, Jesus wouldn't let anyone go in with him except Peter, John, James, and the little girl's father and mother. The house was filled with people weeping and wailing, but he [Jesus] said, "Stop the weeping! She isn't dead; she's only asleep." But the *crowd laughed at him* because they all knew she had died. (Luke 8:49, 51-53)

Some people loved Him. But many more *hated* Him, so much so that they eventually humiliated, tortured and executed Him.

Would I hang out with Him if He was here walking around today? I'd like to say yes but there's that part of me that says no...that shudders...that *distances* from Him. A man acquainted with many sorrows. A man despised. A man rejected. A man laughed at by crowds. *My friend...*Jesus?

Syrian refugee children (Northern Iraq) (June 2015)

Would I Hang Out With Jesus?

Yazidi refugee father with his child
(Northern Iraq) (June 2015)

Story: Visit to a New Refugee Camp: Shia Muslims

Even my close friend, someone I trusted, one who shared my bread, has *turned against me*. (Psalm 41:9 NIV)

*B*ETRAYAL IS *PAINFUL*. Betrayal is a terribly sad thing. To spend time with people who have been betrayed by neighbors…by friends…helps us better understand what it was like for Jesus to be betrayed by His neighbors…and His friends.

JOURNAL ENTRY, IRAQ, JUNE 22, 2015:

"We went to two refugee camps today. The first has about 16 families who are Shia Muslims (the majority of Muslims in Iraq; ISIS is Sunni; Saddam Hussein was Sunni; Sunni is the minority of Muslims in Iraq but the majority of Muslims worldwide). Their leader/elder is Abu Raajii.[33] We visited with him and I learned that these families were living in [a town]

---

[33] Name changed for privacy reasons. *Raajii* is an Arabic name and means "have hope."

near Mosul where ISIS took over. Sunni 'friends' warned them that ISIS was coming to their town in an hour, so they fled to Soran (where I am staying) with what they could quickly grab...so not much. Turned out their Sunni neighbors asked ISIS to come to drive the Shia neighbors out, so they were betrayed. Their homes have since been booby trapped by ISIS and they will probably never return.

"They first moved on to the Refuge property here that is a community center and lived in UN tents, and now they have moved to permanent housing where each family gets two small cement block rooms. We met with him and then looked at his home at the camp and met a 4 year old girl who lives there, she was so cute. He was so proud to show me his family's room.

"I was so inspired by what this man has had to lead these families through during the past year. It is brutally hot here right now in this dry desert region, will be up to 113 next week and can get as high as 120. It was an honor to spend time with him and meet the little refugee girl. It is so hard to imagine what it must be like to be betrayed, lose your home and just about everything else, live in a tent through winter and now cinder block rooms in the dry dusty summer desert days, knowing life as you knew it is over.

"The few Christians who are here are serving these Muslim families and it's awesome to serve alongside them for a few days. One of the American/Australian (she's American, he's Australian) Christian families lives here (I'm staying with them) and they have children ages 1, 2 and 4 who are adorable. Life here is challenging for everyone. There are power shortages [and] electric access is reduced at certain times of the day like it is right now, so no A/C can be on until midnight. There is also a fuel shortage due to political squabbles, so the one gas station that has fuel had a massively long line today. We managed to get there early and get some gas. Some people wait for hours to find out they've run out [of gas]. No ambulances here and no car insurance. Roads have so many holes you'd think they were bombed regularly.

"Please pray for this family I'm staying with...God is impacting many people's lives through them...as well as for the refugees, and for the terrorists to turn from their ways of terror. Thanks y'all"

Would I Hang Out With Jesus?

صــــديقي

My new Shia Muslim friend; He's the leader of the Shia tribe that had to flee their homes because of ISIS (Northern Iraq) (June 2015)

ENCOUNTERING JESUS

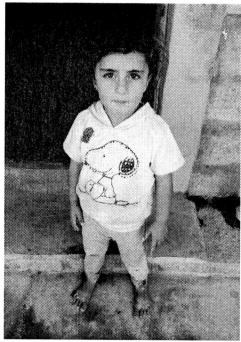

Shia Muslim refugee girl
(Northern Iraq) (June 2015)

Story: The Ski Resort Overlooking the Refugee Camps

But when you give a banquet, *invite* the poor, the crippled, the lame, the blind. (Luke 14:13 NIV)

*T*O BE LOOKED down upon is painful. To be considered less important...like trash...is a terribly sad thing. To spend time with people who have been looked down upon...forgotten...helps us better understand what it was like for Jesus to be looked down upon...to be forgotten...by His neighbors...and by His friends.

JOURNAL ENTRY, IRAQ, JUNE 23, 2015:

"Talk about two extremes and a sad contrast in a land of war, terror, kidnappings, poverty, refugees, as well as fuel and electric and water shortages: a multi-million dollar state of the art ski resort (yes, a ski resort in Iraq) paid for by the Kurdish leader Barzani. His family has ruled this Kurdish area for decades and benefitted greatly from the substantial oil money.

"The resort was built in 2011 and comes complete with a gondola, large villas, a massive and extravagant lodge, and lots of other things like zip lines and playgrounds. The mountains here are breathtakingly beautiful and it does snow for usually a few months a year high up in these mountains.

"What was so sad is that you could see from the resort in the valley down below the Yazidi refugee camp and the Shia Muslim refugee camp lead by Abu Raajii. And also making it a sad experience was the fact that we were the only people at the resort today, except for the numerous employees it takes to run a place this big and I believe the manager's wife and daughter. It's as if you were visiting Disney World, but you were the only visitors there…a strange feeling. If you transplanted me to that resort after telling me to close my eyes, and then had me open them, I would have guessed we were in a ski resort in the mountains of Utah or Colorado. It was an amazingly beautiful and sad place. Relatively very few people go there anymore. They used to come from Baghdad and Mosul. Saddam Hussein had a massive villa on the mountainside that we could see that had now been taken over by President Barzani.

"There is an observatory up on the mountain that was damaged by missiles back during the 2003 war in Iraq.

"A beautiful and equally depressing place. I felt so bad for the new management who have been brought in to increase business. We talked with them during our visit. I felt so bad for them as they explained how they planned to try to get the regional Kurdish people to visit the resort. Needless to say, they were glad to have some visitors. It was an extreme example of the mis-allocation of resources to the loss of people in desperate need who could be seen down in the valley below.

"They had a paintball room and the ad for it on the wall of the resort looked like a scene from the war in Falluja, Iraq (see pic below). It was a sad exclamation mark on the experience to see that as we left. So few in the world have so much and so many in the world have so little. I don't know if I've ever seen such a striking example of that before."

מֵרֵעַ

The ski resort overlooking the refugee camps down below (Northern Iraq) (June 2015)

Tim and I with new friends at the ski resort (Northern Iraq) (June 2015)

10 Playing Tag With Jesus

Every year *Jesus' parents* went to Jerusalem for the Passover festival. When Jesus was twelve years old, they attended the festival as usual. Then he returned to Nazareth with them and was obedient to them. And his mother *stored all these things in her heart*. Jesus grew in wisdom and in stature and in favor with God and all the people. (Luke 2:41-42, 51-52)

*J*ESUS...THE *HUMAN* Jesus...had *parents*. And I have parents. And I know how much fun it is to be loved by our parents. My parents are very loving and I have enjoyed being very loving to our children. Children are a joy. I can picture Jesus's mother *storing the memories* of her son in her heart...precious gems of memories.

My new Arab Palestinian Christian friend in Nazareth who graciously interpreted the Arabic service into English for me as we sat together during the service (Nazareth, Israel) (March 2014)

Story: Playing Tag with Our Son

Children are a *gift* from the LORD; they are a *reward* from him. (Psalm 127:3)

ONE OF OUR son's favorite games is to play tag with me. He laughs and giggles as I chase him around the yard or in the swimming pool. Sometimes I catch him and tickle him and he laughs even more. I wonder if Jesus and His dad Joseph played tag. I think they did…and I think they laughed and giggled too.

It's an awesome *privilege* to be a parent…to be a father. What a joy it is to laugh and hug your child. To enjoy a *friendship* with them. To love them and be willing to do anything for them, including *die* for them. And God loves us *more* than that…*way more* than we can even begin to imagine. So much so that He came to dwell among us through His Son Jesus…to become a human and live among us…to reach out to us…and to die for us. We miss out on a *special* part of Jesus when we miss out on a *friendship* with Him. Imagine that…Jesus…"Immanuel…*God with us*" (Matthew 1:23 NIV).

Refugee children in class at a camp (Northern Iraq) (March 2014)

Playing Tag With Jesus

Our son and I have enjoyed many wonderful times together like visiting this mountain lake at 10,000 feet elevation...I wish every child could visit such a beautiful, peaceful place (America) (2015)

Story: Game with the Little Refugee Girls

See that you do not despise one of these *little ones*. (Matthew 18:10a NIV)

ONE OF MY favorite memories from the trip to Lebanon was visiting with a Syrian Muslim refugee family in Southern Lebanon near the Israeli border. An area where two wars have been fought in the last 15 years. They lived in a cinder-block "house"...it was just two small cinder-block rooms next to each other. That's all it was. Imagine building two little rooms out of cinder-blocks. That's it...that's their *home*.

One room was for sleeping and cooking, and one room was for visiting with friends...the social room. I visited there with five new Lebanese friends I had made along the journey that started when I landed in Beirut. Three of them were Pastors, one was a Pastor's wife, and one was the teenage son of one of the Pastors. We all sat in chairs along the wall as the refugee father and mother hosted us. They of course made us tea in the way of the gracious hospitality that is the Middle East. It was *delicious*.

While the parents visited with the other adult visitors, I took interest in the two little girls...refugee girls...who had joined us and were sitting in a single chair in the corner of the room across from me. They were holding a little baby...a refugee baby...a real baby, not a doll. And the two girls were just *adorable*. I love visiting families in the Middle East. Children often poke their heads in the room excited to see this stranger who has travelled there from some far off land...a land across an ocean. They don't get a lot of visitors from America so it's a special treat for them to see me sitting there in their home.

Like I do with young children, I could not help smiling at them and would do a little wave to them of my hand. They smiled back. I sat there continuing to do that as the other adults talked. And then God *prompted me* to go over to the girls, so I did. I slowly walked over and knelt down on one knee in front of them. They were excited at the approach of this nice man from a distant land. They did not speak English, so we couldn't chat much. So God graciously prompted me to play a game with them that requires no words. I held out my hands towards them, indicating that they should do the same. They hesitated, eyes glistening at the excitement of this unexpected gift. I crossed my hands over and then grasped them together, and turned them in towards me. It's a fun game that my dad taught us when we were young. The idea is that then, while your hands and fingers are all clasped and interlocked together, another person points at one of your fingers without touching it and you have to wiggle just that finger. It's a fun game and is challenging and results in a lot of laughs and giggles as the person pointing to the finger enjoys watching the other person try to wiggle that one finger. Everyone has fun with that game and I enjoy playing it with our children.

The girls got the idea and the younger of the two joined in with me while the older girl held their little baby brother. She began to point at my fingers and I was able to wiggle the right one some of the times and some of the times I wiggled the wrong one. They both giggled. It was a fun and very unexpected moment in life. Time stood still, all wars and pain were forgotten, as we sat there *giggling together*.

I learned later that day about that family's story. That refugee family...those precious little girls...had fled ISIS in Syria. ISIS was on the way to their town so they had to flee...*quickly*. Their parents and they headed towards Lebanon. There is a mountain range that runs along the Lebanese/Syrian border. Not a hill. A *mountain*. As in thousands-of-feet-up-kind-of-mountain. As in the mountain range where battles are fought between the Lebanese military and Hezbollah against ISIS and other Sunni-rebel groups. So it's not just a mountain...it's a *war-torn mountain...a battlefield*.

As I remembered the precious, smiling faces of those beautiful little girls, I listened on about how their family crossed that mountain at *nighttime* to escape. What do you say to your children as you flee in the night across a war-torn mountain...desperately trying to save them from the war...from militants that want to enslave or kill them...or worse. I imagine you reassure them that

Playing Tag With Jesus

everything will be okay...that they just have to go on a little farther...that they're going to make it. And you desperately fight to hold back your own tears...you desperately try to hide the fact that you are *terrified* and that you are *walking on the brink of death*...as you guide your children through the night *fleeing a war*.

Thank God that they made it. And thank God that the Pastor and his wife there in that little town in war-torn Southern Lebanon are caring for their family. They are including the girls in the Sunday school classes at the local church. Loving them and encouraging them. I miss those little girls and think about them often. I'm glad they got to meet a stranger who smiled and played with them and giggled with them.

מֵרֵעַ

The two little refugee girls in Southern Lebanon (June 2015)

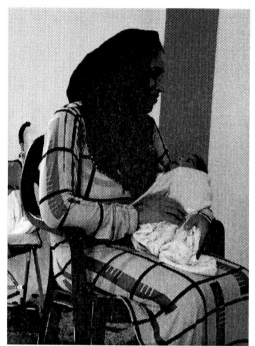

Syrian refugee mother with her baby
(Southern Lebanon) (June 2015)

11   Hammering Nails With Jesus

> Then they scoffed, "He's *just a carpenter*, the son of Mary and the brother of James, Joseph, Judas, and Simon. And his sisters live right here among us." They were *deeply offended* and *refused* to believe in him. (Mark 6:3)

*J*ESUS WAS SO human that *His own brothers* didn't believe at first that He was the Son of God:

> But soon it was time for the Jewish Festival of Shelters, and Jesus' brothers said to him, "Leave here and go to Judea, where your followers can see your miracles! You can't become famous if you hide like this! If you can do such wonderful things, show yourself to the world!" For even *his brothers didn't believe in him*. (John 7:2-5)

Imagine being Jesus's brother and hearing people in their hometown of Nazareth *despising* Jesus…*scoffing* about Him: "He's just a carpenter's son…how dare he try to teach us as if he's some religious expert!":

> Then they *scoffed*, "He's just the *carpenter's* son, and we know Mary, his mother, and his brothers—James, Joseph, Simon, and Judas. All his sisters live right here among us. Where did he learn all these things?" And they were *deeply offended* and *refused to believe in him*. (Matthew 13:55-57)

I can hear those painful words right now as I sit here typing…"He's just a kid that grew up here like we did…how *dare* he act like some religious expert…how *dare* he tell us that he was sent here by God…he's *just* the son of the local guy who builds things out of wood!"[34]

But later, Jesus's brother James did believe that Jesus was who He said He was. In fact, James ended up believing *deeply* in that. In fact, God wrote the book of James through Jesus's brother, James. How powerful that James became such a believer in the deity of his brother Jesus that he starts off the book of James declaring himself not a brother but a *servant*…and not just of Jesus, but of the *Lord* Jesus Christ. James does not even *tout* that he was Jesus's *brother*.

---

[34] The Greek word translated to carpenter is *tekton*, which connotes a craftsman in wood.

James, a *servant* of God and of the *Lord* Jesus Christ, To the twelve tribes scattered among the nations: Greetings. (James 1:1 NIV)

But step back in time before James believed. Back before Jesus taught in the synagogues. Back before Jesus was scorned…despised…hated for what He said. What was His life like growing up in that small, dusty town…growing up in His dad's carpentry shop…growing up eating meals prepared by His mom…knowing that He was *born to die* and many would hate Him…even to the point of *crucifying* Him?

Imagine living your entire life *knowing* many of your friends would *betray* you and you were going to be *brutally tortured* after having done nothing wrong:

But some of you do not believe me. (For Jesus *knew from the beginning* which ones didn't believe, and he knew who would betray him.) Then he said, "That is why I said that people can't come to me unless the Father gives them to me. At this point many of his disciples *turned away and deserted him*. (John 6:64-66)

Why didn't you arrest me in the Temple? I was there among you teaching every day. But these things are happening to fulfill what the Scriptures say about me. Then *all* his disciples *deserted him and ran away*. (Mark 14:49-50)[35]

I wonder if Jesus ever thought about that in His dad's carpentry workshop as He hammered nails into a piece of furniture. I wonder if He ever *winced* as He swung the hammer and the nail went *deeper into the wood*. If He did, did anyone see Him and ask Him if He was okay?

---

[35] Paul also experienced the same abandonment by his friends. I love that Paul asked God to please not hold that against his friends: "The first time I was brought before the judge, no one came with me. *Everyone abandoned me*. May it not be counted against them" (2 Timothy 4:16).

Hammering Nails With Jesus

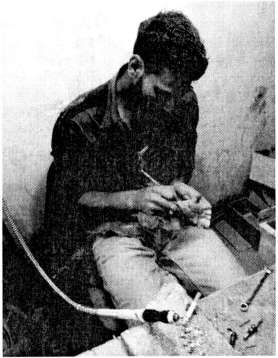

A wood-carver in the West Bank (Bethlehem, Israel) (May 2012)

Story: Visiting Jesus's Childhood Town

"Nazareth!" exclaimed Nathanael. "Can *anything good* come from Nazareth?" "Come and see for yourself," Philip replied. (John 1:46)

Y OU CAN LEARN a lot about a person by visiting the town where they grew up as a child. Jesus grew up in an unassuming, run-of-the-mill kind of town. And it was wonderful to visit that town...Nazareth.

Journal Entry, Israel, May 15, 2012:

"We then drove to the Mount of Precipice (also known as the leaping mountain) overlooking Nazareth. At the base of it in a cave have been found Neolithic remains dating back to 10,000 B.C. We hiked up to the top and the panoramic view was amazing! It overlooks Nazareth, Mount Tabor (also known as the Mount of the Transfiguration) and the Jezreel Valley with Samaria off in the distance. Jesus would have gone to this overlook to pray, play and get some solitude both as a boy and a man. This is also the peak where the town members brought Jesus to throw him off of it for declaring in the synagogue after reading from the Scroll of Isaiah that the reading about the Spirit of the Lord had been fulfilled in their hearing. Jesus got away from the crowd on top of this peak, and there we were standing on it overlooking Nazareth. Another wow moment...there have been a lot of those on this trip.

"We then drove over to the Church of the Annunciation in Nazareth. Wow, is it a beautiful church. It is very large and built over the cave in which Mary, Joseph and Jesus lived, in which an altar had been built. There are many inscriptions on the walls of the cave/grotto mentioning Mary. I visited with a nun from Italy who appeared to be sitting watch over the cave. After viewing the cave/house, we walked upstairs and the doorway opened into an enormous church built in 1969 with a large opening in the floor in front of the altar that looks down to the cave below. There was a very large mosaic painting a couple of stories tall behind the altar. This latest church was built on the ruins of four previous churches dating back to the fifth century, although worship has been held at this location dating back to the first century. Nearby is the Church of St. Joseph, which tradition holds is the location of Joseph's carpentry shop."

Hammering Nails With Jesus

Amazing time with my parents following in the footsteps of Jesus (Mount Precipice) (Nazareth, Israel) (May 2012)

Story: Standing where Jesus was Nailed to the Cross

When they came to a place called The Skull, they *nailed him* to the cross. And the criminals were also crucified—one on his right and one on his left. (Luke 23:33)

*M*Y FRIEND JESUS was *nailed* to a cross. He was *humiliated* in front of family, friends, strangers and enemies. And He did all of this *for me...for you...*so we wouldn't have to suffer the punishment that *we deserve*. To have a friend do that for me, and then to stand next to where it was done...where Jesus bled on the cross...was a powerful experience...a very *personal* one with my friend Jesus.

Journal Entry, Israel, May 20, 2012:

"11th station: Jesus is nailed to the Cross. The book we were using [as we walked the Via Dolorosa through Jerusalem] had a powerful statement in it: 'Nails did not hold Him to the Cross, love did.' Walking up the steps and into the section of the church that was built over the rocks on which they believe Jesus was crucified is hard to describe. Glass encases the stones/cliff edge and the sections of the rock where Jesus was believed to be crucified as well as the criminals on each side of Him are all here. A special altar is built over the spot where Jesus' Cross was believed to have been inserted in the rock, and you can kneel down and touch the opening in the floor where the base of the Cross may have been. The Greek Orthodox are in charge of this section of the Holy Sepulchre, so it is ordained in intricate detail and ornamentation with beautiful paintings and burning candles. I lit a candle for [my wife] and the kids and left it burning in this holy place. I then knelt and prayed in a corner of the room in eyesight of the place [where] Jesus was crucified. I had a vision of Jesus walking along a dirt path with me and Him saying, 'walk with me'…'you have been walking with me this week'…'come sit at my feet'…The words that came to me at that moment were that, 'I want to know Christ and Christ crucified and the power of His resurrection.' I prayed, *'Lord, help me stop focusing on myself.'*"

Hammering Nails With Jesus

Rock on which it is believed that Jesus was crucified
(Jerusalem, Israel) (May 2012)

Story: Building a Pinewood Derby Car with Our Son

Isn't this the *carpenter's* son? (Matthew 13:55a)

ONE OF THE blessings of being someone's child and also being a parent is being able to better relate to the love not only that God has for me and for Jesus, but also to the human-level love that Joseph and Mary had for their human son Jesus. That helps me have a more personal relationship with Jesus as I picture Him…my friend…spending time with his dad in his dad's shop building things out of wood.

Our son and I spent five years together in Cub Scouts before he moved on to Boy Scouts.[36] In Cub Scouts, one of the fun projects you get to do with your son is build a little model pinewood derby car that you can race down a track against the cars built by other Cub Scouts. The cars are small…about the size of your two open hands. They are very fun to design and build.

I'm not a carpenter and I don't have a wood-working shop. There is a local carpenter…in fact, his dad was also a carpenter…who has been very gracious to

---

[36] www.scouting.org

open up his carpentry shop to the local Cub Scouts so they can build their cars. It's a fun place to visit...lots of tools, wood and piles of sawdust. It's a place where things are *created*. Where blocks of wood turn into a beautiful chair...or even a little pinewood derby car.

There is a special electric saw that is used in that man's shop to carefully cut the shape of the car out of the wood block that the boys are given. The carpenter stands behind the Cub Scout and the Cub Scout places his hands on the carpenter's hands as the carpenter gently and expertly guides the saw blade through the wood. I can picture Joseph doing the same things for his son Jesus...*guiding his hands* as he taught his son how to safely cut wood. How to safely *drive nails* into wood without drawing any blood.

Depiction of the last supper with Christ (carved in olive wood)
(Israel) (May 2012)

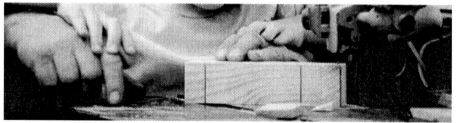

Two pairs of hands cutting the pinewood derby car in the carpenter's shop
(America) (January 2013)

12 Jesus My Brother?

> Then Jesus' mother and brothers arrived. Standing outside, they sent someone in to call him. A crowd was sitting around him, and they told him, "Your mother and brothers are outside looking for you." "Who are my mother and my brothers?" he asked. Then he looked at those seated in a circle around him and said, "Here are my mother and my brothers! Whoever does God's will is my *brother* and *sister* and *mother*." (Mark 3:31-35)

I HAVE A brother and he's a great guy. It was a lot of fun growing up with him. I live in a different state now and miss him. Brotherly love…I've got a lot of that for him.

Have you ever considered *Jesus* as *your brother?* Jesus had *physical* brothers here on this planet. Their names were James, Joseph, Judas, and Simon (Mark 6:3). But He also has *spiritual* brothers:

> For whoever does the will of my Father in heaven is my *brother* and *sister* and mother. (Matthew 12:50)

> Therefore, it was necessary for him to be made in every respect like us, *his brothers and sisters*, so that he could be our merciful and faithful High Priest before God. Then he could offer a sacrifice that would take away the sins of the people. (Hebrews 2:17)

When we receive Jesus into our heart, we are *adopted* by God into God's *family*:

> So you have not received a spirit that makes you fearful slaves. Instead, you received God's Spirit when he *adopted you* as *his own children*. Now we call him, "*Abba, Father.*" (Romans 8:15)

Once you receive Jesus as your Lord and your Savior, you become a *child of God*. And a brother of Jesus:

ENCOUNTERING JESUS

See how very much our Father loves us, for he calls us his children, and that is what we are! But the people who belong to this world don't recognize that we are *God's children* because they don't know him. (1 John 3:1)

And because *we are his children*, God has sent the Spirit of his Son into our hearts, prompting us to call out, *"Abba, Father."* (Galatians 4:6)

And how amazing that Jesus…the Savior of the world…refers to God as "Abba, Father," or "Daddy, Father," and we can now do the same as well:

"Abba, Father," he cried out, "everything is possible for you. Please take this cup of suffering away from me. Yet I want your will to be done, not mine." (Mark 14:36)

And we become brothers and sisters with other members of God's family. We become part of a *big* family! Jesus *my brother*. That's a *personal* way of relating to Him.

My new Taiwanese Christian friend and brother (face blurred for privacy reasons) (Jericho, West Bank) (April 2013)

Jesus My Brother?

Story: My Brother Who Lives in the West Bank

> If one member suffers, *all* suffer *together*. (1 Corinthians 12:26a ESV)

*I*N 2013, I returned to the Middle East to serve the refugees in Camp Aqabat Jabr in Jericho. God led me to a ministry in Jerusalem that had some people serving in Jerusalem, and they were gracious enough to let me join them for eight days.

I arrived in Jerusalem and spent the first night there at their communal-style house near the Damascus Gate of the Old City of Jerusalem. It was not far from the hotel that the tour group had stayed in the year before, when I first visited Israel. However, this time I found myself sleeping on a top bunk bed over a former Russian soldier who had met Jesus and was now serving Him in Jerusalem. He sure was an interesting guy. He was married to a kind woman and they had adopted two precious girls.

After a couple of days, I headed to the West Bank as Jericho is located there. A woman drove us as far as a gas station in the desert that was on the highway from Jerusalem at the intersection of the road that you turn onto to drive to Jericho. I remember being surprised that not only were there some gas pumps there, but there was also a *camel!* That was as far as the woman was comfortable driving as it was too risky for her to drive into Jericho for reasons I did not fully understand...I think it was because there were Israeli license plates on the car. A taxi drove up out of the desert from the direction of Jericho, picked us up, and then headed back through the desert to Jericho.

Later that day, I met the man I was going to spend my time with in Jericho serving the refugees. His name was Nadir.[37] I learned that he was formerly a Muslim and now followed Jesus and it had *cost him a lot* to follow Jesus, including some time in prison for leaving Islam...as in *years* of time in prison. He had also been a chef, having been trained in Baghdad. Following Jesus cost him his livelihood too. He has a great smile and loves to laugh. I liked him immediately and wow does he *love* Jesus. Our *brother* Jesus.

I so enjoyed my time with Nadir that week spending time visiting with refugees and providing them with food as well as diapers and milk for their babies. You learn a lot about someone when you spend a week with them in a small desert town like Jericho. We not only served refugees, but also took some time one day to visit the nearby Dead Sea. He had never visited the Dead Sea as

---

[37] Name changed for privacy reasons. *Nadir* is an Arabic name and means "dear."

a tourist. We wiped Dead Sea mud all over ourselves and I about passed out from the desert heat wave that day! We laughed a lot that week and we cried too. He's afraid of heights and I convinced him to ride the cable car up the mountain to a monastery that is carved into the mountain…the same mountain called the Mount of Temptation where it is believed that Jesus was tempted by the Devil. We had so much fun that day as he conquered his fear of heights and saw the beautiful, breathtaking view from way up there over Jericho and into the desert towards Jordan…a view he had never seen before. And, being a trained chef, we ate some delicious food together that he prepared for us. And we of course drank some great Middle Eastern tea and coffee together. It was a *wonderful* week.

I was so thankful to get to know Nadir as a brother in God's family. My *brother* who lives in the West Bank. I miss Nadir very much. Please say a prayer for him as it has cost him dearly to follow Jesus. He sure loves Jesus a lot. And I know Jesus loves him even more.

מֵרֵעַ

My new Palestinian Christian friend and *brother* Nadir (Dead Sea, West Bank, Israel) (April 2013)

13   Jesus the Miracle Man

> As Jesus was walking along, he saw a man who had been *blind from birth*...Then he spit on the ground, made mud with saliva, and spread the mud over the blind man's eyes. He told him, "Go wash yourself in the pool of Siloam" (Siloam means "sent"). So the man went and washed and came back *seeing*! (John 9:1, 6-7)

A FRIENDSHIP WITH the Son of God. With the person who has all authority in Heaven and on Earth. *All* of it. A friendship with a person who makes blind eyes see...deaf ears hear...lame legs walk...leprosy skin clean...and dead people alive (Matthew 11:5). And Jesus sends *us* with His *full authority* (Matthew 28:18-20). So why then are we *worried*? Why aren't we *trusting Him*?

Think about that for a minute. Do you *really* believe that God can make *blind eyes see*? Deaf ears hear? Lame legs walk? Leprosy skin clean? *Dead people alive*? You may have read stories in the Bible over the years about Jesus doing such things. But do you *really believe* Jesus does those things? That Jesus can do those things *today*? Do you really believe? Or is there that part of you when you pray for someone...maybe someone with cancer or blindness...that doesn't think the person can be healed? That they are too far gone...too far down the road of cancer or blindness...to be healed? Do you include in your prayer of healing, "...if it's God's will..." Do you include some type of a hedge in your prayers...an "out"...in case the prayer is not answered...in case the healing does not occur? Do you really, confidently believe that Jesus can make blind eyes see? It's a *critical* question.

Jesus not only made blind eyes see, but he also made *seeing eyes blind*. We can read these stories about Jesus quickly...really just pass them by...without stopping and reflecting on...without believing...that Jesus actually did these things. He actually made seeing eyes blind. And we just pass them by and miss out on the opportunity to search in our own soul as to whether we truly believe that Jesus can make seeing eyes blind. In one instance, Jesus didn't just make one set of eyes stop seeing...he made an *entire crowd's eyes*...a mob's eyes...stop seeing Him:

When they heard this [teaching by Jesus], *the people in the synagogue* were furious. Jumping up, they mobbed him and forced him to the edge of the hill on which the town was built. They intended to push him over the cliff, but *he passed right through the crowd and went on his way.* (Luke 4:29-30)

Jesus can make an *entire crowd's eyes stop seeing.* Do you believe that? Have you allowed God to lead you to and through situations in your life where you have to trust God...where you have to *completely* rely on *Him?* One of the core challenges for many Christians in America is that they think they can rely on *themselves* for much of their life's needs...food, transportation, shelter, safety, healthcare...so we sadly miss out on getting to see Jesus make blind eyes see, make the lame walk...make seeing eyes *blind.* It's no wonder that the Church in areas of the world where it is persecuted...actually *thrives*...because it is having to rely *completely* on Jesus. They are getting to know Jesus at a much more *intimate* level as He makes deaf ears hear, the dead alive...and seeing eyes blind.

And in another situation, Jesus spent hours with two men...two of His followers...walking with them and talking with them...while He made their seeing eyes blind to the fact that the Son of God...the One they followed...was *right there walking and talking with them.* Shortly after Jesus was crucified, two men were walking back to Emmaus from Jerusalem, no doubt disappointed that Jesus had been crucified along with their hopes of a messiah who would save them from the bondage of the Romans. And Jesus joined them...but for a time made seeing eyes blind:

As they talked and discussed these things, Jesus himself suddenly came and began walking with them. *But God kept them from recognizing him.* (Luke 24:15-16)

They walked for miles and arrived at their home. They invited this nice man who had joined them for a meal...and much to their surprise their eyes that Jesus had made blind that day were allowed to see:

As they sat down to eat, he took the bread and blessed it. Then he broke it and gave it to them. Suddenly, *their eyes were opened,* and they recognized him. And at that moment he *disappeared!* (Luke 24:30-31)

Brother Andrew, the founder of *Open Doors*,[38] learned to trust Jesus and His awesome powers...His awesome authority...as Brother Andrew smuggled Bibles

---

[38] www.opendoors.org

into closed Communist countries...right by border guards and checkpoints...sometimes with *Bibles in plain sight*. Brother Andrew learned to pray before going through a security checkpoint that God would make *seeing eyes blind*:

> Just ahead was the Yugoslav border. For the first time in my life I was about to enter a Communist country on my own instead of in a group invited and sponsored by the government...Now here I was with car and luggage literally bulging with [Gospel] tracts, Bibles, and portions of Bibles. How was I to get them past the border guard? And so, for the first of many times, I said the Prayer of God's Smuggler: "Lord, in my luggage I have Scripture that I want to take to Your children across this border. When You were on earth, You made blind eyes see. Now, I pray, *make seeing eyes blind*. Do not let the guards see those things You do not want them to see." (*God's Smuggler*, pp.107-08)

In one of the many border crossings made by Brother Andrew, he during another trip approached the Rumanian border. Rumania was not only a communist country, but the government had severely cracked down on Christians and many suffered greatly. Christians were oftentimes arrested, had their property seized and were prohibited from sharing about Jesus. Rumanian Bibles were very difficult to find and were routinely confiscated by the government. And Rumania was filled with security checkpoints. So there was God's messenger...God's smuggler...approaching the Rumanian border driving a car that had been packed with hidden Rumanian Bibles. As Brother Andrew waited in the line of cars, he could see ahead that the border guards were *ruthlessly* questioning passengers and searching every part of the cars, even removing hub caps, *taking engines apart* and removing seats...desperately trying to find any contraband. Inspections were taking up to an hour *per car* as every nook and cranny of the vehicles was searched. It's hard to imagine the level of *anxiety* and *fear* that Brother Andrew faced sitting there in his car waiting for his turn...surrounded by Bibles that he had hid in it.

When there was finally only one car ahead of him in the line, he prayed for a miracle:

> "Dear Lord," I said, as there was just one car ahead of me, "What am I going to do? Any serious inspection will *show up* those Rumanian Bibles right away. "Lord," I went on, "I know no amount of cleverness on my part can get me through this border search. Dare I ask for a miracle? Let me take some of the Bibles out and *leave them in the open where they will be seen.*

Then, Lord, I cannot possibly be depending on my own stratagems, can I? I will be depending utterly upon You." (p.166)

After finishing his prayer, he took several Bibles out from where he had hid them and placed them on the passenger seat...*right there next to him*. And then it was his turn to drive his little VW car to the checkpoint next to the guard who inspected the passports. Brother Andrew, figuring that he would not only have to turn off the car but get out, tried to do that but the guard pushed his door closed with his knee and waved him on to enter Rumania...all occurring in *less than 30 seconds*. Shocked, Brother Andrew started the car and inched forward into Rumania seeing in his review mirror that the car behind him had not only been stopped, but the driver had been asked to get out of it and the hood had already been opened by one of the guards as they prepared to search the engine. Brother Andrew explains:

My heart was racing. Not with the excitement of the crossing, but with the excitement of having caught such a *spectacular glimpse of God at work*. (p.166)

Brother Andrew believed that Jesus could make seeing eyes blind. And *Jesus did*.

Corrie ten Boom and her sister Betsie experienced Jesus making seeing eyes blind at the Ravensbruck concentration camp in Germany during World War II. Prior to arriving at Ravensbruck, Corrie had been given a precious miniature copy of some of the books of the Bible...it was a gift that they *cherished* more than gold. It was oftentimes their *lifeline* in such a dark place. On the third night after arriving at Ravensbruck, they were ordered along with the other new arrivals to go through a degrading security check and shower. They had to strip naked and walk past the scrutiny of a dozen German guards into the shower room, and then put on a thin prison dress and shoes. All other items they had with them had to be surrendered to the prison guards. After dressing in the prison gown, they were then searched by more guards before going back to the prison barracks.

Corrie prayed her own "smuggler's prayer" before they entered the first security check: "Dear God...You have given us this precious Book, You have kept it hidden through checkpoints and inspections. You have used it [to help] so many..." (*The Hiding Place*, p.203). It was at that critical moment that Betsie staggered against her, trying not to faint. Betsie was in very ill health and dying. By God's gracious miracle, Betsie and Corrie to her surprise bypassed the first security check due to Betsie's condition. God had answered Corrie's prayer. Corrie explains in *The Hiding Place* that, after miraculously bypassing the first security checkpoint with the tiny Bible in hand, she and Betsie were "[r]ich in this new evidence of the care of Him who was God even of Ravensbruck" (p.204).

However, the second security check after the shower room when they would only have the prison dress on was yet to take place. Corrie described the bulge that the tiny Bible made as it hung around her neck under her prison gown and what she believed God expected her to do:

> It made a bulge you could have seen across [the marketplace back home]...there was no real concealing it beneath the thin cotton dress. And all the while I had the incredible feeling that it didn't matter, that this was not my business, but God's. That all I had to do was walk straight ahead." (p.205)

Corrie continued as she described the miracle that God was about to show her:

> As we trooped back out through the shower room door, the S.S. [guards] ran their hands over *every* prisoner, front, back, and sides. The woman ahead of me was searched three times. Behind me, Betsie was searched. *No hand touched me*...and so Betsie and I arrived in Barracks 8 in the small hours of that morning, bringing not only the Bible, but a new knowledge of the power of Him whose story it was. (p.205)[39]

And Brother Yun experienced Jesus making seeing eyes blind at a high-security prison where Brother Yun and other Christians were being held. Brother Yun was crippled from being beaten by the guards and held in solitary confinement. Yet, God told Brother Yun through a vision to *walk out of the prison...to just go...*so Brother Yun went. He describes how the Lord made the prison guard blind:

> Somehow the Lord seemed to blind that guard. He was staring directly at me, yet his eyes didn't acknowledge my presence at all. I expected him to say something, but he just looked through me as if I was invisible! (pp.256-57)

---

[39] Corrie describes in *Tramp for the Lord*, the sequel to *The Hiding Place*, how God miraculously got her and numerous copies of her book, *The Hiding Place*, into communist Cuba, where Christians had been put in prison for passing out Christian literature. See Chapter 28, pages 161-62, for more encouragement about how awesome is God.

ENCOUNTERING JESUS

One of the other Christians in that prison was Brother Xu who, along with other prisoners, witnessed Brother Yun miraculously escape. He describes in *The Heavenly Man*:

> This act of God's mercy and power [Brother Yun's miraculous escape] greatly encouraged us. We once again saw that nothing is impossible for God—*absolutely nothing*. He holds our lives in his hands...Within a few minutes of Yun's escape the guards discovered he was missing and a huge manhunt was launched. A thorough investigation was held by the authorities to find out how a crippled prisoner in a maximum-security solitary confinement could walk out of the prison and disappear! Interestingly, the investigation concluded that Yun had received no human help from any of the prisoners or guards during his escape. I testify that this is entirely true. It was all the sovereign hand of our Almighty God. (p.261)

And it's one thing to *read* about miracles or to *hear* about them. It's a whole other thing to *experience* them...to witness them...to *be part of them*...like Brother Andrew and so many others have. And that's just what God had planned for me as I prepared to return to the Middle East while carrying into Muslim countries six copies of the book *Vacation in Iraq* that was full of the Gospel, God's Word and stories about awesome things that *Jesus* was doing in the Middle East.

Jesus the Miracle Man

Israeli soldiers at road checkpoint in Israel (May 2012)

Story: Jesus Makes Seeing Eyes Blind

Now all glory to God, who is able, through his mighty power at work within us, to accomplish *infinitely more* than we might *ask* or *think*. (Ephesians 3:20)

*D*URING ALL OF the trips to the Middle East...through so many checkpoints and security checks...even while being detained at the Israeli border crossing...I don't recall ever praying for Jesus to make seeing eyes blind. Part of this...I would say the biggest part...for not praying this was that I *did not believe* Jesus could do that. Make the seeing eyes that are looking right at me and questioning me and searching my bags...*blind*? Really? Thank God that God is a gracious God. He allowed me to experience Him making seeing eyes blind at a security check in the Middle East. And it's a lesson...an experience...that I pray I will never forget because I learned something about Jesus that day...my friend Jesus who is always with me.

I've learned from travelling to the Middle East and within the Middle East that a man travelling by himself in that area of the world is a red flag...a security concern...and rightfully so given all of the suicide bombings and general level of distrust in that area. If I was in charge of a checkpoint and a man arrived with a lot of bags and was travelling by himself, I would be more concerned than if a married couple arrived with their four-year-old daughter or son. I've never run a security checkpoint, but it seems reasonable to me that a man travelling by himself raises red flags.

In fact, it can be such a flag that I was pulled aside and questioned by security at the airport in Tel Aviv as I was walking into the airport…I believe for that exact reason I was a man travelling by myself getting ready to walk into their airport. An airport that has no doubt received many bomb threats…a town that had missiles shot at it from the Gaza Strip not too long ago.

And I've also learned from travelling in the Middle East that oftentimes the first checkpoint you go through before entering a country in the Middle East is at the *departure* airport gate before you've even flown to that country. When I travelled "by myself"[40] to Israel in 2013 to return there to serve the people in refugee Camp Aqabat Jabr, not only was there a metal detector in the boarding area for the flight from America, but there was an Israeli soldier or police officer (he looked more like a soldier) standing by the door that led down the walkway to the airplane. There I was travelling by myself…and although many others passed him by…he stopped me and questioned me. I had not expected that level of security when we had not yet even left America…so I was nervous and caught off guard as he questioned me.

When I travelled "by myself" in 2014 as I crossed the land bridge from Jordan into Israel with Iraqi and Jordanian stamps in my passport, once again the red flags went off…a *bunch* of them. I was detained for over three hours and questioned into the evening by five different people while another five people searched my bags and tried to make sense of why I had a Bible, a Jewish prayer book, and a Quran in my backpack.[41] It was an *amazing opportunity* to see God's kindness and goodness show up in such a hostile situation, and is one of my favorite stories in *Vacation in Iraq*.[42]

So, there I was returning once again to the Middle East "by myself" in 2015. The flight from America first flew to Istanbul, Turkey. I had never been to Turkey. Turkey is somewhere between 96 to 99% Muslim depending on who

---

[40] Note to self: Jesus is *always* with us…and that's a *promise* (Matthew 28:20).
[41] God told me early on in my travels to the Middle East to carry a Bible, Jewish prayer book, and a Quran with me. That way, God explained, whoever is searching my bags will find a book that they can relate to. And, sure enough, that's what happened at the Israeli border crossing. They were *perplexed*. God's ways sure aren't our ways (Isaiah 55:8-9).
[42] Chapter 32, Story entitled, "Israeli border crossing: the 4th questioner."

you ask, and is predominantly a Sunni Muslim country.[43] Suffice it to say that Turkish security is not a good place to get caught carrying a Christian-based book about Jesus, praying for terrorists and sharing the Gospel with Muslims. *Vacation in Iraq* is over 400 pages long and has lots of pictures in it of me with Palestinian police, Muslims, refugees, former Muslims, and lots of other friends. Six copies of it weigh about 10 *pounds*. Needless to say, my backpack was large and heavy. I was also carrying a small backpack *and* an additional bag as I didn't want to check anything through to Iraq since I was travelling that 30-hour leg of the journey through five airports in three countries. Suffice it also to say that I was a walking, living, breathing Middle Eastern security *red flag*.

It was a Saturday evening and time to board the flight on Turkish Airlines to Istanbul. I had never flown to Istanbul so I didn't know how they handled security at the departure gate in America. At the gate, there were no security officers from the destination country like I experienced on the flight to Israel. I gave my boarding pass to the attendant and was thankful that no one pulled me aside or searched my bags. I breathed a sigh of relief and started to walk down the long walkway to the airplane. As I looked down the long walkway, I caught my breath as I saw that there were not one...not two...but *three* Turkish police officers questioning three passengers at that moment and looking through their travel papers. Each police officer was questioning someone. It was a *narrow* walkway, so everyone had to pass by them...*closely by them*. They would pull people out of the slowly-moving line after looking carefully at the people walking toward and then past them. It became a quiet line as I imagine most people tensed up about whether they would be pulled by security.

And there I stood waiting to walk past the officers, knowing deep in my heart that one of my biggest desires for that trip was to deliver copies of the *Vacation in Iraq* book to some of my friends in Iraq who are refugees at the camp there, especially to my closest refugee friend Lokman, whose family is pictured in the book and written about. I had found out the week before leaving for Iraq (by way of the flights through Turkey) that I was supposed to see my friends at the refugee camp the very next day...the day after flying through the Istanbul airport...which is a miracle as it's a UN camp and is not easy to just come and go from for security reasons. So there I stood with my big, heavy bags wanting so badly to deliver those books to my refugee friends...to hopefully encourage

---

[43] Most of the world's Muslims are Sunni Muslims. Saudi Arabia, for example, is another predominantly Sunni Muslim country. Iran, on the other hand, is predominantly a Shia Muslim country, as is Iraq.

them that people were reading about them and remembering them…that they were not forgotten.[44]

As I finally approached the three police officers, two of them were still questioning passengers they had pulled out of the line. The third officer had just finished with someone and so I figured I was next for him as I was getting ready to have to walk *straight towards him* in that narrow walkway that at that moment felt even more narrow. If I wanted to board the plane, I had to get past him and his eyes that were eagerly beginning to look for the next person to pull. It was at that moment that God whispered to me, "Look at the officer's eyes and walk straight towards him." I knew that *I knew* that it was God whispering to me. It made no sense to me to do what God had just asked, but I've learned on these trips to do what God whispers, regardless of how *crazy* it seems. I was about to find out why God wanted me to look directly at the security officer's *eyes*: God didn't want me to *miss His miracle*.

And the most amazing, unexpected, unexplainable thing happened. I looked at the officer *directly in his eyes* as I walked directly towards him…five feet away…four feet…three feet…two feet…and I *said hello to him*. And for the first time in my life I saw *eyes that were not seeing*. He was looking right through me like I was invisible. I almost waved my arms in front of his eyes because I could not believe what I was seeing…and what he was *not seeing…me*. He didn't say anything back to me…he didn't acknowledge me in any way whatsoever…I was invisible to him with my large backpack and two other bags. I was the invisible red flag. So I just kept walking and was never stopped. God had made *seeing eyes blind*. And that is an experience I don't ever want to forget. For the first time in my life, I believed…truly believed deep down to the depth of my soul…that God…that Jesus…not only can but did make seeing eyes blind. Right before my seeing eyes.

God was amazingly gracious to me…and to my friend Lokman…by allowing those books to get through security. Due to my unbelief, I had not even thought to pray for God to do something like that…to make *seeing eyes blind*. But, in His grace and mercy, He knew the desire of my heart and answered the prayer that I had not even thought to ask. He is an awesome Heavenly Father and Jesus is an amazingly faithful friend.

Some of the Scriptures that come to life for me through an experience like that…that grow me in my faith that God truly is the Living God and that Jesus truly is always with me…are:

---

[44] "Your love has given me much joy and comfort, my brother, for your kindness has often refreshed the hearts of God's people" (Philemon 1:7).

I the LORD *search the heart* and examine the mind, to reward each person according to their conduct, according to what their deeds deserve. (Jeremiah 17:10 NIV)

And when you pray, do not keep on babbling like pagans, for they think they will be heard because of their many words. Do not be like them, for *your Father knows what you need before you ask him.* (Matthew 6:7-8 NIV)

And be sure of this: I [Jesus] am *with you always*, even to the end of the age. (Matthew 28:20b)

But Jesus spoke to them at once. "*Don't be afraid*," he said. "Take courage. *I am here!*" (Matthew 14:27)

And they rose up and drove him out of the town and brought him to a brow of the hill on which their town was built, so that they could throw him down the cliff. But *passing through their midst*, he went away. (Luke 4:29-30 ESV)

صــديقي

Eyes not seeing…a sleeping cat in Israel (May 2012)

My dear friend Lokman; he got tears in his eyes when he saw the *Vacation in Iraq* book with his family's pictures in it (Northern Iraq) (June 2015)

14   Thank You Jesus For the Gifts!

> Whatever is *good and perfect* comes down to us from God our Father, who created all the lights in the heavens. (James 1:17a)

GOD IS NOT only a living God, but also a *giving God*. God gives *abundantly*. God gives when we don't deserve. God gives as only a good, perfect, loving *Father* can give. I love the story of the Prodigal Son in Luke 15:11-32. The father in the story represents God and the *wayward* youngest son represents…*us*…as does the older son who is *ungrateful* for what the father gives the youngest son. He *despises* how gracious and giving the father was to the youngest, rebellious son. I encourage you to read and re-read that story…please meditate on what God is showing you about Him in that story…it is a powerful reminder of how *crazy-gracious* God is to us…gracious in a way that we cannot possibly understand. And whether we're the child who runs away from God…who *squanders* all that God has given us…or we're the child who stays closer to God but is *ungrateful* for what God has given us and who *despises* what God is giving to people who "don't deserve it"…*God loves us all in a crazy-gracious-only-God-kind-of-way*. Every good and perfect gift we have is from Him…our Father.

God's greatest and most sacrificial, I-love-you-no-matter-what kind of gift, was *Jesus*. His only Son. A gift we cannot possibly comprehend…a gift that all we have to do to receive it is open our heart. A perfect gift.

As you focus on the gracious and loving character of God…of our Heavenly Father…I encourage you to focus on the gift of His *Fathership*…His *loving* and *perfect* and *intimate Fathership*. Our *Abba*. Our son's favorite band is the Swedish band from the 1980's called Abba. He plays their songs often and we enjoy singing them together. It's a fun time with him enjoying that music. For the band, the word "Abba" stands for the first initials of each of the band member's names.

"Abba" in the Bible is a Greek term of *tender endearment* for a father…it's the difference between calling someone a "father" and calling someone a *"daddy"* or *"papa."* There's a big difference between the two. *Very big*. "Father" can be a bit more distant and less personal…less intimate…than "daddy"…"papa." Anyone who is a dad has hopefully experienced the amazingly precious moments in life when you get home from work or a journey or an errand…and you walk in the door or are seen from a distance and you hear those amazing words..."daddy!" as your child runs to you with open arms and a smile as big as a sunset and eyes twinkling with sparkles of love. That is an *amazingly precious moment in life*. And there is God...our Heavenly Father...wanting to be our Abba...our *Daddy*...just like He was Jesus's Abba...*Jesus's Daddy*.

> And because *we are his children*, God has sent the *Spirit of his Son into our hearts*, prompting us to call out, *"Abba, father."* Now you are no longer a slave but *God's own child*. And since you *are his child*, God has made you *his heir*. (Galatians 4:6-7)

> He [Jesus] went on a little farther and fell to the ground. He prayed that, if it were possible, the awful hour awaiting him might pass him by. *"Abba, Father,"* he *cried out*, "everything is possible for you. Please take this cup of suffering from me. Yet I want your will to be done, not mine." (Mark 14:35-36)

> So you have not received a spirit that makes you fearful slaves. Instead, you received God's Spirit when *he adopted you as his own children*. Now we call him, *"Abba, Father."* For his Spirit joins with our spirit to affirm that *we are God's children*. And since we are his children, *we are his heirs*. (Romans 8:15-17a)

Wow. Amazing. Incomprehensible. What a *gift*. The gift of a good and perfect and loving Heavenly *Daddy*. Have you received that wonderful gift? If not, please ask Him for it...for Jesus...for your *Heavenly Daddy*...today...right now.[45] Then, as you pray the Lord's prayer,[46] I encourage you to pray, "Our *Daddy*, who is in Heaven..." That has made my relationship with God much more *personal*.

Another amazing gift that God gives us when we give our heart to Jesus, and which is part of receiving God as our Heavenly Daddy, is the gift of the Holy Spirit, a gift that *lives in us*. Wow, what a connection with our *friend* Jesus and our Heavenly Daddy! The Holy Spirit *dwells in us*. The Holy Spirit is described as a *helper* and a *counselor*.

> And I [Jesus] will ask the Father, and he will give you another Advocate, who will *never leave you*. He is the Holy Spirit, who *leads into all truth*. The

---

[45] "If you declare with your mouth, 'Jesus is Lord,' and believe in your heart that God raised him from the dead, you *will* be saved" (Romans 10:9 NIV); "And everyone who calls on the name of the Lord *will* be saved" (Romans 10:13 NIV, Joel 2:32a).
[46] Matthew 6:9-13.

world cannot receive him, because it isn't looking for him and doesn't recognize him. But you know him, because *he lives with you now and later will be in you* [once the day of Pentecost occurred for the disciples]. No, I will not abandon you as orphans—I will come to you...But when the Father sends the Advocate as my representative—that is, the Holy Spirit—*he will teach you everything* and *will remind you of everything I have told you*. (John 14:16-18, 26)

There is so much more I [Jesus] want to tell you, but you can't bear it now. When the Spirit of truth comes, *he will guide you into all truth*. He will not speak on his own but will tell you what he has heard. He will tell you about the future. He will bring me glory by *telling you whatever he receives from me*. All that belongs to the Father is mine; this is why I said, "The Spirit will tell you whatever he receives from me." (John 16:12-15)

When we receive salvation through receiving the gift of Jesus in our heart, we receive the Holy Spirit as a "deposit *guaranteeing* our inheritance" (see Ephesians 1:13-14).

God also gives us the wonderful gift of a *room in Heaven*. Wow, what a gift!:

> My Father's house *has many rooms*; if that were not so, would I have told you that I am going there to prepare a place for you? And if *I go and prepare a place for you*, I will come back and take you to be with me that you also may be where I am. (John 14:2-3 NIV)

Any time in life that you feel like you have no place to rest your head (Luke 9:58), you can rest reassured that Jesus *promises* that as a follower of His...as a child of God...He has gone ahead to prepare a room *just for you*. Can you even begin to *imagine what your room will look like in God's House*?

Again, the ultimate gift that God gives us is salvation, forgiveness, unconditional love, amazing grace...*all* through His Son Jesus:

> God saved you by his grace when you believed. And you can't take credit for this; it is *a gift from God*. Salvation is not a reward for the good things we have done, so none of us can boast about it. (Ephesians 2:8-9)

So, have you *received* His gift to you? If not, you can receive His gift of Jesus...of salvation...of unconditional forgiveness, love, grace and mercy...right now. All you have to do is open your heart and receive. And your life...your destiny...will be changed *forever*.[47]

מֵרֵעַ

Pastor Kadin and Pastor Muneer; friends are a great gift (Zahle, Lebanon) (June 2015) (faces blurred for privacy reasons)

---

[47] Check out www.harvest.org/knowgod/

Thank You Jesus For the Gifts!

My new friend Rick and I enjoying a meal after walking the Via Dolorosa together (Jerusalem, Israel) (May 2012)

Story: Dying in a Shanty in Nairobi

> Religion that God our Father accepts as *pure and faultless* is this: to look after orphans and widows in their distress and to keep oneself from being polluted by the world. (James 1:27 NIV)

*A*FTER RECEIVING GOD'S amazing gift of forgiveness in February 2004 at the age of 37 and beginning my journey of wanting to follow Jesus, I found myself in the Mathare Valley slum of Nairobi, Kenya four months later. That slum is nicknamed "Little Mogadishu" because its residents consist primarily of refugees who have fled the war in neighboring Somalia. Somalia's capital is Mogadishu. There are *hundreds of thousands* of people trying to survive one hour at a time in the slums of Nairobi. I had never seen conditions of poverty and abject lack of hope as I did in those slums. An ocean of shanties as far as you could see in all directions. Man-made "creeks" of raw sewage flow among the shanties. Trash everywhere piled layer upon layer. Shanties built *on top of trash dumps* out of tin, wood, sticks, plastic and anything else that could be found to build something to try to survive in. Children wandered around barefoot among the sewage creeks and filth. There was a putrid smell in the air of car exhaust, pollution, sewage...and hopelessness. You could smell and see the hopelessness. People were no doubt dying every day from AIDS.[48] God broke my heart...*shattered* it to pieces...in that slum on those hot Kenyan days of summer that we spent there visiting with people who were slum dwellers.

We were accompanied by our hosts...the son of a pastor as well as one of the assistant pastors from a local Christian church, both of whom are Kenyans. The church was located in the slums and took in children off the streets to share the love of Jesus with them, give them a place to live and to go to school, and give them hope and a future.[49] When you rescue a child off the streets of a slum like Mathare Valley, you oftentimes don't know when the child was born. I remember looking at a handwritten list of the children at that program that was written on a board. Most of the children had *"unknown"* listed next to their age and birthday. I thought of our children and how we celebrate their birthday every year and it is such a special time for them. They are the star of the show that day and receive so many wonderful gifts. These children don't have a birthday to celebrate. I love what the local program does there for the kids...they have a big birthday party each year to celebrate *all of the children's birthdays*. How awesome is that!

We were also accompanied by a soldier carrying a machine gun. That was a new experience for me. The slums can be very dangerous so they wanted to help us feel safe.

As we walked among the shanties...one after another as far as you could see to the horizon...we stopped by the stand-alone shanty of a woman. The tin-walled and tin-roofed shanty stood there in the slum by itself. Oftentimes shanties share walls and are connected one to another to another to another. This shanty was different. It was sitting there in the orange Kenyan clay...by itself. Our host opened the tin door after knocking on it and we were invited in. It was dark inside so our eyes had to adjust at first. As I began to be able to see more and more of what was in that tiny shanty...it was no bigger that a small tool shed that you might have in your yard to store tools in...I could see that there was a woman lying on the small make-shift bed, which was more of a homemade cot made from scrap wood and canvas. I could see her eyes and they were *desperately sad*...the eyes of someone who has fought a long fight and knows the battle is about over.

I came to learn as the pastor's son knelt by her side that she was dying of AIDS, so that explained why she and her tin shanty were isolated from the other shanties.[50] And I also came to learn that she had a little daughter...sounded to be

---

[48] Acquired Immune Deficiency Syndrome.
[49] Jeremiah 29:11.
[50] There is a great fear in Africa of "catching" AIDS as if it was contagious like a cold or the flu.

Thank You Jesus For the Gifts!

about six or eight years old. Her daughter was not there as she was at the local slum school that some Christians were running there in the slum...God bless those people who run that school...we did not get to meet them. The woman on the cot in that dingy, dark, isolated tin shack started to weep as she talked in Swahili with the pastor's son. After they talked for a minute...as she wept...he explained that she was asking the pastor's son to please take her daughter in to their program after she dies. I asked him if they would do that and he said that they would and had assured her of that. Here was a mother dying in a tin, sweltering shack *begging* a young man to please care for her daughter after she dies. You can see the tears of God's eyes in a place like that at a moment like that. I fought back tears, struggling with what I was experiencing.

After a short visit, we stepped out of that tin shack into the blazing Kenyan summer sun and our eyes had to adjust once again. My eyes were trying to adjust to seeing a different world than I had ever seen in my life. I remember standing there looking back at the closed door of that isolated tin shack. I never saw that woman again. That local program honored their word and took that little girl into their school with loving arms. What an *awesome gift from God* to a dying mother that her daughter...her precious child...would be cared for after she died.

The slum built on a trash heap
(Nairobi, Kenya) (June 2006)

Thank You Jesus For the Gifts!

The isolated shanty in which a mother was dying from AIDS (Nairobi, Kenya) (June 2006)

Story: The Gift of the Holy Spirit

So if you sinful people know how to give good gifts to your children, how much more will your heavenly Father give the *Holy Spirit* to *those who ask him*. (Luke 11:13)

ONE OF THE greatest gifts that we receive after we ask Jesus into our heart is the *gift* of the Holy Spirit:

And when you believed in Christ, he identified you as his own by giving you the Holy Spirit, whom he promised long ago. The Spirit is God's *guarantee* that he will give us the *inheritance* he promised and that he has purchased us to be his own people. He did this so we would praise and glorify him. (Ephesians 1:13b-14)

[God] has identified us as his own by *placing the Holy Spirit in our hearts* as the first installment that *guarantees* everything he has promised us. (2 Corinthians 1:22)

And there is clearly a difference between a baptism by *water* versus a baptism by *Spirit*. John the Baptist referred to the difference, telling some of his followers that, "I baptize you with water, but [Jesus] will *baptize you with the Holy Spirit!*" (Mark 1:8)

When Jesus appeared to the disciples after the resurrection and was eating with them, he told them to "not leave Jerusalem until the Father sends you the *gift* he promised, as I told you before" (Acts 1:4). Jesus continued by explaining to them that:

> John baptized with water, but in just a few days you will be *baptized with the Holy Spirit*. (Acts 1:5)

The Greek word translated to "baptized" in both places in Acts 1:5 is *baptizo*, which connotes being made *fully* wet…to *submerge*…to *immerse*. To be *immersed* in the Holy Spirit.

And sure enough, on the day of Pentecost in Jerusalem 50 days after Jesus had been resurrected from the dead, the disciples were gathered together. And they had a *power-encounter* with God as they were *filled with the Holy Spirit*:

> On the day of Pentecost all the believers were meeting together in one place. Suddenly, there was a sound from heaven like the roaring of a mighty windstorm, and it filled the house where they were sitting. Then, what looked like flames or tongues of fire appeared and settled on each of them. And everyone present was *filled with the Holy Spirit* and began speaking in other languages, as *the Holy Spirit* gave them this ability. (Acts 2:1-4)

I asked Jesus into my heart while I was in my car in February 2004 in a large city. A Pastor named Greg Laurie[51] had a radio show during the time I drove to work. I *unexplainably* turned on that Christian radio station one morning after driving past a billboard advertising a Christian radio station. Interestingly, I had never listened to Christian radio before that moment. I was 37 years old and began to soak in what the Pastor was sharing about…what he was sharing about Jesus. And finally, at the end of one of those 30-minute radio messages, I accepted the Pastor's invitation to ask Jesus into my heart and to forgive me…and *I was set free* (John 8:32). My life immediately began to change. Shame was replaced with forgiveness. Condemnation was replaced with grace. Hate was replaced with love. Enslavement was replaced with freedom. It was like fresh,

---

[51] www.harvest.org

Thank You Jesus For the Gifts!

cool water from a mountain river pouring over my parched soul. I was *renewed* from the inside out!

About eight months later, I was attending a church program about the Holy Spirit. The visiting Pastor[52] taught about the Holy Spirit from the Bible, including the *baptism* of the Holy Spirit. And at the end of the second evening program, everyone who *wanted* the baptism of the Holy Spirit was invited to come up front to the altar; and they would lay hands on you and pray for you to receive the baptism of the Holy Spirit. I was the first one up there and I experienced something I don't ever want to forget. As they prayed and laid their hands on me…and as I *hungered* for the Holy Spirit…I became *immersed* in the Holy Spirit. And I've never been the same since.

God tells us in Luke 11:13 that He *will* give the Holy Spirit to *those who ask*:

So if you sinful people know how to give good gifts to your children, how much more will your heavenly Father give the Holy Spirit to those who ask him.

He also tells us that, "Everyone who calls on the name of the LORD will be saved."[53] And we are further told:

If you *confess* with your mouth that Jesus is Lord and *believe* in your heart that God raised him from the dead, you *will* be saved. (Romans 10:9)

What amazing *promises* from God! So, regardless of whether you believe the deposit of the Holy Spirit at the time we are saved and the baptism of the Holy Spirit are one in the same, or you believe they are different, or maybe you even believe they are different but can occur at the same time…what we *can* agree on is that God *graciously* gives the amazing gifts of salvation and the Holy Spirit to *those who ask*. Wow is He a gracious gift-giver.

So, have *you* asked Him for the gift of Jesus and the gift of the Holy Spirit? Have you asked God to *immerse* you in…to *fill* you with…the Holy Spirit? He's a gracious gift-giver…so go for it.

---

[52] Rev. Gary Dalmasso of Renewal in Christ Ministries, www.ricm.org
[53] Joel 2:32a, Acts 2:21, Romans 10:13.

ENCOUNTERING JESUS

Watching my mother about to be baptized in the Jordan River by Pastor H (West Bank, Israel) (May 2012)

Story: Gifts with My Friend...Who Happens to be Muslim

After David had finished talking with Saul, he met Jonathan, the king's son. There was an *immediate bond* between them, for Jonathan loved David...And Jonathan made a solemn pact with David, because *he loved him* as he loved himself. (1 Samuel 18:1, 3)

I HAVE BEEN so fortunate to become friends with a man named Ahmad. We met in May 2013 at the local mosque. It was one of those times in life when you meet someone and you become *instant friends*...there is an *immediate bond*. His friendship has been a great gift to me and my family. He moved back to Saudi Arabia with his wife and daughter this past summer (2015) since he finished the university studies he had come to America to take. I miss him and think of him often, and we keep up with each other through a great App for our smartphones called "WhatsApp." I hope that my friendship with him has been a great gift to him too. Here are a few entries from the journal I keep about some of the wonderful times we have spent together:

Thank You Jesus For the Gifts!

JOURNAL ENTRY, AMERICA, AUGUST 18, 2013:

"Was so blessed to spend about an hour and a half with Ahmad…I asked him to come over to show me how to make the great tea that he makes. I bought an electric hot water heater/kettle and already had sugar and cinnamon sticks. This was Ahmad's first visit to [my home]. It was such a great time with him. We made tea (it was delicious!) and sat on the couch and talked about Islam and Christianity."

JOURNAL ENTRY, AMERICA, JUNE 2, 2014:

"I picked up Ahmad at his apartment at 6pm yesterday. It was a beautiful sunny day in the high 70's. He brought a thermos of hot tea and some cups. I brought a blanket to sit on for the picnic and some snacks, including a fig cookie from Saudi Arabia that I bought at the local *halal*[54] store. This was his first time to ride in the jeep and there were no doors on it and the top was pulled back. We first went to [a local yogurt store] and I bought him some yogurt. It was funny to watch him figure out how the yogurt machines work. He got some different flavors…and loved it! He said he is going to bring his *zawjah* (wife) to this yogurt store 'every weekend.' She arrives from Saudi to DC on Thursday *inshallah* (God willing). He is excited to see her and she will be here for it sounds like the rest of his schooling (he has one year left). She has been in school in Saudi. He loved the yogurt! We sat outside and enjoying talking and laughing. We then headed on to have a picnic like we did when we first met together. He suggested going to [a local recreational area], which is a beautiful recreational outdoor area that the Cub Scouts have used for their [model rocket launching] each September.

"We set out the blanket in the shade by one of the ponds and enjoyed the delicious hot tea that he made. He said it was a secret as to what leaves he used for it but told me they are like mint a little and are from Saudi. He has not been able to find them here in the US. The tea was wonderful! We enjoyed having tea and talking and he told me how much my friendship has meant to him and how I'm the only friend he has made in the US that

---

[54] *Halal* means "lawful or permissible" in Arabic. It refers to foods that Muslims are permitted to eat under Islamic *Shari'ah* law, including how particular foods must be processed. For example, Muslims are prohibited from eating pork, so pork is not *halal*. Interesting that Muslims and Jews have that in common.

has continued the friendship. He also told me that many people ask about me…about Abu William. ☺…I told Ahmad how much his friendship means to me and how fun it has been to be friends with him.

"After having tea, it was time to head on as the park was closing at 7:30pm. We drove outside of the gate and then I let Ahmad drive the jeep and I took video of him after taking some still pictures of him with the jeep inside the park. We were laughing so much as he drove the jeep around on the pavement and then in the dirt. What a fun friend he is!

"I then took him back to his apartment and we had some water and he showed me an App for my phone called WhatsApp, which is a great way to share pictures and videos with a group instead of having to do an email. He set it up for me and he sent me the videos of the jeep riding by using WhatsApp."

Journal Entry, America, January 31, 2015:

"William and I spent a fun day together while [our daughter] and [her friend] painted pottery at [a local pottery shop] (we love going there!). William and I (mostly William ☺) hosted Ahmad at the condo for Arab-style tea and chocolate chip cookies. William did such a great job cooking the cookies and helping serve Ahmad. Ahmad brought some sweet bread that his *zawjah* (wife) made…it was delicious! I love Ahmad like a brother…his friendship is a blessing. We love to see each other and smile so big when we do. He will be moving back to Saudi Arabia in July after he graduates in June from [the local university]. I will miss him so much. He and I have been friends for almost two years and we have had a lot of laughs together and many wonderful meals and conversations."

Journal Entry, America, March 1, 2015:

"Message from Ahmad on WhatsApp about the food that the kids and I delivered to Ahmad on Saturday for him and his wife (*zawjah* in Arabic) to enjoy:

> 'The meal and cookies you brought us taste delicious, we had them in our dinner, my wife say thank you very much for yall for being

Thank You Jesus For the Gifts!

nice to us. *Wallahe*[55] the only thing I'm gonna miss when I leave the states is you and your amazing lovely family'

"The friendship between Ahmad and me is such a wonderful gift from God. He is moving back to Saudi Arabia with his wife in July after he finishes school at [the local university]. I will miss him terribly. God willing (*inshallah*), I will visit him in Saudi as soon as 2016…wow what a wonderful time that would be!"

How fun it has been being friends with Ahmad, a friendship that continues to this day. Another funny story about our unique friendship involved Christmas gifts and a one-of-a-kind surprise gift.

In December 2013, as Christmas was approaching, our son and I took a gift to Ahmad and his wife at their apartment. The gift was wrapped in Christmas paper with a bow on it. Ahmad was excited about this new surprise in his life. I got the sense that he had not been given a Christmas gift before, at least not one wrapped in holiday paper with a bow on it. William proudly handed him the package and Ahmad asked if it was common to put a "flower" on top of the gift. William and I chuckled as we explained to him that it was a "bow" and, yes, that was the custom for gifts at that time of year.

A week or so later, Ahmad surprised *us* with a Christmas gift wrapped in holiday paper with a bow on it. He handed me the gift and I was perplexed to discover that *warmth* emanated from within the wrapping paper onto my cool winter hands. We sat down on the couch and I gave William the honor of opening it. William carefully unwrapped the gift so as not to damage the beautiful Christmas wrapping or bow and, much to our surprise, inside was a *warm rotisserie chicken*! Ahmad beamed with pride at this gracious gift as William and I's hearts warmed in response to Ahmad's kindness.

I still think that is the only Christmas gift I have ever received on which the Christmas wrapping paper was warm to the touch. I sit here typing this, not only laughing out loud but also close to crying. What a gift of a cherished memory with a dear friend whom I miss very much.

Thank You God for the gift of a dear friend and precious memories.

מֵרֵעַ

---

[55] An Arabic expression meaning, "I promise by God."

My dear friend Ahmad as we said goodbye; I miss him very much (America) (July 2015)

Ahmad and me enjoying a meal together (America) (2014)

15   Hanging Out at the Shopping Center With Jesus

> Truly I tell you, whatever you did for one of the least of these brothers and sisters of mine, you did *for me*. (Matthew 25:40)

SOMEHOW, SOMEWAY, BEYOND my understanding…when we feed the hungry, give a drink to the thirsty, show hospitality to a stranger, provide clothes to the naked, or visit the sick or people in prison…somehow, we are *spending time with Jesus*…we are doing those things *to Jesus*:

> Then the King will say to those on his right, "Come, you who are blessed by my Father; take your inheritance, the kingdom prepared for you since the creation of the world. For I was hungry and *you gave me something to eat*, I was thirsty and *you gave me something to drink*, I was a stranger and *you invited me in*, I needed clothes and *you clothed me*, I was sick and *you looked after me*, I was in prison and *you came to visit me*." Then the righteous will answer him, "Lord, when did we see you hungry and feed you, or thirsty and give you something to drink? When did we see you a stranger and invite you in, or needing clothes and clothe you? When did we see you sick or in prison and go to visit you?" The King will reply, "Truly I tell you, whatever you did for one of the least of these brothers and sisters of mine, *you did for me*." (Matthew 25:34-40)

I don't understand how that works. But I do know that I do get to know Jesus better…more *personally*…when God does those things through me. When God serves those precious people through me…and through you…we are getting to know *Jesus* better.

Leading the Yazidi refugee children in songs and games
(Northern Iraq) (June 2015)

Story: Beggars in the Parking Lot

If someone has enough money to live well and sees a brother or sister in need but *shows no compassion*—how can God's love be in that person? (1 John 3:17)

THERE IS A large parking lot in a shopping center here in the town where we live. It's a popular location for homeless men and women to stand there asking for help…for money…for food…for *anything*. It is uncomfortable seeing them. How often I look away and *try to ignore them*. Pretend I don't see them. Whatever I do, I so often make sure *not* to look them in the eyes. Because if I look them in the eyes, then they will know I saw them…that I saw them in need…that I saw them begging…that I saw them humiliated standing in the cold or rain or heat asking for scraps as many people *look the other way* and drive past them. I so often hope that we won't have to stop the car next to them because of traffic. It's an awful thing that God has given me *so much*…even His very own Son on a cross…and I so often try to drive by the homeless without giving them *anything*, not even a kind look. And there is Jesus telling us that I am driving past *Him*…my friend and my God…a beggar in distress. He gives me His very

Hanging Out at the Shopping Center With Jesus

life...His *everything*...and I drive past Him in the car He blessed me with while trying desperately not to *look Him in the eyes*.

صــديقي

Spending time with orphans at a rural school in Africa
(near Nairobi, Kenya) (July 2004)

Story: Taking a Homeless Man Shopping

> Suppose you see a brother or sister who has no food or clothing, and you say, "Good-bye and have a good day; stay warm and eat well"—but then *you don't give that person any food or clothing*. What good does that do? (James 2:15-16)

TWO LAWYERS IN a big city in America were living in the fast lane. Making lots of money. Wasting lots of money. Working too much. Focusing very much on themselves. And then they met Jesus and their lives...their hearts...were *dramatically changed*. I was one of those lawyers and my dear friend Rob was the other one. We worked together in the downtown of a large city and therefore were in proximity to homeless people who lived on the downtown city streets. After God changed our hearts, we began to have *compassion* for the homeless.

One day, we stopped to talk with a homeless man. He was dirty, smelled and was hanging on to life...surviving on the streets. So much wealth around him in the expensive high-rise office towers. So many expensive cars driving by him. And instead of passing him by, we had stopped to talk with him...to see how he was doing. Definitely not something I would have done before meeting Jesus. Jesus has a way of changing people from the inside out...and He was sure doing a number on me and my heart.

Before we knew it, God had my friend and I ask the man if we could take him shopping for some clothes and food. We learned more about his story. Turns out he was living in some bushes next to the highway...secretly so that he had better odds of other homeless people not finding his few possessions and taking them. The man who was living in the bushes on the side of the highway. Hungry and alone. The *Jesus* who was living in the bushes on the side of the highway. My *friend Jesus*.

The man got in my friend's car and we drove to a clothing store. I remember walking into the store and then just standing there as the man began picking out clothes. He was so excited. I was numb and didn't know what to say. I was experiencing this man on a personal level...an up-close-and-personal level...and somehow was getting to know Jesus better because of this homeless man. My heart broke as he picked out clothes. He picked out clothes quickly, no doubt probably at least a little bit concerned that we might change our minds. We bought him the clothes and bought him some food. And then we drove him back to the bushes where he lives next to the highway. He got out of the car and we said goodbye and we drove away. I don't know what happened to him. But I do know that I got to know Jesus in a *more personal way* that day.

מֵרֵעַ

My great friend Rob (America) (June 2015)

16 Hanging Out at the Homeless Shelter With Jesus

As they were walking along, someone said to Jesus, "I will follow you wherever you go." But Jesus replied, "Foxes have dens to live in, and birds have nests, but the Son of Man has *no place even to lay his head.*" (Luke 9:57-58)

*J*ESUS GAVE UP His life...*for us*. And He made Himself nothing...*for us*. He didn't have a place to lay His head...*for us*. Imagine that level of humility that the Son of God...the One who holds *all* authority in the Universe...would come here and live like that...*for us*. And if He was here walking around in the flesh today...the Man who gave His life for us...for you...how would we react? What if He lived in a shanty or was homeless? Would we react differently to our Savior...our friend...if He was a successful, well-to-do Savior, as opposed to living in squalor in a shanty or living at the homeless shelter? Would our friendship be a comfortable one...or an *uncomfortable* one? Would we be comfortable taking our friend to church, work or home with us?

Hanging Out at the Homeless Shelter With Jesus

Underground prison in Jerusalem where Jesus may have been held the night before He was crucified (Israel) (May 2012)

Story: Living in a Shanty...in America

For we know that when this earthly tent we live in is taken down (that is, when we die and leave this earthly body), we will have a *house in heaven*, an eternal body made for us by God himself and not by human hands. (2 Corinthians 5:1)

I HAD NEVER been in a shanty until I first went to the slums of Nairobi, Kenya in 2004. It was shocking and life-changing to experience people up close who were barely surviving in shanty after shanty after shanty *as far as you could see* in every direction. I have always lived in nice homes. A roof over my head. Running water...and clean water at that. Soft bed. Clean bathroom. On and on. So, what does God do to help me have *compassion* for the millions of people around the world who live in shanties and abject poverty? He nudged me to go to Nairobi and then return to America and build a shanty out of scrap metal and wood…out of rusty appliances…out of trash…and *live in it* for a few days. And He woke me up in the middle of the night one night with a vision that I would have to walk three miles each way from that shanty to get water. God also made clear that the shanty should be built on a friend of ours farm about 20 minutes outside of the town where we lived. Some of the property there was being mined for sand, so there was a small pond forming from where they had already dug out the sand. It was a fairly barren place right up next to a forest. And so, with God's guidance and some great friends, including my brother-in-law who graciously drove from another state to join us, we lived in a shanty for a few days. It was a life-changing experience.

The plan for the property after the sand mining would be finished was to have a Christian camp set up on it. That in fact has become a reality. The man who was planning to be the camp director…and who is still the camp director to this day…helped our daughter and I build the shanty. It was very gracious of him to do that.

As to building the shanty, we used materials that were there at the property, which was near a forest used for many years as a trash-dumping ground. A lot of the trash that had been dumped there over the years had recently been cleaned out of the surrounding area (old wood, sheet metal, old refrigerators and other appliances, etc.), which was piled up in a massive trash pile as large as several trucks. Foraging for supplies to build a shanty is just how so many people in Nairobi would have to build a shanty…so we did that too.

After we moved into the shanty, we sometimes ate crispy (burnt) rice and half a sweet potato each for dinner that we cooked over a fire. We would sing songs, read our Bibles, host visitors and experience a lifestyle that none of us were accustomed to. It was a simple life and the experience impacted us in a powerful way. People came from all over the area to visit the shanty. I hope the experience was a blessing to them too.

We were also given $1 *per day* to live off of for buying food while we lived in the shanty.[56] That didn't go very far and we found ourselves cherishing a granola bar and saving part of it for later, instead of eating it all at once. Fortunately, my wife brought us some food during the project, so we nicknamed her the "United Nations." It was wonderful to see her arrive! It's amazing how much you

---

[56] "Almost half the world — over three billion people — live on less than $2.50 a day… Almost two in three people lacking access to clean water survive on less than $2 a day, with one in three living on less than $1 a day." www.globalissues.org/article/26/poverty-facts-and-stats

appreciate people caring for you and coming to visit you when you are living in a difficult situation like that.

As God would have it, the three miles we would have to walk for water each day put us smack dab in the middle of a little town down the road that had a history of being a fighting town over the years…in other words, a town with a history of conflict. And so that was the town that we walked to each day with a walking stick carrying the gallon-size water jugs. I enjoyed some interesting conversations in that little town during the time we lived in the shanty, including with one man who said he hated missionaries that go to Africa…and then he found out that I go to Africa to help people. We ended up becoming *friends*. God is full of surprises!

One night, a storm rolled in. Some of us slept on cots and one of our friends who stayed one night with us slept on the ground *under* one of the cots. As the storm moved in, we laid a tarp over us and our belongings inside the shanty as the roof leaked. At one point, our friend under the cot had to move to a different spot in the shanty in the middle of the night as he was getting extremely claustrophobic. The storm arrived shortly after he moved spots. One of the tarps sprung a leak and the person under that tarp woke up soaking wet. We had to rearrange ourselves around 4am that morning. Things were wet…we were tired…it was just *miserable*. And to think that people live that way *every day*, sometimes for their *entire life*.

Here are some journal entries about that shanty experience.

JOURNAL ENTRY, AMERICA, MAY 2, 2007:

"I am a bit anxious about this one because I think [God] is going to break my heart in a new way. I have not stepped into other folks' shoes like this before. The thought of heading out to that land tomorrow to start building a shack to live in just breaks my heart as there will be fathers around the world doing that exact same thing at that exact same time while their little children stand next to them ready to sleep on the dirt floor of that shanty tomorrow night. [Our six-year old daughter] has been asking a lot of questions about me living in a shanty and told a friend of hers at school today while I was there that, 'My daddy is going to live in a shanty pretty soon.' [She] also asked me if anyone would offer to help me while I was out there, like give me some food, or ask to give me a ride when they see me walking down the side of the road carrying water in jugs…Children are so amazing and God is so present in them in such special ways."

Journal Entry, America, May 7, 2007:

"We arrived at the back of the property and parked next to the two large piles of trash, consisting of couches, vinyl siding, dirt, scrap and sheet metal, bricks, wood, old plastic toys, a baby seat, and other items that had been removed from the woods around the property as part of the clean-up of the property…I looked at the large pile of trash and figured that there was not much we could use in it. By the end of the day, I was climbing all over the trash heap and pulling out all sorts of materials that could be used to build the shanty….[the] vinyl siding, sheet metal, fence posts, tree limbs, refrigerators and dryers, an [air conditioning] unit, etc. It's amazing how your perspective changes when you are building the structure that will house you.

"[The future camp director and our daughter] and I exchanged hello's and unpacked some tools from our [car] trunks. We then joined hands and prayed. The first thing we built was a large cross that we placed in the ground at the 'point' overlooking the lake that is being formed as a result of the sand mining. There were a few pieces of construction equipment out on the sand next to the lake, but they were quiet since it was a Saturday and the crew was not working. The cross was beautiful.

"[Our daughter] took off her shoes and began digging in the piles of sand and having a good time. I set up her pink chair and she got out her 'Hello Kitty' pink umbrella to give herself shade from the sun when she sat in her chair drinking juice. [The future camp director] and I began pulling materials out of the trash heaps to use to build a shanty, which we had never built before. [Our daughter] joined in after a short while and pulled some of the materials across the 20 feet or so to the place where we decided to build the 'shanty town.' By this time, the sun had come out and it definitely felt hotter.

"[Our daughter] made a cross on her own out of wood, and hammered the nails herself (I held the wood for her while she hammered), and she dug the hole herself in front of the shanty for the cross. She is amazing!

"[As] we dug through the trash heap to find building materials, and [as] our six-year old daughter helped out, it really struck me that there are dads and moms around the world building real shanties in real slums at that very same moment while their children help out, as they get ready to live in that shanty that night, possibly for the rest of their lives. Many people who live in large slums like those in Nairobi don't ever leave the slums, so that is the only life they know. When rains come, shanties can be flooded or washed away. When the people living in them cannot come up with the $12 of rent each month to pay their shanty landlord, then they are evicted. More times than we would want to imagine, bulldozers will arrive to demolish the shanties (with no notice to the parents and children living in them), so that the land can be seized and used for the personal gain of others.[57] When the sun goes down, the shanty doors are closed and padlocked due to how dangerous life can be in the slums at night time. The children typically sleep on the dirt floor breathing in the dusty dirt as they sleep. And this happens every day around the world involving millions of people (again, over 1 million people in the slums of Nairobi alone).

"It's hard to comprehend that $12 would keep a family in a home (shanty) for a month and that, today at this very minute, families are being evicted and left to survive in the streets because they could not come up with the $12 today. Experiencing some of what people in the slums experience is at the heart of the purpose of the shanty project: to provide a personal experience for us so that we can be more compassionate for those millions of people in the world who have to live in shanties and, as such, open our hearts to them to want to reach out to serve them, all to God's glory. When we don't personally experience their suffering, it is so much easier (and human nature) to want to ignore or not think about what families like them are enduring today. When I first arrived in the Nairobi slums three years ago, my heart was shattered at what I saw....children caring for children in the slums and even households where the oldest member of the

---

[57] This happened to the ministry in Nairobi that we partnered with to provide medical camps in the Nairobi slum there. I first visited the Fountain of Life Church and Children's Home in 2004. I returned in the summer of 2006 with six friends, including my dad. Later that year in December 2006, a gang of men showed up at nighttime and bulldozed the property, demolishing the children's bunk dormitories and destroying the school and church as well as the water well that had recently been installed on the property. Many of the possessions of the 60 boys living there (ages 4 to 14) were looted during the demolition. The children had to spend the night in the cold having lost almost everything. These "land grabs" occur often throughout the world in places such as slums. The people living on the property are considered disposable trash and worth very little compared to the value of the land. See https://www.ijm.org/casework/property-grabbing for more information about land grabbing as well as a wonderful ministry named International Justice Mission that helps stand up for the rights of people caught in these situations.

family was 10 years old, left with no parents but with younger siblings to care for.

"Not only are there families in the slums who live in shanties and who have little if anything to eat, but many of those people also have AIDS, which makes many of them bed-ridden, so that they cannot work...and hence the domino effect on the rest of their lives and children (no work means no money means no rent means eviction and life on the streets for children as young as our son William, who is three; the thought of William being on his own left to dig through trash with pigs and goats to find a scrap of food just breaks my heart, and I thank God that He has opened my eyes and heart in this way....to realize in a personal way that children are having to dig through trash for food right now at this very minute).

"Thank You, Lord, for breaking my heart more."

God taught us many lessons during those few precious days living in that shanty. One of them was that we should not feel sorry for the people in the shanties so much as we should feel sorry for the way *we* live our lives in America with *so much excess*. That was a hard lesson to take in. God also showed us what it is like to live a beautifully simple life at the shanty...so much so that we had mixed emotions about leaving the shanty at the end of the project. The shanty had truly become our home and we were so happy to host guests in it. We were reminded that a home is less about the structure and more about the love in it. Another lesson that hit us deeply was that, if Jesus was here in the flesh on this planet today, He may very well be living in a shanty...and how many of us would want to *live there with Him*?

Please keep the people living in the Nairobi slums and all other slums in the world in your prayers, especially the children.

Hanging Out at the Homeless Shelter With Jesus

The shanty we lived in (America) (May 2007)

Walking three miles for water (America) (May 2007)

Story: Little Boy at the Homeless Shelter

Whoever is kind to the poor *lends to the LORD*, and he will reward them for what they have done. (Proverbs 19:17 NIV)

ONE OF THE things I used to be *scared about doing* that I now *look forward to doing* is helping serve the meal at the local homeless shelter. The church we attend provides and serves the meal to the shelter residents once a month. I have gone from being afraid to go to the homeless shelter…which is in an impoverished and fairly high-crime area of town…to looking forward to going there. It is one of the places in life where each time I'm there, I know in my spirit that, "This is just the kind of place where Jesus would be." And I get to know Jesus better by being there serving the residents and by getting to know the residents more *personally*.

Journal Entry, America, June 22, 2012:

"I was blessed to help serve dinner at the homeless shelter on the evening of June 22, 2012. There were about six children there ages 10 months to 8 years old. I played hot wheels cars and visited a while with 5-year old Robbie[58] and two other children. Robbie is a sweet kid, has two hot wheels, probably about all he's got to play with…and he loves those two little cars. His mom was there with one or two other children, no dad around from what I could tell, same with the other kids there…mom around but dad apparently out of the picture. I was reminded that, as much as I screw up being a dad at times (we all do), at least most kids have a dad in their lives who loves them and they know it. Robbie was so hungry to receive my attention and affirmation and smiles that evening at the shelter. He talked about living at another shelter before this one…and he's only 5. I watched a mom feed her coughing 10-month old as her other two children were on their own near her or at another table…she's only one mom capable of only doing so much and she looked really tired and hopeless. I was so blessed to get to bring her seconds of spaghetti tonight, I wondered if the dad of her children was ever kind to her like that.

---

[58] Names changed for privacy reasons.

Hanging Out at the Homeless Shelter With Jesus

"I also visited with John, who is a kind man about 50 years old. He told me, in answer to my questions, that you can stay at the shelter for free for 30 days but are on your own during the day...have to leave at 8am and can't check back in until 6pm. After 30 days, you have to pay $3 per night but he said some people can't afford that...because times are tough right now. I waste that much money in a second lots of times each day. He said that even though times are hard right now, he is thankful for what he does have. He thanked us for feeding them tonight because he said we did not have to do that. God chose to bless me (and hopefully the people at the shelter) abundantly that night like He always so graciously does for us as His children. I hope Robbie sleeps peacefully tonight...I wonder if he will dream of his dad if he can even remember him. Please pray for all of the children going to bed tonight in homeless shelters, streets, shanties, sewers and all sorts of other places here and around the world. Our children are so blessed...they know that their mommy and daddy love them and that their Daddy in Heaven loves them even more. I wonder if Robbie even knows he has a Daddy in Heaven who loves and adores him. I wonder if anyone will ever make the effort to tell him. I hope he finds out. Please keep all of the people at the shelter in your prayers. Thank you."

מֵרֵעַ

Children in the Mathare Valley slum
(Nairobi, Kenya) (June 2006)

Story: Lego Pieces at the Homeless Shelter

Yes indeed, it is good when you obey the royal law as found in the Scriptures: "*Love* your neighbor as yourself." (James 2:8)

I LOVE SPENDING time with the children at the homeless shelter. They are precious and are oftentimes there only with their mom…as their dad is usually no longer around…*gone*. The mothers look tired…and I love treating them with *respect* and *kindness*.

Journal Entry, America, July 27, 2013:

"There was a mother there tonight with four children ages about one to six. One of her girls was excited to show me her two little toys…it was just two lego pieces that fit together…that's it. She was so proud of them. Her little sister, the one year old, watched me and her big sister while teething on a plastic container lid from what looked to be a peanuts container. Their mother looked so tired. She was very careful to keep her kids close by and made sure they were all eating. I cannot imagine what it must be like to be homeless with four little children. The homemade dessert that we brought tonight was a big hit with her children…ice cream oreo cake. The woman from church who makes the desserts each time for our group to serve at the shelter sure makes a lot of people happy. I hope [the homeless mother's] kids sleep well tonight and I hope she can get some rest too."

Hanging Out at the Homeless Shelter With Jesus

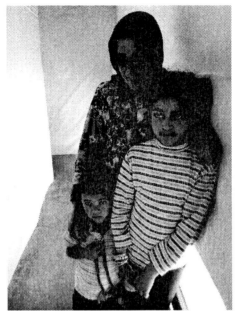

A refugee mother and her children
(Zahle, Lebanon) (June 2015)

Story: Showing Respect and Kindness to a Prostitute

The *generous* will themselves be blessed, for they share their food with the poor. (Proverbs 22:9 NIV)

*J*ESUS SHOWED COMPASSION to the down-trodden…the people who had been chewed up and spit out by society…the people who were viewed by many as trash…as *throwaways*. I love that Jesus loves *everyone* no matter what they've done.

JOURNAL ENTRY, AMERICA, JULY 27, 2013:

"There is typically at least one woman at the shelter each time (usually a few) who very much appear to be prostitutes and I try to treat them with a special amount of respect and kindness. What is so sad is how they look…not just how they dress…it's that look of a person who has lost most if not all of their dignity…it is so sad. They oftentimes eat by themselves...probably glad to have some of their own space for a change. They have a hard time looking at you in the eyes and oftentimes just look down. I enjoy checking on them while they eat to see if they would like a refill of juice or another dessert and say yes ma'am and no ma'am to them and that I hope they enjoy the meal. I try to help restore some of their dignity. It makes me so sad to see them and I wonder how they got to this point in their life and can only imagine the tough road they have had to walk."

صــديقي

Precious refugee mothers and their children gather around a truck delivering water to the refugee camp (Zahle, Lebanon) (June 2015)

Story: A Little Homeless Girl Says Grace

They asked Jesus, "Do you hear what these children are saying?" "Yes," Jesus replied. "Haven't you ever read the Scriptures? For they say, 'You have taught children and infants to *give you praise.*'" (Matthew 21:16)

ONE OF THE children I grew very fond of at the shelter was a little girl with a very outgoing personality...and a *beautiful smile*. She was only about five years old when I first met her at the shelter. She was born homeless as her mother struggled with addictions. She was homeless for the *first several years of*

Hanging Out at the Homeless Shelter With Jesus

her life. I can't imagine what that's like as a child or as a parent. I have so enjoyed spending time with that little girl and her mother at the shelter.

Journal Entry, America, June 28, 2013:

"Hi y'all, I hope you're having a fun summer. Once again I was privileged to serve at the homeless shelter tonight. The church provided the 4th Friday of the month meal tonight for the shelter residents like the church does each month. I have been noticing a cute little girl named Sarah[59] at the shelter for about four months now, who it turns out is six years old. She is very outgoing and full of life. Last Sunday we took some leftover donuts over to the shelter after church and Sarah and her mother were sitting on a blanket outside the shelter in the sweltering summer eat trying to stay cool in the shade. Sarah had a few toys to play with. It was hot out. The shelter residents have to leave at 8am each day after having a bite to eat and can't check back in for the night until 6pm. They are on their own during the day. The farther they walk away from the shelter the farther they have to walk back, so some of them just stay right outside the shelter all day...with no meal...waiting for it to open back up.

"Sarah's mom is very kind and obviously committed to raising Sarah to feel loved and to have good manners and to learn Christian values. I have never seen anyone around them who appeared to be a dad to Sarah or a husband to her mother. Her mother always makes sure to thank us for feeding her and Sarah when we provide the Friday evening meal. She looks to be a committed mother. I left the shelter last Sunday thinking to myself, 'Sarah deserves better than having to live at the homeless shelter and having to sit out in the heat all day.' Thank goodness she has such a great mother. Unfortunately, her mom told me tonight at my asking that Sarah's dad 'is not in her life.'

"Tonight Sarah and her mom were there as usual. They were so excited to hear that we had brought cake and ice cream for dessert. Sarah loves ice cream. While Sarah's mother waited in line by the kitchen for their meals, I went over and spent some time with Sarah at the dinner table she was sitting at by herself. She was working hard on a little word find of Christian words. The first word she found was Jesus. She was so excited to find more and more words. She was so focused on her puzzle. She is a very

---

[59] Names changed for privacy reasons.

smart young lady. I told her what a great job she was doing and how I could tell she was very smart. She looked up as she held her purple crayon, smiled, and then went on finding more words. She told me that word finds are her favorite kind of puzzle to do. She finished finding the words and was excited to show me all of the words she found. Her mother was still in line.

"As residents started bringing their meals back to the tables in the large meal room with benches and tables, I was reminded that I had not said the blessing yet for the meal. I enjoy doing that and get to do it most of the times I am there with the Friday night meal team. As I stood up from the table that Sarah was at to say the blessing for the whole room, the thought occurred to me to ask sweet little Sarah if she wanted to say the blessing...so I bent down and asked her. Now Sarah is the youngest resident at the shelter right now and I've never heard her say a blessing, but I have seen her and her mother bow their heads before prior meals to say a quiet mommy-daughter blessing together. Sarah looked at me and considered the proposal. She is definitely a thinker. She decided that she would like to do that, looked up at me again, and with a big smile told me a big 'yes!' I was a bit surprised and told her we would have to make sure her mommy approves of her doing that. Just then her mom returned to the table with two big meals and Sarah jumped right in to ask her if she could say the blessing for the whole room. Her mom was surprised at such a question but was glad to nod her approval. I told Sarah I would try to get everyone to quiet down for her as I figured she would at best get out a whisper of a blessing that few could hear, even in a quiet room. After all, she is only six and lives in a homeless shelter. Well, I figured wrong.

"I went over and turned off the TV and announced to the 40 or so residents in the meal room that we were going to say the blessing now. As the residents quieted down and stopped what they were doing, I motioned to little Sarah and explained to the room that this beautiful little girl was going to say the blessing. As if Sarah had done this a hundred times before, she took a breath and began singing in a loud and clear and beautiful voice, 'God our father, God our father, we thank you, we thank you, for the many blessings, for the many blessings, aaaaaaamen, aaaaaaamen.' And with that she gave a big smile and the residents of the homeless shelter began cheering and clapping at what they had just witnessed. I have never heard such a collective cheer in all my visits to the shelter. I looked over at Sarah and she looked at me. She began walking towards me on one of the benches

Hanging Out at the Homeless Shelter With Jesus

and opened her arms as wide as she could indicating she wanted a hug. I was not expecting that. I walked over and could tell her mom was okay with this and I gave her a big hug as she enveloped me in her arms. I told her, 'I knew you could do it, I'm so proud of you.' She was beaming. I was humbled. As I walked back towards the kitchen, I wondered if a man had ever told her those words before...I knew you could do it, I'm so proud of you. I felt so undeserving to share in such a precious moment with little Sarah. She is an amazing young lady and she blessed me big time tonight.

"I talked with her mom after she and Sarah had eaten and Sarah was off talking with one of the volunteers. I asked her how things are going for them. She said it's been a hard time but that they will eventually get out of the shelter. She said she hoped they could find a place to live in six or so weeks. I got the sense that this was more of a dream to her than a soon-to-occur reality. She then, as she always does, thanked us for providing her and her daughter with a good meal.

"I plan to buy Sarah some word find books tomorrow and take them over to her. She will probably be sitting on a blanket with her mom in the hot day. To Sarah it will probably seem like just another regular day in her life. Sarah deserves better than that but I am so thankful that she has such a loving and caring mommy. Maybe seeing her and giving her a present tomorrow will put a smile on her face. I know it will put one on mine.

"Please say a prayer for Sarah and her mother. Thank you so much."

Yazidi refugee children, so adorable
(Northern Iraq) (June 2015)

17 Becoming Friends With Jesus: Go On a Trip Together

Blessed are the pure in heart, for they will *see God*. (Matthew 5:8 NIV)

*M*AKES SENSE, DOESN'T it? Want to know someone better? Then spend *time* with that person. Get some *one-on-one time* with them. Go to a museum with them…to a picnic…on a walk…out for lunch…or even go on a trip with them to somewhere like…*Beirut?* It had been almost two years since I told Jesus that I wanted to see Him…I wanted Him to appear to me…so He answered…by sending me to Beirut.

God *always* honors His promises. And he promises us in His Word that if you "Come near to God…he *will* come near to you" (James 4:8a NIV). So I went near to Him by asking Him to appear to me. And, sure enough, He did…on the way to Beirut.

Like with Iraq, I had never been to Beirut before. And that was not one of the places high up on my list of *vacation* destinations. In fact, like with Iraq, it wasn't on my vacation list at all. But there was God tugging me…nudging me…to *go*. Unbeknownst to me, God was going to help me get to know Jesus better…more *personally*…on my way to and also in that war-torn, beautiful city.

My first picture taken in Lebanon, outside the Beirut airport
(June 2015)

Information about Lebanon

> Then Jesus left Galilee [modern day Israel] and *went north* to the region of Tyre [modern day Lebanon]. (Mark 7:24a)

I KNEW VERY little about Lebanon. Most of what I knew was what I had read in news headlines about the militant group Hezbollah, about the long civil war in Lebanon, about the clashes at the Lebanon/Syria border with ISIS, about the *millions* of Palestinian and Syrian refugees that now live there in camps and anywhere else they can find, and about it once being one of the jewels of the Mediterranean. I knew it was a very small country surrounded mostly by Syria to the North and East as well as by the Mediterranean Sea to the West, and Israel to the South. Lebanon had fought some wars with Israel, in fact recently.[60] I also knew that Jesus…my friend Jesus…had spent time in the town of Tyre, which is now in modern-day Lebanon (Mark 7:24). In fact, he cast out an evil spirit from

---

[60] In fact, Lebanon has been involved in at least five wars during the past 40 years, as well as numerous armed conflicts not classified as wars. There have also been numerous bombings and assassinations in Lebanon that have killed civilians, including politicians and journalists.

a woman's daughter there (Mark 7:25-30). Jesus then proceeded north to Sidon, another town in modern-day Lebanon (Mark 7:31). But I didn't know anything *personal* about Lebanon. Like with a person, it's hard to know anything *personal* about a place without spending *time* there. The same goes for getting to know Jesus…you've got to spend *time* with Him.

I first travelled back to Iraq in June 2015. I then travelled on to Beirut. After being in Lebanon for three days, I wrote in my journal some of the things I had learned about Lebanon…about the people there…about the *experiences* that had made Lebanon and the Lebanese people more *personal* to me.

Journal Entry, Beirut, June 26, 2015:

"Lebanon is a beautiful country situated on the Mediterranean Sea. Unfortunately, it's also situated next to Syria and therefore very close to the war. It's also a critical part of the world's response to the refugee crisis caused by so many wars in the Middle East.

"2 million refugees in Lebanon (1.1 million from Syria, 700,000 Palestinians, [the] rest [are] Iraqi refugees). 4 million Lebanese citizens in Lebanon, so 1/3rd of the country is refugees.[61] Staggering numbers, especially given that Lebanon is 1/3rd the size of Maryland. The refugees take any types of jobs, usually very low-paid labor, which puts a further strain on the country and its citizens and what jobs are available. The refugees from Syria that brought money/wealth with them live in apartments in Beirut or immigrate to Germany, Canada and other places.

"Telling people here that I am helping the refugees through the church gets a mixed reaction…you can tell that so many refugees puts a massive strain on a country this size, and there is so much hatred between the Lebanese and Syrians due to past wars. Lebanon is in debt of $65 billion due to refugees, international pressure being put on it to make refugees citizens, which due to number of them would dramatically change the Muslim/Christian makeup of the country. Iran supports Hezbollah since Iran is a Shia Muslim country and Hezbollah is a Shia Muslim militant group. Many of Syrian refugees are Sunni Muslims so Saudi Arabia as a Sunni Muslim country would like for Syrians to become Lebanese citizens and Sunni Muslims could potentially influence government here.

---

[61] In fact, while I was in Lebanon, I was told that it was common knowledge that as much as *40%* of the people in Lebanon are refugees.

"Currently the President of the country has to be a registered Christian (they say he's not really a Christian), President/government apparently very corrupt, involved with both legal and illegal businesses here.

"Major language [in] schools…is French because Lebanon used to be a French colony. Signs in highway are in Arabic and French, that surprised me ('*beyrouth*' instead of Beirut).

"Civil war 1976 to 1990. War was between Christian militias and Muslim militants like Hezbollah and Syrians who sacked (took over) Zahle. Pastor I am with is also 48 years old. Fought in one of the three Christian militias (civilians fighting in the war) from ages 14-21 (so from about 1980 to 1987), a miracle that he survived the civil war. He began following Jesus at age of 23. There are many gun shops here, he said most people have a gun. Reminds me of the Kurds in Northern Iraq.

"If a non-Lebanese citizen is found by Lebanese government to have gone to Israel, that person is never allowed into Lebanon and their name is recorded in a computer. If a Lebanese citizen is found to have gone to Israel, [and] if that person has political friends, they will just be punished by life in prison. If no political friends, will be hanged.

"Can check NASCAR off my list of things to do after riding in a taxi on the highway in Beirut! Wow, highway lane lines are more of a suggestion. I am learning that there are entire conversations taking place on the roads as cars speed around and weave through the old narrow Roman Empire-origin roads, as the cars honk at each other, it's impressive how they let each other know where they are by use of horns. Cool! Since the road layout in much of Lebanon was primarily built by the Roman Empire, the roads twist and turn like noodles in a bowl of spaghetti. They are very narrow too. In many places only one car can fit through, amazing to see how the cars navigate each other!

"Passed police station in Beirut and lots of soldiers with machine guns there, a heavily fortified station. Lebanese military and police have a heavy presence in the country.

"Passed a building yesterday in Hezbollah area, looked like it had been through a war, full of what looked to be bullet holes in the concrete, I asked the taxi driver what happened to that building and he would not answer me. I saw another building like that this morning on way to [suburb of Beirut] to meet the Pastor, they are like war memorials."

Boarded up, war-torn building
(Beirut, Lebanon) (June 2015)

Story: Unknown Plans in Lebanon: Jesus Leads the Way

Lead me in the right path, oh LORD...Make your way plain for me to follow. (Psalm 5:8)

FINDING PEOPLE TO connect with in countries in the Middle East is an interesting process. An interesting time of learning to better trust *God* as He leads the way. A level of trust has to exist for the person going as well as for the person hosting. The person there in the Middle East is taking on risk by hosting an American...a foreigner...someone who sticks out in that environment. Sometimes the connections are made by God through a friend of a friend of a friend...

Prior to going to Iraq, Jordan and Israel in 2014, God asked me if I could handle showing up in Jordan with no plans, no connections, no hotel...and instead just arriving to find out what God had planned. I had to wrestle with that for *weeks* before I finally conceded to God that, if that was *His* plan for me in Jordan...even though it wasn't *my* plan...then I was good with that. And it was *that very night*...in the middle of the night...that I got an email from a friend of a friend in Israel telling me who I was going to connect with in Jordan...who the friend in Jordan of the friend in Israel of the friend in America was. So that's how it oftentimes goes.

So here I was a year later back in Iraq...getting ready to fly to Beirut in a couple of days...and still *waiting on God* to confirm a connection for me in Beirut. A connection with someone...*anyone*. But things were quiet. No email from Beirut telling me that someone...anyone...would meet me at the airport when I arrived. Instead, it was radio silence from Beirut. And I was nervous. I had been nervous enough about going to Beirut in the first place. But now, sitting on a couch in Iraq getting ready to fly to Beirut on Turkish Airlines in a couple of days...and not having heard from *anyone* in Beirut...the *nervousness* was surrendering itself to outright *fear*.

I have been learning through these Middle East journeys to rely more on God...to trust Him more...to seek direction from Him more through prayer and His Word. And so as I sought direction from God while sitting on that couch in Iraq, He led me to the book of Romans.

JOURNAL ENTRY, IRAQ, JUNE 22, 2015:

"Encouragement from God's Word when I still don't know what connections and plans are in Lebanon. *Lord please glorify your name through me. Amen*

"For those who are *led* by the Spirit of God are the *children* of God...

"In the same way, the Spirit *helps us in our weakness*. We *do not know what we ought to pray for*, but the Spirit himself intercedes for us through wordless groans...

"And we know that *in all things God works for the good of those who love him*, who have been called according to his purpose...

"What, then, shall we say in response to these things? If God is for us, *who can be against us?*...

"No, in *all* these things we are more than *conquerors* through him who loved us. For I am *convinced* that neither death nor life, neither angels nor demons, neither the present nor the future, nor any powers, neither height nor depth, *nor anything else in all creation*, will be able to separate us from the *love of God that is in Christ Jesus our Lord.*" (Romans 8:14, 26, 28, 31, 37-39 NIV)

God's Words in Romans were comfort to my aching soul. God gave me *peace* for the moment. And I *slept well* that night in Iraq as I waited for God to lead the way to Beirut.

מֵרֵעַ

The town in Iraq where I stayed (Northern Iraq) (June 2015)

Encountering Jesus

Story: Trip to Erbil: The Journey to Beirut Begins

So be strong and *courageous*! Do not be *afraid* and do not *panic* before them. For the LORD your God will *personally* go ahead of you. He will neither fail you nor abandon you. (Deuteronomy 31:6)

So, THE JOURNEY began from Northern Iraq through Turkey to Beirut. The first leg of the journey was to travel from Soran, Iraq near the Iranian and Turkish borders to Erbil…a drive of about 90 minutes that winds through a mountain pass as well as numerous checkpoints…and beauty. How comforting it is to know that God *personally* goes ahead of us and that He will not fail us and will *not abandon us*.

Journal Entry, Iraq, June 23, 2015:

"Hi y'all, we drove from Soran to Erbil today as I fly to Beirut early tomorrow morning. I'm staying in a nice hotel across from the 'Mega Mall,' which is a modern large mall, hence the name. You have to go through a metal detector for security reasons. We shopped in the local Bazaar in downtown, which reminded me of the Old City of Jerusalem area…lots of shops in cavernous stone walkways with the smell of spices and espresso, and Arabic and also Kurdish being spoken. We could not find an open restaurant due to Ramadan, so we had to settle for TGIFriday's, where everyone who works there is Filipino and speaks English. They had a special part of the menu for observers of Ramadan. It was a surreal dining experience.

"Northern Iraq has a lot of oil money and there has been a big effort to build it up like a Dubai of sorts. Problem is there is a war taking place 20 miles from here with ISIS, and the U.S. consulate was car-bombed here in April so, like the ski resort, many commercial and residential buildings are empty or filled with refugees (in half-finished buildings). It's kind of like painting a torn-up couch…it has a pretty color but is still visibly torn up. This nation is a torn-up nation from so many years of civil war and terrorist wars. Due to Ramadan, I was one of maybe 15 people in the massive fancy mall (has five or so levels). It's kind of a sad sight.

Becoming Friends With Jesus: Go On a Trip Together

"One thing about this trip that I am very excited about is the two missionaries who were also staying at Tim's house told me today that it had been very encouraging to spend time with me. That made my day as one of the reasons I go on these trips is to encourage the missionaries as it's a hard life for them in an environment like this with moving around so much. We had a fun breakfast in Soran and lunch in Erbil before I bid everyone goodbye as they needed to get back to Soran.

"On the drive to Erbil, we drove through a town named Shaqlawa, which is 45 minutes from Erbil. It used to be a Christian community and a refuge for Christian refugees. However, many Arabs from war-torn Falluja, Iraq have recently relocated to Shaqlawa, which is now nicknamed Shaqluja. An ISIS cell was uncovered there recently, presumably planning attacks on the Christian community or tracking what Christians and Westerners are doing in Iraq, like the US State Dept warning yesterday about militants/terrorists monitoring these types of groups. Please pray for the church and missionaries over here, including Tim and his wife and three children.

"I've been thinking about the refugees today and wondering how they are doing. Thanks for praying for them too."

Tim and me in Erbil (Northern Iraq) (June 2015)

Encountering Jesus

New friend in Iraq: a police officer we met at a coffee shop in Erbil (Northern Iraq) (June 2015)

Story: Feeling Alone in Iraq: Jesus the Faithful Friend

Give all your worries and cares to God, for *he cares about you.* (1 Peter 5:7)

AFTER A FUN day with new friends in Erbil, Iraq, I stood there on the front steps of the hotel waiving to them as they got in their car and drove off. And the ugly head of *fear* instantly began to rear itself. I was now "alone" again in Iraq. I had been invited to attend a church service that evening in a suburb of Erbil, but I was tired and weary from the journey. A lot had happened in three days in Iraq…many emotions swirled around in my soul. I was missing my good friend Lokman who was still living in the refugee camp, now the father of three children with their newborn baby. I had been through many security checks and checkpoints. The day before, I had received a US State Department security warning email about Iraq. I glanced through it and decided I had seen enough…it seemed to generally be the same types of warnings I was used to reading…terrorists, kidnappings, explosive devices, the need for personal security guards, the warning to not travel to Iraq unless you *have to*...so I stopped reading it. I turned and walked into the hotel and up to my room.

And so there I sat on the edge of the bed in that quiet hotel room in Iraq, wondering *who* God was going to connect me with in Beirut. And *how* He was going to do that. And *when*. I had been told about a month before by a new friend in America that I could connect in Lebanon with a Lebanese Pastor friend of his, but I had heard nothing from his friend. I decided to get some sleep and went to bed at 6:30 p.m., falling asleep to the sound of the minaret from the local mosque chanting something over and over in Arabic for the Islamic holy month of Ramadan. It sounded very close by and was loud...*very loud*...as it echoed through the city, so I put in ear plugs and drifted off to sleep.

I slept for two hours, awaking at 8:30 p.m. I couldn't go back to sleep. It was now dark in Iraq and the flight departed for Istanbul in 10 hours. I unplugged my phone from the charger...and began sending emails to friends requesting prayers given that the plans for Lebanon were not in place yet. I wanted *so badly* to know what God had planned there. It's funny...and kind of pathetic...that so often we, or at least I, don't request people to pray until *I'm desperate*. And as I sat there in that room in the darkness of the Iraq night, I had indeed become *desperate*. Even just to hear from someone...*anyone*...by email would be a great gift. How quickly we forget that Jesus is right there with us...our *brutally faithful friend* Jesus. So I began sending the emails...hoping, praying...that doing so would somehow help.

Prayer from back home in Scotland was a great source of encouragement and power for Mary Slessor as she followed Jesus through the cannibal jungles of Africa, and I was going to find out that would be the case for me too. Be encouraged by Mary Slessor's experience:

> Mary Slessor's achievements are inspiring evidence of the power of prayer. "I have no idea how and why God has carried me over so many hard places...except in answer to prayer at home for me. It is all beyond my comprehension...Pray on—power lies that way." (p.138)

Below are excerpts from some of the emails I sent from that hotel room. Emails from a *desperate guy in Iraq*...a guy trying not to appear in the emails to be on the verge of *panic*. I just started laughing out loud as I type this and reflect back on that moment in that room so far away as I now go back and read these emails. How often we try to *appear* to be the calm and cool Christian "trusting" God to lead the way...while we *secretly panic*. *That's* funny...*really* funny.

Encountering Jesus

Emails from Iraq, June 23, 2015:

"Hi [friend in Jordan], it is Brian from [America]. I trust you and your family are well in the Lord. I am in Erbil and fly to Beirut tomorrow. I would like to serve the refugees there and am trusting God to provide me those opportunities with a group there. Is there someone you know who I should go see there about helping out? I will be in Lebanon until Sunday morning and don't know right now what the Lord has planned. The Lord put it on my heart to contact you tonight. Thank you and God bless you. Brian

"Hi [friend in America] from Iraq, I hope you and the [local] church family are having an awesome week with Jesus! Would yall please pray for me? I fly to Beirut, Lebanon in the morning (it's night in Iraq right now) and right now I don't know if anyone will be meeting me at the airport, where I will stay, or anything else. I am trusting Jesus to lead the way. I leave Iraq at 11pm tonight [Eastern Standard US] time and arrive in Beirut at 7:30am tomorrow [Eastern Standard US] time. Please pray for opportunities for me to serve the refugees in Lebanon, to grow closer in my relationship with Jesus, and to encourage the church. I'm praying for you and your family and the [local] church family right now. Thanks for being a blessing!"

"[Friend in America], would you please text or call [our mutual friend] with the prayer request about Lebanon? I'd love for him and the [youth group] team to join us in prayer about this. I emailed him and [his wife] tonight about it but don't know if they will see it before I arrive in Beirut. Praise God when the body of the Church prays together across nations! Thanks!"

As I emailed friends in America and Jordan during the Iraqi night, I felt like a sailor on a sinking ship *desperately* tapping out a *call for help* across the radio lines. How quickly our friendship with Jesus...our personal relationship with Him...our faith that He is with us always...can *falter*. Thank God that He *never* gives up on us.

Becoming Friends With Jesus: Go On a Trip Together

City center in Erbil, a long way from home (Northern Iraq) (June 2015)

Story: Encouragement in Iraq: Jesus Wakes Me Up

The *earnest* prayer of a righteous person has *great power* and produces *wonderful results*. (James 5:16b)

So WHAT DOES a *brutally faithful friend* do? A friend like that stays with you no matter what. What a friend we have in Jesus. He gives us peace. He stays with us. He loves us...*no matter what*. And that's just what He did for me that night in that Iraq hotel room.

Unbeknownst to me, people had indeed received the emails and *had already begun to pray* that night about God's plan for Beirut. I was *enveloped* in peace and fell asleep. Then something happened to me that I hope I never forget. I was woken up in that hotel room in Iraq by *someone tapping me on my shoulder*. I was startled, it was so *real*. But *no one was there*. As God would have it, I looked at my email after being woken up that way and was so blessed by *encouraging* emails from friends, including a video message that our kids sent to me from Italy, where they were on vacation.[62] God is good!

In the Bible, the story is told about how Daniel had a vision and the man who appeared to him touched him as *encouragement in answer to prayer*.

> Just then *a hand touched me* and lifted me, still trembling, to my hands and knees. And the man said to me, "Daniel, you are very precious to God, so listen carefully to what I have to say to you. Stand up, for I have been sent

---

[62] Okay, so they vacation in Italy...while I vacation in Iraq. God's ways *definitely* are not our ways (Isaiah 55:8-9). God is so amazingly gracious...I was so glad that they got to experience Italy...wow what history, great food, people and beauty!

to you." When he said this to me, I stood up, still trembling. Then he said, "Don't be afraid, Daniel. Since the first day you began to pray for understanding and to humble yourself before your God, your request has been heard in heaven. I have come in *answer to your prayer*. (Daniel 10:10-12)

That man was Jesus.[63] Wow must Daniel have been encouraged!

At one point, Peter the disciple was imprisoned by King Herod after the King had the disciple James killed by sword. Peter's death was *imminent*. Peter was not only be guarded by 16 Roman soldiers, but he was also chained in the prison cell between two of those soldiers. And, in *impossible* circumstances from an *earthly perspective*, an angel of the Lord appeared in that cell that night as Peter slept and *struck Peter on his side* in order to wake him up. Not only was God going to encourage Peter through this angelic awakening…but God was going to miraculously rescue Peter as *encouragement in answer to the prayers* of many faithful followers of Jesus:

> About that time King Herod Agrippa began to persecute some believers in the church. He had the apostle James (John's brother) killed with a sword. When Herod saw how much this pleased the Jewish people, he also arrested Peter. (This took place during the Passover celebration.) Then he imprisoned him, placing him under the guard of four squads of four soldiers each. Herod intended to bring Peter out for public trial after the Passover. But while Peter was in prison, *the church prayed very earnestly for him.* The night before Peter was to be placed on trial, he was asleep, fastened with two chains between two soldiers. Others stood guard at the prison gate. Suddenly, there was a bright light in the cell, and an angel of the Lord stood before Peter. The angel *struck him on the side to awaken him* and said, "Quick! Get up!" And the chains fell off his wrists. Then the angel told him, "Get dressed and put on your sandals." And he did. "Now put on your coat and follow me," the angel ordered. So Peter left the cell, following the angel. But all the time he thought it was a vision. He didn't realize *it was actually happening*. They passed the first and second guard posts and came to the iron gate leading to the city, and this *opened for them all by itself*. So they passed through and started walking down the street, and then the angel suddenly left him. Peter finally came to his senses. "It's really true!" he said. "The Lord has sent his angel and saved me from Herod and from what the Jewish leaders had planned to do to me!" (Acts 12:1-11)

---

[63] See description of Jesus in Daniel 7:13 and Revelation 1:12-13.

Becoming Friends With Jesus: Go On a Trip Together

So, do you *really* believe that this happened to Peter? Do you believe it can happen to you? I admit that I had less faith about these types of miracles until they started happening to me during the trips in the Middle East. It seemed that the more difficult the circumstances I faced…the more that God showed up.

After I was woken up in that dark room in Iraq by someone tapping me on my shoulder, I was very *encouraged* and believe that Jesus wanted me to see those messages…and He wanted to *reassure* me that I was *not alone*…so He tapped me on my shoulder as an extra reminder that He *truly* is *always* with me. Even in a hotel room at night in the Middle East. In answer to the prayers of the faithful back in the United States.

Here are some of those encouraging emails…those *great gifts*…that had arrived while I slept.

Emails to Iraq, June 24, 2015:

"Hey my friend! Awesome to hear from you. I have been following your progress. You have had multiple Pray Warriors praying for you on a pretty constant basis here in [America]. I love you my brother! We cannot wait to get a firsthand account of this awesome journey."

"It is wild that this is when you asked for specific prayer as part of your journey. On the surface, everyone focuses on the Iraq leg. The Lord has laid on my heart, from day one, the Lebanon leg of your journey. I pray that His awesome plan for you and your journey will glorify His name, to His glory, at the time and place of His choosing. I love you my brother!"

"Praying God's Waterfall of Grace upon you and your time in Beirut.
Faith pleases God, He rewards those who diligently seek Him.
You are walking by faith, not by sight.
Your God will supply all your needs.
The steps of a righteous man are ordered by God.
He is Jehovah Jireh.
He is making your paths straight.
He is the Illuminator.
Greater is He that is in you than he that is in the world.
Praying for you bro."

"We are praying, bro. We are ALL praying. He has led you there and has promised to never leave you nor forsake you. Jesus will be your peace, the Spirit will be your comforter and the Father will be your provider.

'Don't take care. Take risks' Love you, bro."

"It is our joy, honor and privilege to pray for you! Thank you for the emails and the blessing of your awesome book! We have worship at 8:00 and will lift you up in prayer with leaders at 11:00 too. God bless you, Brian!"

"Hi Brian,
We had an awesome time of prayer last night and a group from [our home church] at [the youth group service project] organized a prayer time for 7:30 am this morning for you. We are praying that you can discern God's plan for you in Beirut. Please continue to let us know how we can pray for you and can't wait to hear about your visit!"

"Will continue to pray for you and specifically for tonight and tomorrow."

Talk about *encouragement* with a capital "E"! Wow was I encouraged as I sat there in the hotel room reading these *wonderful* messages…my *desperate soul* was filled with encouragement, peace and joy.
Jesus the *brutally faithful friend*. I prayed for guidance. I asked others to pray for guidance. I desperately asked Jesus to please lead the way. He *heard* me. And He *guided* me:

I love the LORD because he *hears my voice* and my prayer for mercy. Because he *bends down to listen*, I will pray as long as I have breath! (Psalm 116:1-2)

Pray in the Spirit at all times and on every occasion. Stay alert and be *persistent* in your prayers for *all* believers *everywhere*. (Ephesians 6:18)

What a gracious gift from my friends…the gift of their friendship, encouragement, faithfulness and prayers. It's hard to describe how much that meant to me that dark, lonely night in Iraq.
I love my friends. And I love Jesus…my *brutally faithful friend*. Just like God's Word says, a true friend is always loyal…always there in our time of need…loves us at all times…and stands with us during times of adversity:

A friend is *always loyal*, and a brother is born to help in *time of need*. (Proverbs 17:17)

Becoming Friends With Jesus: Go On a Trip Together

A friend *loves at all times*, and a brother is born for *a time of adversity*. (Proverbs 17:17)

I was so encouraged about my *personal friendship* with Jesus. Here God was answering the prayer I had offered two years earlier…to please show Himself to me…and there I was in that hotel room getting to know Jesus better.

I emailed one of my friends that night:

Jesus is an awesome and faithful friend. The Lord woke me up from sleeping to read [your] encouraging messages…someone tapping on my shoulder…His presence is that *real*.

And I typed in my journal the next day:

Jesus is indeed always with us. He gives us peace that surpasses all understanding. I experienced that last night and today…crazy peace.

Friendship. Peace. Encouragement. *Jesus*.

מֵרֵעַ

Sun setting over refugee camp in Northern Iraq (June 2015)

Story: Driving to the Iraq Airport at Night: Jesus Watches

A song for pilgrims ascending to Jerusalem. I look up to the mountains—does my help come from there? My help comes from the LORD, who made heaven and earth! (Psalm 121:1-2)

*B*EFORE I WENT to bed in the hotel in Iraq, I asked the man working at the front desk how I could get a ride to the airport at 3:30 a.m. He told me that a man he knew could take me. I thanked him in Arabic...*shukran jaziilan*...and trusted that God would send the right person for the job. I didn't know *any* of these people.

When I think of the Middle East, it's easy now to picture Land Rovers rushing along the city streets...and across the desert and mountain roads. Land Rovers are a popular vehicle in the Middle East. I imagine they are reliable. And reliability of your vehicle is *critical* in a place like that.

So, as I walked into the hotel lobby at 3:30 a.m. that morning, I was introduced to the man who would drive me through the night to the airport. And, sure enough, he was driving a Land Rover.

As this stranger and I drove through the night along the quiet roads...as we zoomed past buildings with Arabic signs...I looked out the window and had one of those moments where you realize deep within your soul that God's Word is indeed *God's Word*. One of those moments when Words in a Book come true before your very eyes:

Now all glory to God, who is able, through his mighty power at work within us, to accomplish *infinitely more* than we might *ask or think*. (Ephesians 3:20)

I never in my wildest imagination during the first 46 years of my life asked or thought that I would someday be riding in a Land Rover with a stranger along the dark, quiet roads of Iraq...wondering whether someone would be waiting for me at the airport in Beirut in 12 hours. God is an *awesome* God and Jesus is an *amazing friend*.

Journal Entry, Iraq, June 24, 2015:

"Erbil airport security early this morning, checkpoint first, then bomb check mile or more from airport with pat down at next station, then a couple more checkpoints, and passport control, then airport security check with bags searched. So much security, but God is the only one true security.

"I wonder Lord what your plans are for Lebanon. Thank you for sending me there. May you be glorified.

"Plane takes off for Istanbul in 30 minutes at 6:10am, friends are going to be praying for me at the same time (will be late last night in the US). *Thank You Lord for their prayers. Please bless and keep them in the palms of Your hands. Amen*

"It's a different experience to be arriving in Beirut, Lebanon, a war-torn country where the primary terrorist/militant group is the Shia Muslim Hezbollah group...not knowing if anyone is going to meet me at the airport. I have not received an email from anyone confirming that someone will be there, and I have no hotel reservation or even a hotel name or a phone number for anyone there. But God is faithful and He told me to go to Lebanon, so I am going and will see what He has planned. He has given me an amazing amount of peace and I am so thankful to Him for doing that. That is the fruit of prayers of friends!

"God led me to wear my Christian leather bracelet (has a cross on it) the whole time I was in Iraq. Perfect love casts out fear (1 John 4:18). I was not ashamed to be a Christian or afraid to wear a bracelet like that in Iraq, because God is with me. God is good!

"The vehicle in front of us this morning at the bomb check/pat down checkpoint at the Erbil airport had a UN license plate on it. I made note of the man who got out of it at the checkpoint. As God would have it, he stood next to me on the transfer bus at the Istanbul airport, so I struck up a conversation with him. Turns out he is from Nigeria and is the Director of Education for the UN/UNICEF in Iraq and he is familiar with the high school that was started at Camp Baserma that Lokman my friend is in charge of! Praise God! I told him about my involvement with that camp and seeing the high school and knowing Lokman. He was touched that I go help refugees for no pay and on my vacation time. I told him I'm paid by God. We exchanged cards and he asked me to contact him to discuss Camp Baserma further and maybe helping to get computers in Erbil to donate to the camp high school. Praise God!"

ENCOUNTERING JESUS

Driving through the night on the dark streets of Iraq (June 2015)

Story: Digging into God's Word: Jesus Leads the Way

Your word is a *lamp* to my feet and a *light* to my path. (Psalm 119:105 ESV)

A FUN AND exciting part of the Middle East journeys is making new and unexpected friends from countries all over the world. At the house I stayed at in Iraq, there were two missionaries also staying there for a visit. One was Italian and one was Polish. They were both now living in England and serving God there and around the world on multiple continents as He would lead them. They were very interesting to meet and a joy to spend time with.

The last morning in Iraq before I left the house, I ended up unexpectedly having breakfast with these two new friends. They had already sat down at a small table in a small upstairs kitchen in the house to eat. I was walking past that room and stopped by to say good morning. I ended up sitting down at the table.

After some general chit-chat, the woman originally from Italy explained to me with her Italian accent that it's not to our eyes, but to our steps that we should take our path. She explained that we step in faith *without fully seeing* because we should trust the Lord with *all* our heart and lean not on our own understanding. She said that in *all* ways we should acknowledge Him and He would make our paths straight (referring to Psalm 119:105 and Proverbs 3:5-6). How amazing that God would share that with me through her as, unbeknownst to these two new friends, I was *struggling* with anxiety about not knowing the plans for Beirut...with not being able to *see* the plans.

So there I was focused on those verses in Iraq before flying to Beirut. Wow does God know *exactly what* we need and *exactly when* we need it!

God reminds us over and over how critical it is to *know* His Word and to *remain* in it:

The grass withers and the flowers fade, but the word of our God *stands forever.* (Isaiah 40:8)

If you *remain in me* and my words *remain in you*, ask whatever you wish, and it will be done for you. (John 15:7 NIV)

The Greek word translated to English as "remain" is *meno*, which connotes staying, dwelling, *enduring*. Hanging on to Jesus. God sees what we don't see...and He keeps His loving eye on us as He shows us the way we should go:

I [God] *will* instruct you and teach you in *the way you should go*; I will counsel you with *my loving eye on you*. (Psalm 32:8 NIV)

Corrie ten Boom took great comfort in this promise of God, explaining in *Tramp for the Lord* that Psalm 32:8 was "God's pledge to guide me in all my journeys" (p.33). What comfort and assurance we can have in knowing that God's loving eye *is on us* as He leads us where to go!

After boarding the flight to Istanbul, I struggled with the ticking clock in my mind as the seconds and minutes passed by as I got closer to the time I would arrive at the Beirut airport later that day. I struggled with what I could do on that plane to help figure out what was going to happen in Beirut...to figure out what my next steps needed to be. And I was reminded about what the missionary had told me the day before in Iraq...that we *step out in faith* without fully seeing...that *His Word* is the light to our path. So I got out my Bible on that flight to Istanbul *very hungry* for some light.[64]

---

[64] Corrie ten Boom shares in *Tramp for the Lord* about seeking out comfort and direction in God's Word as she found herself alone in New York...God having told her to go there even though she didn't know anyone there...so she went. See Chapter 5, pages 33-44, entitled, "A Great Discovery."

Journal Entry, Flight to Istanbul, June 24, 2015:

"It's a new experience (unfortunate to say) of getting ready to go where God has called me and having to rely on *God's Word* to guide my path through the Holy Spirit. As an American, I'm so used to planning everything out...as opposed to just going and showing up in a foreign war-torn country to see what God has planned. So, I opened up God's Word on the plane to guide my path, not really sure how that would work as I knew the Bible does not say things like, 'Stay at the Hotel Lebanon,' 'Take the blue taxi from the airport,' 'Don't trust the man in the green taxi,' 'Go to the XYZ Church in XYZ city to meet with Pastor XYZ.' Like I said, this was new to me (*but shouldn't be*). So I began perusing through God's Word and read some verses in the Old Testament about Lebanon and the cedar trees there. Was God telling me to go see the famous cedar trees? I was led to the book of Matthew and there things started to get clear in my spirit. I read verses like the following:

"Matthew

Let your light shine before others. (5:16)

Love your enemies and *pray* for those who persecute you. (5:44)

The Lord's Prayer. (6:9-13)

Do not worry about your life. (6:25)

Do not worry about tomorrow. (6:34)

Your Father in Heaven *will* give good things to those who ask Him. (7:11)

Do unto others what you would have them do to you. (7:12)

Ask the Lord of the harvest to send out laborers into His harvest. (9:38)

Jesus gave the disciples *authority* over unclean spirits, to cast them out, and to cure every disease and every sickness. (10:1)

Becoming Friends With Jesus: Go On a Trip Together

Jesus sent the twelve out and told them to proclaim the good news, to cure the sick, raise the dead, cleanse the lepers, and cast out demons...whatever town or village you enter, find out who in it is worthy, and stay there until you leave. (10:7-11)

I am sending you out like sheep in the midst of wolves, so be *wise* as serpents and *innocent* as doves. (10:16)

When you are handed over to the authorities, don't worry about what to say because *God will speak through you* with the Holy Spirit. (10:19-20)

When they persecute you in one town, flee to the next. (10:23)

Have no fear of them, instead fear God. (10:26, 28)

Don't be afraid, you are of more value than many sparrows. (10:31)

Whoever acknowledges Jesus before others will be acknowledged by Jesus before God. (10:32)

Whoever welcomes you welcomes me. (10:40)

Whoever gives even a cup of cold water to a little one will not lose their reward. (10:42)

Whoever welcomes a child welcomes Jesus. (18:5)

The Kingdom of Heaven belongs to little children. (19:14)

Love the Lord your God with all your heart, soul and mind, and love your neighbor as yourself. (22:37, 39)

All authority in Heaven and on earth has been given to Jesus, so go therefore and make disciples of all nations, baptizing them in the name of the Father and the Son and the Holy Spirit, and teaching them to obey everything Jesus commanded of His disciples. And remember that Jesus is with us always. (28:18-20)"

And then I was led on by God to the books of Luke, Acts and others, as my spirit soaked in the encouragement, peace and guidance.

"Luke

Do not be afraid (Zechariah) for your prayer *has been heard.* (1:13)

Love your enemies, do good to those who hate you, bless those who curse you, pray for those who abuse you. (6:27-28)

Give to everyone who begs from you. (6:30)

Whatever house you enter, first say, "*Peace* to this house!" (10:5)

Whenever you enter a town and its people welcome you, eat what is set before you; cure the sick who are there, and say to them, "The Kingdom of God has come near to you." (10:8-9)

"Acts

You will *receive power* when you receive the baptism of the Holy Spirit. (1:5, 8)

Everyone who calls on the name of the Lord shall be saved. (1:21)

Ask God to grant to His servants to speak God's Word with boldness, while they stretch out their hands to heal, and signs and wonders are performed *through the name of Jesus.* (4:29-30)

Many *signs and wonders* were done through the apostles. (5:12)

Pray and *lay your hands* on people. (6:6)

"1 Corinthians

I have made myself a slave *to all.* (9:19)

"Galatians

Bear one another's *burdens.* (6:2)

Don't grow weary in doing *what is right.* (6:9)

"**Ephesians**

Put on the whole *armor of God.* (6:11)

"Interesting that what I did not see going through God's Word is what I have almost always done in the past: plan, plan, plan...instead of pray, pray, pray and go. Jesus even told the disciples that he sent out to not take any overnight bags or money. Wow that's different than what I do."

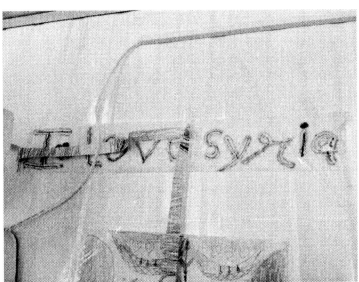

Handwritten sign made by Syrian refugee children in Lebanon that says, "I Love Syria" (Zahle, Lebanon) (June 2015)

Encountering Jesus

Story: Flight to Beirut: Jesus Leads Through Kindness

> Or do you show contempt for the riches of his kindness, forbearance and patience, not realizing that *God's kindness* is intended to lead you to repentance? (Romans 2:4 NIV)

*I*ARRIVED IN Istanbul and found some great stores at the airport to buy souvenirs for friends and family. I also bought some Turkish delights candy to give as a gift to *someone* in Lebanon, but I didn't yet know who that would be. Airports in the Middle East are *fascinating* places. I've always enjoyed "people-watching" in airports, and all the more so in the Middle East as you see people from so many different cultures and you hear so many different languages. Announcements over the airport speaker systems are oftentimes made in both Arabic and English, with Turkish included in Istanbul.

I found the departure gate for the flight to Beirut and tried to get a quick nap, but there was just too much going on there to sleep. People bustling around. Lots of languages being spoken. Restless children who had been cooped up too long on airplanes and at crowded gates.

I checked for wi-fi again like I did the first time I came through the Istanbul airport on the way to Iraq. And, once again, there was not wi-fi that I could figure out how to use and I didn't want to submit my debit card number as I wasn't sure what I would be charged and whether I would even get connected to the wi-fi. So I sat there *without any connection to the outside world*…no phone, no internet, no email, no text…*nothing*. Once again, I had that feeling of immense *vulnerability*. And, add to that, I would be in Beirut in about *three hours*.

It's moments like those where it helps greatly to have read some of the stories about people who have followed Jesus wherever He led them…trusting that He would lead the way and always be with them. In *Tramp for the Lord*, Corrie ten Boom explained how God made clear to her that she should never ask for money, travel expenses, speaking fees or even for a place to stay. Instead, she should "trust in [God] believing that [He] will never forsake [her]" (p.84).

So there I was in Istanbul…with my Loving Daddy watching over me. And it was time to board the flight to Beirut. God was again gracious through the security check and I was let on to the plane without *anyone* searching the heavy backpack and additional backpack that I was carrying. In fact, *I wasn't asked a single question*. God knows how much we can handle…! (1 Corinthians 10:13).

And there I was walking onto the plane for the two-hour flight to Beirut. It was a big plane. I was assigned to one of the side sections of the plane where there are two seats by a window. Next to the two seats was an aisle, and then four seats in the middle of the plane, and then another aisle followed by another section with two seats by the window on the other side of the plane. I found my seat and saw that there was a young Muslim veiled woman sitting in the seat in-between me and the window. With her was a precious little girl about two years old squeezed in between the woman and the seat in front of her. I helped the mother put up her suitcase and stroller in the overhead compartment and then settled in to my seat. In the back of my mind, the clock kept ticking as I got closer to the arrival in Beirut...now only *two hours away*.

I told the woman next to me that, after the flight took off, if there were open seats on the flight (which it looked like there would be), I would be glad to change seats so her daughter could sit in my seat. She was *relieved* to hear this...it looked like she had already had a challenging travel day with her little girl. She looked *exhausted*.

Her daughter played with the cross on my bracelet and with the magazines I was perusing before I moved seats. It was fun making big smiley faces to her as she smiled back at me. And it was fun treating her mom with *respect* and *dignity*. I wondered what their lives were like...and what the little girl's life would be like in the days and years ahead.

The people on the flight were a combination of veiled women as well as women dressed very Western, as well as men dressed Middle-Eastern conservatively as well as very Western too. A man in line at the departure gate told me that Beirut is very "Westernized," and I was seeing a hint of that on the flight. I was excited to get to experience Lebanon soon...!

So as I sought out each step of the path I was on, I stood up on the plane that was now in the air and looked around for an empty seat to sit in. There was one several rows behind us on the other side of the aisle that we were on, so I walked back to it and took a seat. It seemed to be the one I was supposed to sit in.

So I sat there wondering what the next step would be. And then the stewardess walked down the aisle passing out the passport control cards. I took mine and looked at it, and was glad to see that it was in both Arabic and English. But I was not so glad to see that you were *required* to not only list *where* you would be staying, but the *address* for it as well. My immediate thought was, "*You've got to be kidding me.*" Ugh, I thought as I stared down at the security card in my hand...I had *no idea* where I would be staying and did not know the name of *a single hotel in Beirut*. And there was no wi-fi on the flight to look one up. That was an *unsettling feeling* as the plane raced towards Beirut.

I found that the man who was now across the aisle from me...my new neighbor, a very *large* Arab man...was enjoying life as he laughed and talked fairly loudly. He had a fun personality and I struck up a conversation with him. We spoke in English and I learned that he and his wife and other family members were returning from vacation in Turkey. He was wearing shorts, which you don't see in the conservative Muslim areas of the Middle East. And he had a fun personality.

As I waited for a nudge from God about the next step, God prompted me to ask him if he could recommend any hotels in Beirut...desperately thinking in my mind that I very badly needed a *name* of one...and preferably *an address*...! His wife was sitting next to him and seemed uncomfortable about this stranger asking her husband if he could recommend any hotels in Beirut. After all, we were landing in about 90 minutes and I expect it would have seemed unusual to most people for someone to be planning their trip to Beirut *an hour before landing there*...!

While we were talking, he reached down into his bag and pulled out what I quickly recognized as a bottle of Jagermeister (a German liquor that tastes like licorice) and poured himself some more in his cup. It was about 1 p.m. and I realized at least some of the reason why he was having such a good, loud time on that plane. As is customary in the Middle East, he offered to pour some into my cup that I had been drinking coffee out of. I wanted to decline but declining an offer of hospitality in that area of the world is a *major insult*. God nudged me that I shouldn't be rude...that I should honor his kind gesture, so I begrudgingly said okay and he poured me a drink.[65] I don't drink much alcohol...maybe a glass of wine or two *per month*, so I figured I could just kind of take a sip. But no, he wanted to *toast and drink together*. So, there on a plane somewhere over the Mediterranean as the clock ticked towards the arrival in Beirut, we toasted, me and my new large and loud Arab friend. I had to *laugh* at that unexpected moment in my life...and I'm laughing as I type this. I could just imagine how it was going to go at airport security now...me arriving *alone* not knowing *where* I was going or *who* I was going to be with...*and* with *alcohol on my breath*...*nice*! Sometimes you just have to laugh...or you might cry instead.

My new friend did finally end up recommending some hotels. And, in fact, got quite *excited* to recommend many of them in Beirut as well as in another town that was apparently also on the Lebanese coast. Due to his thick accent, I was not sure how to spell any of them, so I asked him to please spell *one* of them...*any*

---

[65] Amazingly, after I returned to America, I met a friend for coffee and he recommended that I read a book called, *"God's Smuggler"* about Brother Andrew and his smuggling of Bibles into closed Communist countries. I bought the book and read in it that Brother Andrew experienced the same situation at a pub in one of those Communist countries...whether to accept the gift of a glass of beer. And God nudged him to do the same thing that God nudged me to do...to accept it and not decline the offer of hospitality and kindness. What affirmation that was about accepting my new friend's offer on the flight to Beirut!

Becoming Friends With Jesus: Go On a Trip Together

one of them. I don't even remember if I asked him if he happened to know the *address* of the hotel...! Well, at least I had the name of one, even if terribly misspelled! I figured that was much better than writing, *"I don't know."* However, I didn't yet write the name of the hotel on the customs card in the hope that the walkway to the security area would have advertisements along the way for hotels complete with pictures of them *and addresses*.

The announcement came on shortly after that...the plane was beginning its *descent into Beirut*. It was time to learn some more about the path that God had me on...like how difficult the questioning in the passport line would be...and whether I would be admitted into the country. And, if I was denied entry, where would I go?

מֵרֵעַ

The bracelet God told me to wear every day during the trip to the Middle East (June 2015)

Encountering Jesus

Story: Passport Control in Beirut: Jesus Whispers

"My thoughts are *nothing* like your thoughts," says the LORD. "And my ways are *far beyond* anything you could *imagine*." (Isaiah 55:8-9)

THE FLIGHT PATH into Beirut takes you in low as you approach the coastline. It's a beautiful sight to see the *deep-blue* of the Mediterranean Sea give way to the skyscrapers of Beirut. The plane flew over an impoverished area and landed and I said goodbye to my newest friend as I walked up the aisle of the plane to the doorway into Beirut. The other passengers and I walked the long walk to security...and I came to find out that there wasn't a *single* advertisement for a hotel along the way. And it was time to go through security.

Journal Entry, Beirut, June 24, 2015:

"It's an interesting moment during a trip in the Middle East when you approach the passport control lines...as you approach the person who will decide if you are allowed into the country. There I was at the Beirut airport looking at the different stations and the people at them...I had no idea where I would be staying, only had one incomplete local phone number for someone I've never met and who did not know I had [part of] their number and did not know me (Lokman at Camp Baserma in Iraq has a sister in Beirut and gave me her number and some gifts for her, but turned out the number was not complete...!), did not know what I would be doing in Lebanon or whether anyone was going to pick me up.

"I stood there going through what I would say if I was questioned like I was at the Israeli border last year...and then pushed all that aside as I was reminded that the Lord will tell me what to say. There was a woman at one station who looked nice and the rest of the stations were run by men with a manager being brought in when an issue arose. One of the men looked particularly tough and serious and seemed to be [thoroughly] questioning people's documents, etc. God nudged me to get in *his line*, although I wanted to get into the lady's line. So I got in the serious/tough looking guy's line...because God is always right. I quickly wrote the name of a hotel on the passport/customs card but had no address for it and hoped I spelled the name of it right! I had no reservation info to show security and no phone number other than one for a total stranger (which was not even a complete number...!). I had hoped there would be signs in the walkway after we got off the plane showing names, addresses and phone numbers of hotels, but there weren't any. So I waited in his line and I think (I hope!) I prayed. I thought about what I would do if I was denied entry. Would I go back to Istanbul? I didn't know how that would work. Thank God people of faith were praying at that very time because my faith was weak.

"Last year when I approached passport control in Iraq, I was told my passport was fake (turned out he was messing with me...!). What would this man do here in Beirut?

"It was my turn and I walked up to his window. I smiled at him and he didn't smile at me. I handed him my passport and he looked down at it...and immediately smiled and said, 'United States...I love United States! My fiancé is from America and I want to live there!' I was relieved and shocked (oh yee of little faith...!), and smiled a real smile and laughed. He ended up asking me what America is like and we had a fun visit and talked about marriage and what the Bible says about a man and a woman getting married. I wished him a blessed marriage!

"Once again I was in awe of God and how faithful He is. So I walked into Beirut to get my bag. I was in!"

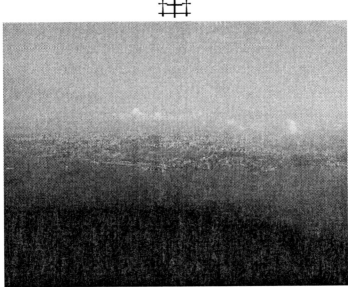

First view of Beirut…as the plane prepared to land
(Lebanon) (June 2015)

Story: Hezbollah's Turf: Jesus Drives with Us

God's way is perfect. All the LORD's promises *prove true*. He is a shield for all who look to him for protection. (Psalm 18:30)

I AM LEARNING more and more from these trips to the Middle East *with Jesus* to rely on God and not myself. After all, He's the one who can raise the dead:

In fact, we expected to die. But as a result, we stopped relying on ourselves and learned to *rely only on God*, who raises the dead. (2 Corinthians 1:9)

And God reminds us over and over as we trust in Him that He truly is able to do *immeasurably more* than we might ask or imagine:

Now to him who is able to do *immeasurably more* than all we *ask or imagine*, according to his power that is at work within us. (Ephesians 3:20 NIV)

So there I was walking past the customs/security area towards the baggage area. I checked to see if there was wi-fi, fully expecting that there would not be…and to my surprise, there was! At the airport, you got 30 minutes of *free wi-fi*. I was so thankful to get briefly reconnected with the outside world. What a gift from a gracious God!

As I waited for the piece of luggage that I checked from Iraq that was given to me by my new friend in Iraq and that was full of gifts to take back to America, I signed on to wi-fi and searched for the Lebanese Pastor's name that I had been given by a new friend in America. I had his name as well as the name of the Beirut suburb where the church he pastored was supposed to be located. I ran the search on Google and found the church website, but saw that there was *no address or phone number* listed for it, presumably for security reasons. But, it did have a small picture of the church. So I left that image on the screen and turned off the iPad for the time being.

The woman who I had initially sat next to on the flight was there with her daughter and a luggage cart…trying to keep her daughter from running around and once again looking very frazzled. I walked over to her and offered to help as she waited for her bags to arrive. She was once again relieved at a gesture of *kindness* and I had fun smiling with her daughter again. When the bags started arriving on the conveyor belt, she pointed to hers and I put them on her luggage cart and she and her daughter were off to Beirut. Our paths had crossed for those short moments and I hoped that *God's* kindness shown through me would be a continued blessing to her.

My bag arrived, which is always great to see when travelling overseas. I got it and headed to the airport exit. It was time to step out into Beirut to see what God had planned next.

I walked out and was immediately approached by some taxi drivers speaking Arabic. I had *no idea* what they were saying. I wasn't sure how I was going to go about asking them to take me to a church that I *only had a picture of*. Before I could begin trying, much to my surprise and relief, the big Arab man who sat next to me on the plane walked up and asked me what I was doing. I explained to him that I was trying to find a church and gave him the name of the suburb where it was supposed to be. He responded with words that were wonderful as he gently pushed me to the side, "*Okay, let me handle this.*"

I learned quickly as I listened to him and one of the taxi drivers speak in Arabic that Lebanese men are *very* animated as they talk…like Italians but in Arabic…they are a hoot! He and the taxi driver got into what appeared to me to be a heated and very excited conversation…on and on they went back and forth with lots of hand gestures. And then, as quickly as their verbal jousting had started, it was over. My friend turned to me and God gave me some more comforting words through him: "Okay, *he's going to take good care of you* and charge you a good price." Wow what soothing words to my shaken spirit…!

The taxi driver asked me to follow him and we walked across the street and down the sidewalk. I was in Beirut! We passed a beautiful tree and I found that he spoke a good amount of English, albeit with a heavy Arabic accent. I asked him while also motioning if it would be okay to take a picture of the tree. He was surprised and said okay, so I did. My first picture in Lebanon.

We got into his taxi, me joining him up front in the passenger seat, and he drove away from the airport. There we were heading into Beirut as I wondered how he was going to find the church. Beirut is a large city, as in over a million people big.

Within about 10 minutes as we drove along the highway, he told me that he knew a "good shortcut" that many taxi drivers don't take, which sounded good to me. After all, I was excited to find the church and hopefully find the Pastor there as well before the sun went down. He turned off the highway and we soon were approaching a *checkpoint* in the street. He stopped and the soldier waived us through. It turned out the shortcut was through *Hezbollah's* (the Shia Muslim militant group in Lebanon) *turf*! No wonder not everyone took this shortcut…I imagine none of the tour buses would!

The area we were driving through looked like what the Gaza Strip looks like on TV. It was probably the most impoverished city area I have ever seen other than the slums of Nairobi. It was terribly run down with lots of cables crisscrossing over the narrow street like a scene out of what I imagined Cuba might have looked like during the Cuban Missile Crisis. I took the opportunity to pray for the members of Hezbollah and reflected on what a *privilege* it was to be there praying for them as we drove through their turf. I could not resist taking a picture as we drove past the run-down buildings and he warned me rather energetically to not take any more pictures!

As we drove on, he asked me if I knew who the man was at the airport that had talked to him for me. I told him I did not, realizing that I didn't even know that man's name. He smiled and told me that he is *friends with that man's brother*. Wow, I thought, God is amazing and faithful! Of all the people I would sit down next to on that large plane...after having given up my original seat for a two-year old girl and her Muslim veiled mother.

We continued on...I was fascinated with what I was seeing in Hezbollah's area of Beirut. We passed a building that looked like it had been through a war, full of what looked to be *bullet holes* in the concrete. I asked the taxi driver what happened to that building and he would not answer me. It stood there like a silent, no-name war memorial.

The taxi driver arrived in the area of Beirut where I had been told the church was located. But *there was no church*. The taxi driver drove around and around in circles, stopping often to show someone the picture of the church. No one recognized the church. *No one*. The taxi driver even called his girlfriend and asked her to get on the Internet and search for churches in that suburb. She found some but none matched the one he was describing to her. I could tell he was getting agitated about how long the taxi ride was taking and presumably how much gas he was burning up with all these extra miles. He had apparently agreed on a price with my new friend at the airport, so his profit margin was dropping quickly as we drove and drove around the streets of Beirut.

He finally told me that the church was *nowhere to be found*. And there I found myself having to rely on God to tell me through the taxi driver where I should go. And I was very thankful that I had a connection with this driver through the man on the plane. What a gift that was from God! The man who was going to "take good care of me" decided in that car at that moment where I was going to stay for my first night in Beirut.

He told me he knew a good hotel that charges a fair price, and said he would negotiate the price for me. He also said it was near the waterfront in downtown Beirut. I told him that sounded good to me, so he headed towards the hotel. The taxi driver, who turned out to be a Muslim, parked his car and walked into the hotel with me. He began speaking in Arabic with the man at the front desk and negotiated the price for me. He finished and turned to me and told me how much the hotel was…it indeed sound to be a good price. I was relieved and paid him the fare plus some extra for all that he (and his girlfriend!) had done for me. And I was relieved once more to find out the hotel had *wi-fi that was working.*

I checked in to the room and returned to the lobby to look at my emails. It was early evening. I sat down, logged on to the wi-fi, opened the email program…and was further relieved to find an email from my friend in America who told me about the Pastor in Beirut. The Pastor I had been searching for with the taxi driver. And what did I read? To my surprise and relief, I read that the Pastor was *looking for me* at that moment at the airport. It turned out I had given my friend the *wrong arrival time* for the flight, and he had sent that to the Pastor who I had never heard anything from. What a feeling to know that someone in Beirut was looking for me…*in a good way*! I sat there smiling at the iPhone in my hands. I emailed my friend in America and he responded quickly…probably concerned about my whereabouts. It had been a long travel day and we agreed by email that it would be best if I got some rest and the Pastor would pick me up at the hotel in the morning. What wonderful news! So, it turned out that there had been a miscommunication and I would find out the next day that the Pastor thought he had sent me an email, but it never made it to me. And God used all of this to teach me about having a friendship with my *faithful friend Jesus*, who had been with me *the entire way.*

Picture of a run-down building I took during the taxi drive through Hezbollah's turf in Beirut after passing through Hezbollah's security checkpoint (Lebanon) (June 2015)

Story: Hi From Beirut! Arrival with Jesus

This I declare about the LORD: He *alone* is my refuge, my place of safety; he is my God, and *I trust him*. (Psalm 91:2)

I LEARNED SO much about Jesus, my Heavenly Father and the Holy Spirit during that 36 hour journey from the house in Northern Iraq to the arrival of my friend's email as I sat in the hotel lobby in Beirut. I had taken a trip *with Jesus*, and I got to *know Him* in a deeper, more personal way. I've heard it said that, "You never truly appreciate that Jesus is all you need until He's all you've got." I learned that during that journey. And I learned how to better *trust* my Heavenly Father and His Word. And I experienced the leading of the Holy Spirit in an *amazing* way. One Godly nudge and one step of faith at a time.

Becoming Friends With Jesus: Go On a Trip Together

Emails from Beirut, June 24, 2015:

"Hi bro, what a blessing yalls prayers were regarding Beirut! It was a big step in my faith journey to show up in Beirut with no plans or phone numbers, Jesus is always with us! God did miracles to get me through security and to a hotel in Beirut, no one was waiting for me, excited to see where the Lord leads. Taxi driver took a shortcut through Hezbollah's turf, checkpoint let us in, was what I imagine being in the Gaza Strip is like, I prayed for them to turn from their evil ways as we drove through a tough looking type of place, what a privilege! Praise God brother! God connected me with a Pastor here today by way of a mutual friend in America so, Lord willing, will start spending time with refugees here as soon as tomorrow. Please let the sisters there know how much I appreciate their prayers and encouragement! Thanks again for an awesome time in Iraq."

Emails from Beirut, June 25, 2015:

"Hi yall from Beirut. Wow was last night an amazing time of prayer across the ocean, thank yall so much. What a day of miracles by God as he stretched me in my level of trust in Him."

"Hi from Beirut! Because of the last 36 hours and what God did as part of the journey from Iraq to Lebanon, I am so encouraged in the power of God through the prayers of believers! And in the need to send believers out to share the good news, to pray for healing, and to trust that God will lead the way and provide all that is needed. Turns out there was a Lebanese Pastor who was expecting me but his message never arrived to me. We connected last night by God's grace and travelled to a refugee camp today near the Syrian border. God is so amazingly faithful. Thank you for the prayers…the arrival yesterday in Lebanon when prayers were taking place was a miracle-filled time. What a blessing to look back at what God did and how gracious people were to pray and stand in the gap. Be encouraged…I sure am!"

God is truly the Living God. The Bible is truly the Word of God. The Holy Spirit is truly our Guide. And Jesus is truly a *brutally faithful friend*.
Enough said.

Breakfast at the hotel in Beirut...*delicious* (Lebanon) (June 2015)

18   Eating Pizza With Jesus

> Still they stood there in disbelief, filled with joy and wonder. Then he asked them, "Do you have anything here to eat?" They gave him a piece of broiled fish, and *he ate it as they watched.* (Luke 24:41-43)

HE ASKED FOR something to eat. The Son of God...the Miracle Man...asked people for *something to eat.* And then they *watched him* eat the piece of broiled fish.

I get hungry. Refugees get hungry. We all get hungry. Even *Jesus*...God with us...got hungry:

> The next morning as they were leaving Bethany, Jesus was *hungry.* (Mark 11:12)

> In the morning, as Jesus was returning to Jerusalem, he was hungry. (Matthew 21:18)

> After fasting forty days and forty nights, he was hungry. (Matthew 4:2 NIV)

> As he spoke, he showed them his hands and his feet. Still they stood there in disbelief, filled with joy and wonder. Then he asked them, "Do you have anything here to *eat?*" (Luke 24:40-41)

And what a great time it is enjoying a meal or tea with new friends in the Middle East, whether in a refugee camp or a restaurant or someone's home. There is something special about having a meal or a tea together. Wow how awesome it would be to enjoy a meal with Jesus.

ENCOUNTERING JESUS

Fresh-picked fruits and nuts
(Mountains of Lebanon) (June 2015)

Story: Enjoying Sweets with New Friends in Beirut

Cheerfully *share your home* with those who need a meal or a place to stay. (1 Peter 4:9)

AN AMAZING THING happens when we go somewhere foreign to us…somewhere that is oftentimes in the headlines about wars, refugees and terrorists…and we make *friends* there. The headlines and fear go away and we find ourselves enjoying our new friends…laughing together, learning about each other, having tea together…having a meal together. I found myself one evening in Beirut at the home of the local Pastor. It was a wonderful evening with new friends. And I was reminded about the *joy* that Jesus must have experienced having meals with His friends.

Journal Entry, Beirut, June 26, 2015:

"There was a war between Hezbollah and Israel in 2006, lasted about a month, 1,200 children in Lebanon killed, Israel bombed many areas of Lebanon…similar death numbers for children in war Israel had with Gaza last August. Daniel[66] (13 years old now and so was about 4 during the war) is the son of one of the Lebanese Pastors I am spending time with, he remembers hearing the bombs and fleeing to his grandfather's cottage in the mountains. Kids deal with a lot of things in this area of the world that they don't deal with in the US.

"I spent a wonderful evening with the Pastor and his wife and their two wonderful children (Daniel is 13 and Esther is 6). His wife served sweets as well as a delicious juice that had juice from dates in it. Yum! It's nice to spend time in a host family's home when I'm on these trips so far away from our hometown. It was such a peaceful evening with them, even though the war was so close by and snipers had previously shot at this church premises where they live (upstairs). Jesus is the Prince of Peace and He was with us that evening and it was wonderful.

"Tomorrow we planned to head south near the border with Israel where wars have been fought between Hezbollah and Israel. There are Iraqi refugees there in addition to Palestinian and Syrian refugees. Eating sweets with Jesus one night, visiting refugees with the former-refugee Jesus another day."

---

[66] Names changed for privacy reasons.

Sweets for sale at Erbil city center market
(Northern Iraq) (June 2015)

Story: Teapot on the Kitchen Counter

> And people should eat and drink and *enjoy* the fruits of their labor, for these are *gifts from God*. (Ecclesiastes 3:13)

MY DEAR FRIEND Ahmad from Saudi Arabia moved back there with his wife and newborn daughter about six weeks after I returned from Lebanon. We had enjoyed a wonderful friendship for two years. We laughed many times together and had many meals and cups of tea together. I remember the first time we had tea together down by the river that winds through the town we live in. We sat there on a beautiful spring day drinking tea that he made...enjoying getting to know each other.

I bought a nice teapot during our friendship so that I could make delicious Saudi-style tea for him when he came to visit me. I'm sitting at my computer right now typing this as I look over at that teapot sitting quietly on the kitchen counter. It's been over a month since Ahmad moved back to Saudi. I haven't used the teapot since he left, and I don't want to put it away in a cupboard because it reminds me of him and our friendship. I learned how to enjoy tea with a friend because of him. He taught me how to make tea Saudi-style. He taught me a lot about hospitality and making guests feel like visiting royalty. Something special happens in a friendship as you sit together sipping hot tea and talking about life.

Jesus spent a lot of time talking one-on-one with people…meeting them where they were in life. Showing them *kindness* and *compassion*.[67] Sharing a drink with them…sometimes of cool water at a well[68]…and sometimes of wine at a table.[69] Life can pass by so quickly if we don't take time to slow down and enjoy a cup of tea with a friend. I wonder what Jesus and I would talk about over a cup of tea. I think…no, I *know*…that we'd get to *know each other better*. Just like my friend from Saudi and I did.

מֵרֵעַ

---

[67] See for example the story of how Jesus treated the woman caught in the act of adultery at John 8:1-11.
[68] See for example the story of Jesus spending time with the Samaritan woman at Jacob's well at John 4:1-26.
[69] See for example the story of Jesus spending the Last Supper with His disciples at Matthew 26:17-30.

Delicious Saudi-style meal Ahmad made for our family shortly before he moved back to Saudi (America) (June 2015)

19   Having a Glass of Wine With Jesus

> The Son of Man, on the other hand, feasts and *drinks*, and you say, "He's a glutton and *a drunkard*, and a friend of tax collectors and other sinners!" (Luke 7:34)

THE SELF-RIGHTEOUS religious rulers of the day in Jerusalem *hated* Jesus...they *despised* His popularity and His brutal honesty. He defied their compassion-less, judgmental focus on rules and laws, instead graciously forgiving and loving the people. These people whom Jesus loved and spent time with included the types of people that the self-righteous religious leaders refused to associate with, such as tax collectors, prostitutes and lepers. Jesus saw and still does see past the sin to the precious person created in God's image. I'm *so thankful for that*.

People disagree at times about whether it's okay for a Christian to drink alcohol. What I do know is that Jesus miraculously created over 100 gallons of wine from water at a wedding in Cana in Galilee (John 2:1-11). It would have been *humiliating* to the bride and groom in that culture for the wine to run out at the wedding banquet. I love that Jesus (and his mother) were no doubt concerned for them.

I also know that God clearly tells us not to get *drunk* on wine:

> Don't be drunk with wine, because that will *ruin your life*. Instead, be filled with the Holy Spirit. (Ephesians 5:18)

I used to get drunk on alcohol...and I love that Jesus loved me *regardless*. And then I stopped drinking alcohol and became a self-righteous, judgmental jerk about other people drinking...and I love that Jesus loved me *regardless*. And now I enjoy having a glass of wine every so often...about once a month or so...and I love that Jesus loves me *regardless*. The point is that Jesus loves us...He loves *you...no matter what* (John 3:16, Romans 8:38-39). There is plenty in the Bible about wine...the *allowance* of it by God...the warning by God about the *abuse* of it...the miracle of Jesus *creating wine* from water. And through all of that is Jesus...my *friend* Jesus...spending time with me regardless of whether I'm a drunkard, a self-righteous jerk or a casual glass-of-wine-every-so-often kind of guy. That's a *great friend*.

Encountering Jesus

New friend I made walking "by myself" through an Iraqi town (Northern Iraq) (June 2015)

Story: Glass of Wine at the Hotel in Beirut

I have never turned away a stranger but have opened my doors to *everyone*. (Job 31:32)

THE TRIPS TO the Middle East are *emotional roller coasters*. And I get drained along the way…weary of the journey…physically tired…trying to take in everything that God is allowing me to experience. One day when I got back to the small Beirut hotel, I went down to the little lobby there and sat on one of the couches that faced the front glass doors and beyond to the busy street. It was a great spot to journal the day's activities and decompress. There was a little bar back around the corner from the front desk…it wasn't any bigger than one of those old fashioned phone booths…the ones they still have on the streets of London. It was *tiny*.

Having a Glass of Wine With Jesus

I asked the bartender for a glass of wine. He was a nice Lebanese man and also served as the man who carried your luggage to your room. I got the impression that he served in a lot of roles at that hotel. He asked me how my day was going and I told him it had been a great one. He nodded and gave me the glass of wine and I settled in to the lobby couch watching the cars, motorcycles and bicycles zip by on the small street out front. I reflected on the day...the refugees...the soldiers...the checkpoints...the new friends. I journaled as I *enjoyed* the glass of wine. Jesus no doubt was sitting there with me. After all, He's *always* with us (Matthew 28:20). I so enjoy His friendship. I so enjoy His grace. I so enjoy His passion to not give up on anyone. And I so enjoy His *unconditional, no-strings-attached* love of me and everyone else on this planet.

View of the coastline of Northern Lebanon...*beautiful* and *peaceful*
(June 2015)

20 Hugging Jesus

That which was from the beginning, which we have heard, which we have seen with our eyes, which we have looked at and *our hands have touched*—this we proclaim concerning the Word of life. The life appeared; we have seen it and testify to it, and we proclaim to you the eternal life, which was with the Father and has *appeared to us*. (1 John 1:1-2 NIV)

WHAT A GREAT feeling it will be to *hug* Jesus. I am excited for the day that I die and *immediately* am in His presence.[70] I plan to hug Him…my friend Jesus. I love hugs. I was so excited to hug my friend Lokman when I returned to the refugee camp in Iraq where I met him the year before.

מֵרֵעַ

Lokman, his wife and one of their children…*wonderful* to see them and give them a great big *hug* (Northern Iraq) (June 2015)

---

[70] See the story of the crucifixion of Jesus with the two criminals at Luke 23:26-43 ("Then he said, 'Jesus, remember me when you come into your kingdom.' Jesus answered him, 'Truly I tell you, today you will be with me in paradise.'" Luke 23:42-43).

Hugging Jesus

Story: Return to Camp Baserma: My Friend the Refugee

Love each other with *genuine affection*, and take *delight* in honoring each other. (Romans 12:10)

I HAD NEVER returned to a refugee camp where I now had a special friend living there. And I was not expecting how *wonderful* it would be to see him again…and how *difficult* it would be to hug him and say goodbye…again. It's one thing to visit a refugee camp, spend time with the wonderful people there, and then leave. It's another thing, I found, to return to a refugee camp to see a friend there…and then leave…not knowing if you will ever see that friend again.

JOURNAL ENTRY, IRAQ, JUNE 21, 2015:

"The second camp we visited today is the much larger (about 5,000 people) Camp Baserma, which is where I visited last year and which consists of Syrian refugees. I have friends there and this was my first experience of visiting friends at a camp as a follow up. It was an awesome and emotional time for all of us.

"First, thank you for your prayers. The dream God gave me for this trip was to give copies of the *Vacation in Iraq* books to my refugee friends whose stories and pictures are in the book. God miraculously allowed that to happen. I was hoping my friends would be encouraged to know people are seeing their pictures and reading their stories and praying for them. In other words, they are not being forgotten. I didn't expect the reaction I got from Lokman. He was in tears, I had no idea how much it would mean to him and his wife. They loved it.

"When you have friends who are refugees in a war-torn land, a lot happens during the 15 months between visits. I was shocked and my heart broke to hear some of the things that I just don't think many times make headlines.

"First, great news that Lokman and his wife had a baby girl, she is now 1 and so cute. They now have three daughters.

"Sadly, there was an explosion recently at a hospital in Syria. Apparently with the demise of the economy there, propane tanks are exploding from faulty workmanship. In the recent explosion, Lokman's sister and a nephew were killed. They apparently worked at the hospital.

"On the brighter side, Lokman in his true nature of being a passionate teacher and wanting the refugee children to continue to receive an education, has started one of the first refugee high schools in this area. He worked for free for six months to get it started, as did my friend Muhammad (more on him below). Lokman was so excited to show me the new high school facility. It broke my heart to see what he was so excited about…let's just say it's not much…but it is a high school and he is passionately preparing these kids to possibly get to attend university if they pass the national high school exam this month. He is an amazing guy.

"Muhammad teaches too and also taught at the new high school for free for six months (they now get a paycheck).

"Lokman and I kept hugging each other as we tried to say goodbye, both of us no doubt wondering if we'll ever see each other again. It was terribly hard to leave. I fought back tears and he did too. It is hard to drive away from a refugee camp where a dear friend of yours lives. Harder than I ever imagined."

Hugging Jesus

Lokman and one of his children in front of the new high school at Camp Baserma (Northern Iraq) (June 2015)

Smiling children at Camp Baserma...I had just bought them some candy (Northern Iraq) (June 2015)

21   Jesus Had Compassion for the Crowds of People

When he saw the crowds, he had *compassion* for them. (Matthew 9:36a ESV)

*J*ESUS IS A *compassionate* Lord. A *compassionate* friend. Since He has shown *us* great compassion, we should show compassion *to others*. By doing so, we not only become more like Him but we get to know Him better.

صــــديقي

Rows of refugee tents for precious refugees
(Northern Iraq) (June 2015)

Jesus Had Compassion for the Crowds of People

Story: Veiled Face in Istanbul: Compassion of Jesus

Since God chose you to be the holy people he loves, you must clothe yourselves with tenderhearted mercy, *kindness*, humility, gentleness, and patience. (Colossians 3:12)

I ENJOY SHARING God's kindness and goodness with others. There are *many* opportunities to do that in the Middle East.

Journal Entry, Istanbul, June 20, 2015:

"A completely veiled woman in black with just a slit in her face cover for her dark brown eyes and eye lashes to be visible through stands silently in the cafe line as her eyes and expressionless black-covered face peer out. Her two little girls stand over by the glass wall looking out at the airplanes milling around on the tarmac. They look to be about 4 and 5 years old. She stands silently. I ask the cashier if the woman has been helped. She's like an abused dog that cowers silently and is so difficult to read. I'm so sad for her. Jesus says we shall know the Truth and the Truth shall set us free. I pray that she will know the Truth and be set free. I wonder what her girls think as they drink their sodas and mommy is completely covered in black except for her eyes. I wonder if they want to see their mommy's face right now...to see their mommy's smile. I don't think she's smiling as she sits in silence with them as they gaze out at the airplanes with their backs to her. I wonder if they will be fully veiled at some point in their lives. I wonder if they are nervous about that. I wonder what it's like to be covered in black except for your eyes for the first time. What reason is there to smile if no one will get to see it and share in it."

מֵרֵעַ

Encountering Jesus

Turkish coffee I bought at the airport coffee shop while my heart broke for the veiled Muslim mother (Istanbul, Turkey) (June 2015)

Story: Life in the Middle East Beyond the Headlines

He has told you, O man, what is good; and what does the LORD require of you but to do justice, and to *love kindness*, and to walk humbly with your God? (Micah 6:8 ESV)

L IVING IN AMERICA, it's hard not to focus on the headlines of news articles about the Middle East...to rely on the news articles as our source of all that we know about the Middle East. Many Americans do not have *any* Muslim friends. I was like that four years ago. The Middle East is a foreign, far-away land...and a *scary* one to many of us. One of the joys of travelling in the Middle East is getting to experience life there *beyond* the news headlines...to experience life there up close and *personal*. Somehow, over there, I can more closely relate to Jesus looking out over the crowds having compassion...and showing kindness.

Email from Istanbul, June 20, 2015:

"Salaam (peace) from Istanbul!

Jesus Had Compassion for the Crowds of People

"Hi yall from Istanbul! What a place and experience. Turkish Airlines was great on the flight from Boston to Istanbul. Great service and food, very comfortable plane, great coffee!

"Below are notes about the experience on the flight to Istanbul and the airport in Istanbul...an amazing place!

"Airplanes I have seen since arriving at the Istanbul airport:

"Pegasus air

"Iberia air

"Emirates air with Arabic on the side of the plane

"Arabian air with Arabic writing on the plane and two crossed swords on it

"Saudi Arabian air with Arabic on the plane

"Zagros air...yeah! This is the only Kurdish airlines in the world and the airline I flew on from Iraq to Jordan last year...I booked a ticket on it myself online thinking it was a German airline and found out it was a young start-up Kurdish airline...! It was a great flight and experience, I'm pretty sure I was the only American on that flight last year!

"I love experiencing life here past the headlines of death and terror and war and brutality and suffering...here are some of the experiences I love enjoying here...this area of the world becomes personal and so different than just sorrowful and terrifying headlines:

"Three year old girl speaking Turkish with her mom while standing on her mom's lap on the flight and rubbing noses and giggling with her.

"Lady In her early 20's, airline worker with Turkish Airlines, wearing a head scarf and laughing with a guy friend and texting etc on her phone with him as they laughed and chatted.

"A man praying towards Mecca at the airport in Boston.

"An infant baby girl sleeping on the overnight flight to Istanbul as we flew over Europe, she looked so peaceful.

"Mosque towers and high rise office buildings and apartment buildings as far as you can see as we land in Istanbul, with a sea that I have never seen before, beautiful.

"In flight movie screens with Arabic subtitles on one, another with Mandarin subtitles, so many people groups and languages and life experiences on the flight.

"Women completely covered/veiled in all black except for a slit in their face cover to see through. I wonder what their faces look like. It must be hot wearing those here in the warm terminal area.

"International gate area in Istanbul swarming like an ant hill that has been stabbed by a big stick by a five year old boy. People of all sorts of nationalities in the warm and congested terminal area bumping each other, trying to keep track of their children, with departure cities on the monitors that I've never heard of. An awesome place!

"A Middle Eastern big man traveling with two little girls ages about 4 and 6, they were so cute as the girls held hands to keep track of each other in the ant hill of humanity. I made room for them along the way and he thanked me. I told him he's a blessed man. He was surprised to hear me say that and seemed to enjoy it.

"I found a quiet seat by the window overlooking the runway of Middle Eastern airplanes milling around outside. I'm so thankful to be here right now away from the hectic crowd downstairs. I'm so privileged to pray for people as I sit here and as I rode the bus from the plane and as I walked in the ant hill at the terminal downstairs...it's crazy down there! So many different languages being spoken here."

Jesus Had Compassion for the Crowds of People

Going for a walk in Iraq one morning, excited to make new *friends* (Northern Iraq) (June 2015)

Story: Sights in Beirut: Jesus Loves Everyone

For God so loved *the world* that he gave his one and only Son, that *whoever* believes in him shall not perish but have eternal life. (John 3:16 NIV)

*J*ESUS LOVES EVERYONE. God gave His Son's life…for *everyone*. Knowing this…focusing on this…helps us love others…helps us love *everyone*. Through eyes of love…not eyes of judgment or hatred or bitterness…the people of the Middle East can be loved. We can and should hate *the evil that is done* through some of the people there like the terrorists…but we can and should love *the person that God created* in His image.[71] I enjoy meeting people in the Middle East and hearing their stories, as well as just watching life and people pass you by there. Jesus loves *every one of them*. And we should too.

---

[71] The common adage, "Hate the sin, love the sinner" is exactly what God says in His Word. Check out Romans 12:9 and Luke 6:35 as well as Chapter 42 in *Vacation in Iraq*.

Encountering Jesus

Journal Entry, Beirut, June 25, 2015:

"Wow is this a hopping and high energy city, what a mix of fancy stores and buildings and the very poor area controlled by Hezbollah, traffic is crazy here, tons of it and cars are a few inches from each other and tempers and horns flare/blare with people yelling at each other in Arabic out their windows! UPS delivery man was riding a UPS moped, weaving among the cars. This city is a unique mix of mosques and churches and Hezbollah and veiled women and very Western style women and very expensive cars and very beat up cars and impoverished areas and expensive areas...all right here in Beirut.

"I'm excited to travel around and spend time with the refugees. Damascus, Syria is about 50 miles east of here. The war is raging north of Raqqa, Syria this week between the Kurdish Peshmerga with US support, on one side, and ISIS on the other. So thankful I can be here to pray for everyone involved.

"The US Embassy is near the hotel. So excited to see what God has planned for the time in Lebanon. What a unique city on the Mediterranean."

Jesus Had Compassion for the Crowds of People

Military vehicle full of Lebanese soldiers driving along the road (Beirut, Lebanon) (June 2015)

Story: Traffic Beirut Style: Jesus Loves Us All

You will be *blessed* in the city and blessed in the country. (Deuteronomy 28:3 NIV)

*B*EIRUT IS A fascinating city. Such a mix of history, war, beauty, food, Muslims, Christians and cultures. It's amazing what you can see in just two minutes there.

JOURNAL ENTRY, BEIRUT, JUNE 27, 2015:

"Two minutes of watching traffic in front of the hotel in Beirut: military truck Vietnam war era style with soldiers in it, old beat up cars, shiny new Land Rover, old safari style Land Rover with soldiers in it, scratched up Mercedes, dented up taxis (no meters in taxis here, everything except gas seems to be negotiable, even hotels), very old looking European style yugo or something like that, new BMW with body style I have not seen before, military humvee with machine gun turret and soldiers, one of many of some of the bravest people I've ever seen: men driving little mopeds with no helmets on among the NASCAR-paced vehicles speeding and swerving along...!

"Military humvee just drove by the hotel. Another camouflaged humvee with soldiers in it just drove by the hotel. People ride dirt bikes here also. Then a moped went flying by with a man driving it, a veiled woman sitting behind him, and a toddler in between them...what a fascinating city!"

מֵרֵעַ

Driving along the road in Beirut (Lebanon) (June 2015)

22   Going Through Tough Times With Jesus

> Since he himself has gone through *suffering and testing*, he is able to help us when we are being tested. (Hebrews 2:18)

*J*ESUS SUFFERED. HE suffered *greatly*. In ways that are hard to imagine. Hard to *read* about. Hard to *watch* when His suffering is portrayed in movies or plays. He knows what it's like to *suffer*...to be in *agony*...to be in *distress*:

> He [Jesus] went on a little farther and fell to the ground. He prayed that, if it were possible, the *awful hour awaiting him* might pass him by. "Abba, Father," he cried out, "everything is possible for you. *Please* take this cup of suffering away from me. Yet I want *your will* to be done, *not mine*." (Mark 14:35-36)

> He [Jesus] prayed more fervently, and he was in *such agony of spirit* that his sweat fell to the ground like great drops of blood. (Luke 22:44)

> He [Jesus] took Peter, James and John along with him, and he began to be deeply distressed and troubled. "My soul is *overwhelmed with sorrow* to the point of death," he said to them. "Stay here and keep watch." (Mark 14:33-34)

> This High Priest of ours understands our weaknesses, for he faced *all of the same testings we do*, yet he did not sin. (Hebrews 4:15)

Suffice it to say that Jesus knows what it means to suffer. To be "*overwhelmed with sorrow to the point of death.*" (Mark 14:34a)

During terrible suffering in our lives, it can be very comforting to be with friends. That was the case for Jesus too. As Adam Hamilton put it in *24 Hours That Changed the World*:

> As Jesus approached his death, he found it *comforting* to be with his *friends*...we all need close companions with whom we can share such feelings [fear, anger, grief]. We need our Peter, James, and John. Often, like

Encountering Jesus

Jesus with his companions, we do not need our friends to say anything in our times of sorrow. Jesus did not ask Peter, James, and John for advice, or even for words of encouragement. Like us, he just wanted to know they were there. (pp.28, 36)

And going through suffering can help draw us *closer* to Jesus…help us relate to Him better on a personal level. As we suffer, we can be reminded that Jesus suffered…that His Father suffered…and that He is *always* with us.

Hudson Taylor was a missionary to China in the 1800's. His autobiography is one of my favorite books. He describes about how trials that he went through—and he went through a lot of them—helped him have a more real and intimate relationship with his Heavenly Father:

> My faith was not untried; it often, often failed, and I was so sorry and ashamed of the failure to *trust such a Father*. But, oh, *I was learning to know Him*! I would not even then have missed the trial. He became *so near, so real, so intimate*. (*Hudson Taylor*, p.123)[72]

So, as people suffer in the world…as we suffer…we can pray for them and for us to get to know Jesus in a more personal way through such suffering. After all, He suffered greater than any human ever has or ever will. He "gave himself as a ransom for all people" (1 Timothy 2:6a NIV) as He took on the sin of the *entire world*…past, present and future (1 Peter 2:24)…so that we could be saved. Instead of being bitter towards God or others…instead of harboring unforgiveness…instead of wallowing in our misery…we can *rejoice* that God is *near* to the brokenhearted (Psalm 34:18, Psalm 145:18, Philippians 4:5). He is near to *us*. Jesus is *always* with us (Matthew 28:20). And we can get to know Jesus *more personally* through such suffering.

I read on the BBC Middle East news app on my iPhone on September 3, 2015 about a man…a refugee, husband and father…who was clearly *overwhelmed with sorrow to the point of death*. My heart breaks for him. There is so much suffering in the Middle East right now…terrible losses and tragedies.

---

[72] *Hudson Taylor* by J. Hudson Taylor.

Going Through Tough Times With Jesus

Small chapel along the Via Dolorosa
(Jerusalem, Israel) (May 2012)

Story: A Refugee Child Washes Up on Turkey's Shore

The LORD is *close* to the brokenhearted and *saves* those who are crushed in spirit. (Psalm 34:18 NIV)

*A*S A PARENT, I imagine that the *worst fear* down in the depth of a parent's soul is for their child to die. Children are precious. They are an *amazing* gift from God. That fear of a parent *lurks* in the shadows of our souls. Every so often, consciously or subconsciously, our souls whisper the prayer that we don't want to vocalize: *"Please God, don't let my child...my baby boy...my baby girl...die."* And I imagine this is all the more haunting of a fear for mothers. The relationship of a mommy with her child is beautiful to watch. And a daddy with his child too.

To see pictures and read about a man so far away in Turkey who fled the war in Syria and who tried to flee to Greece by boat from Turkey...with his wife, three-year-old son and five-year-old son. To read about the boat that capsized off the coast of Turkey and the husband and father who struggled to save his wife and two little boys…the husband and father who lost that battle…and the three-year-old lifeless child, his son, who *washed up on Turkey's shore*…leaves me speechless…leaves me numb…*breaks my heart.*[73]

The people of the Middle East cry out in pain, overwhelming sorrow and anguish…and I sit here *numb*. I don't know what to do. Part of me wants to cry. Part of me wants to go there right now to help the refugees. Part of me wants to turn the other way because the pain is just too much to imagine or bear. I don't know what to do. I pray for them. And sometimes I go spend time with them and also send money to help them. But I want to do more.

Please Lord, show me…show us…what we can do…what we should do…to help people who are suffering. And please Lord, be with this man who has lost something so dear to him…his precious, beautiful family.

صــديقي

More children drown

Map showing sea crossing from Bodrum, Turkey to Kos, Greece
(crossing where the man's family drowned)

---

[73] A copy of two of the BBC news articles about this tragedy are in Appendices C and D.

Story: Visit to Refugees in Hezbollah/UN Area

And then, though it is against the law, *I will go* in to see the king. If I must die, I must die. (Esther 4:16b)

HEZBOLLAH IN ARABIC means "Party of Allah." *Allah* in Arabic means God. Bibles in Arabic use the word *Allah* for God because that is the correct translation in Arabic of the Hebrew and Greek words for God, *Elohim* and *Theos*. So *Hezbollah*, or *Hizbullah* as the correct transliteration from Arabic (there is no "e" or "o" in the Arabic alphabet) means "Party of God." Hezbollah is a Shia (as opposed to Sunni) Islamic militant group and political party based in Lebanon. Hezbollah was formed as a result of the 1982 Israeli invasion of Lebanon...when Israel reached and surrounded Beirut...and was intended to offer resistance to the Israeli occupation of Lebanon. Hezbollah was funded by Iran. Its leaders were followers of the Ayatollah Khomeini in Iran and received training from the elite Iranian Revolutionary Guard. After the 1982 invasion, Israel occupied a strip of land in Southern Lebanon. In response, Hezbollah waged a guerilla war against the occupying forces. Israel withdrew on May 24, 2000. To this day, one of Hezbollah's primary goals is the elimination of the State of Israel.[74]

Hezbollah grew into a political party and now has seats in the Lebanese government on both the Parliament and Cabinet of Lebanon. Hezbollah has a paramilitary wing that is believed to be more powerful than the Lebanese Army. Hezbollah continues to receive weapons and financial support from Iran and political support from Syria, given that Iran is a Shia country (the only one in the world) and Syria's leaders, including President Assad, are Shia Muslims.

Countries such as the U.S., France, Australia and Israel have classified Hezbollah as a terrorist organization. However, in 2015 the U.S. Director of National Intelligence removed it from the list of terrorist threats against the U.S.

---

[74] This is also a stated goal of Hamas, the Sunni militant group that rules the Gaza Strip. Hamas means "enthusiasm" in Arabic. Hamas was founded in 1987 as a Palestinian Islamic organization with an associated military wing. It was founded to liberate Palestine from Israeli occupation and to establish an Islamic state. Some countries (such as the United States and the United Kingdom) designate Hamas as a terrorist organization and some countries (such as Iran and Russia) do not.

Hezbollah supports the Syrian government in its civil war with the Syrian opposition, which includes ISIS, Al-Nusra (Al-Qaeda's Syria branch[75]) and other Sunni Muslim military and terrorist groups. Hezbollah is reputed as being among the first Islamic resistance groups in the Middle East to use tactics of suicide bombing, capturing foreign soldiers, assassinations, murders and hijackings.

On October 7, 2000, Hezbollah abducted and killed three Israeli soldiers who were patrolling the Israeli side of the Israeli-Lebanese border in far southern Lebanon. Then, in 2006, there was a 34-day war between primarily Hezbollah and the Israeli military. The conflict began on July 12, 2006, when Hezbollah fired rockets at Israeli border towns and two Israeli armored Humvees. Israel responded with airstrikes as well as a ground invasion into southern Lebanon. The war lasted until August 14, 2006. It is believed that approximately 1,200 Lebanese citizens and combatants were killed as well as 165 Israeli citizens and soldiers. More recently, on February 14, 2015, the former Prime Minister of Lebanon, Rafic Hariri, was killed along with 21 other people when the motorcade he was travelling in through Beirut was struck by a roadside bomb. On June 10, 2015, Hezbollah announced that it had begun to fight ISIS along the rugged Syrian-Lebanese border.

So…fast forward a couple of weeks to June 26, 2015. There I was on a Friday morning in Beirut heading south on the highway towards Israel…towards Hezbollah's turf and a UN monitored zone[76]…towards the most fortified military checkpoint I have ever encountered during the Middle East trips. The Lebanese Pastor was driving the vehicle. In the passenger seat in front of me sat another man, who is Lebanese and serving God in different countries. The Pastor's teenage son sat in the back with me. The little car zoomed along on the highway. Talk about a *rag tag group of guys* following Jesus to an area with a history of many military battles, conflicts and suffering.

Driving in areas like that, you can sense the *tenseness* in the air…the history of conflicts…almost I imagine like living on a volcano. You just don't know when it's going to *erupt* again.

---

[75] *Al-Qaeda* means "the base" in Arabic. Al-Qaeda is a global militant Islamist organization founded by, among others, Osama bin Laden in approximately 1988 and calls for, among other things, global jihad. Al-Qaeda was responsible for the September 11, 2001 attacks on the United States. It regards liberal Muslims and Shia Muslims, among others, as heretics. It is designated as a terrorist organization by the United States, Russia and other countries.

[76] The United Nations Interim Force in Lebanon (UNIFIL) was established on March 19, 1978 and has had troops present in southern Lebanon since March 23, 1978 in an effort to maintain peace in southern Lebanon between Lebanon and Israel. Artillery fire has occurred in the UN monitored zone as recently as January 28, 2015.

As we drove farther south, we arrived at Hezbollah's turf. It was clear that they claimed it because the Hezbollah flags appeared along the highway…yellow and flapping in the wind with the *machine gun* on them.

Journal Entry, Beirut, June 26, 2015:

"Today we drove south through the militant Shia Muslim group's (Hezbollah) main turf into the UN monitored blue line area where the last war between Israel and Hezbollah (Lebanon) was in 2006.

"Driving now through main Shia/Hezbollah stronghold of Southern Lebanon, interesting that no more Lebanese police or military vehicles here, just stopped at the main military checkpoint.

"Hezbollah military hero banners (big ones) along road, banner of Khomeini in Iran, Hezbollah flags flying, they have a machine gun on them.

"Drove through a major checkpoint, most fortified checkpoint I've been through in the Middle East. The Pastor told me that he gave my name to the Lebanese Secret Police earlier this week as he was expecting them to pull us aside and want to see my passport. Praise God, the soldiers waived us right through! The Pastor was surprised. God has blessed me with an easy crossing at every checkpoint in Iraq and Lebanon on this trip, amazing!

"Road eerily quiet in the UN protected zone we are now in. Lots of cement barriers. Passed a bombed building with a picture on it presumably of the man who was killed in the bombing. Land mines warning sign by side of road. Many UN vehicles and UN military trucks in this area.

"During lunch, UN helicopter flying around and military truck with soldiers drove by. Strange environment for lunch with new friends. UN observes the blue line area and reports violations to Israel and Lebanon. The wife of the Pastor at the church here is now an interpreter for the UN. The Lebanese Secret Service took over the Christian radio station she used to work at."

מֵרֵעַ

Encountering Jesus

Sign along road displaying pictures of Hezbollah members who had been killed (Southern Lebanon) (June 2015)

Story: The Pastor and His Wife Spend War-Time with Jesus

Then I will hold my head high above my enemies who surround me. At his sanctuary I will offer sacrifices with shouts of *joy, singing* and *praising* the LORD with music. (Psalm 27:6)

THE PSALMIST IN Psalm 13:5-6 asks God for deliverance from his enemies and *sings* because He trusts God:

But I trust in your unfailing love; my heart *rejoices* in your salvation. I will *sing* the LORD's praise, for he has been good to me. (Psalm 13:5-6 NIV)

We drove farther south in Lebanon...through Hezbollah's turf...to the main checkpoint and, by God's grace, passed easily through it...not even having to stop! We drove on and eventually arrived at the home of another Lebanese Pastor and his wife. I had no idea about the story I was getting ready by God's grace to hear...a story that would remind me now as I type this what Amy Carmichael, the missionary to India in the late 1800's, wrote: "Often when the sea was most unquiet and the boat most tossed about, *song came*" (p.286).

Journal Entry, Beirut, June 26, 2015:

"I was so fortunate to meet a Pastor and his wife in the Hezbollah militant area where wars have been fought with Israel in 2000 and 2006. First time I've ever been in a UN monitored zone.

"I had a discussion with the Pastor's wife, tears in both of our eyes; in 2000 when war broke out, everyone living in the disputed Israel/Lebanon area had to choose very quickly whether to live in Israel or Lebanon; about 5,000 people left in one day, then the border fence was closed; she and her husband witnessed many atrocities, people were arrested and tortured, children were traumatized; Hezbollah searched houses and she lost her job working at a Christian radio station. She was taken in for questioning by Hezbollah three times. They stayed and kept the church going in that war zone. Then, in 2006, war broke out with Israel and lasted 33 days. The church had about 40-50 members and went down to about three; most people left for Beirut or Sweden or other countries; she says during the bombings of that area by Israel as they took shelter in the church, that is the closest she has ever been with the Lord, 33 day war, church building and people were protected, relied on God for everything. Her and her husband stayed again despite the war to keep the church going. She summed it up in tears: 'This is our life.' They are expecting war again.

"The Pastor's wife told me more about the Israeli bombing in 2006. No glass was broken in the church or their house! They and others living in the church during the bombings were in need of food and had a small garden that kept miraculously producing lots of fruit and vegetables...it was a miracle! Her family members (parents and a sister in the US, another sister in Beirut...so would have been easy for her and her husband and children to leave) wanted them to leave, 90% of people in that area did leave. They had a 9 year old boy and a 15 year old girl at the time. She and the Pastor prayed and trusted God, were led to stay with the church family. The church was completely protected as was their home, all other homes suffered damage from bombs or from Israeli soldiers occupying them and causing damage to them. Israelis bombed the area all around and near the church and their home. They would pick up lots of shrapnel around the church after a bombing phase. They were up one time all night long as bombings did not stop and were so close that it was like an earthquake shaking them and the church building. Kids were asleep while parents prayed. She says the Lord was so close to them and gave them amazing peace. Sometimes they would be laughing and singing and thought if people heard them, they would think they had gone crazy. What an amazing story of God's faithfulness!"

The church where they took refuge during the bombings
(Southern Lebanon) (June 2015)

Sign above the altar in the church that says in Arabic, "I am the way and the truth and the life. No one comes to the Father except through me" (quoting John 14:6) (Southern Lebanon) (June 2015)

23 Jesus, I Need Some Quiet Time

> But despite Jesus' instructions, the report of his power spread even faster, and vast crowds came to hear him preach and to be healed of their diseases. But Jesus often *withdrew to the wilderness* for prayer. (Luke 5:16)

NOW, IF JESUS needed to get away to a quiet place to pray, how much more should we? We live in a noisy and technologically-busy world. Constant news feeds, email and texts are at our fingertips. And time can just pass us by in our busy-ness. How wonderful it is to find a *quiet place* in God's creation to listen to the wind, talk with God, and enjoy being in His company. Jesus did that often:

> Immediately after this, Jesus insisted that his disciples get back into the boat and head across the lake to Bethsaida, while he sent the people home. After telling everyone good-bye, he went up into the hills *by himself* to pray. (Mark 6:45-46)

In fact, Jesus prayed all night before choosing the twelve disciples who would be apostles:

> One day soon afterward Jesus went up on a mountain to pray, and he prayed to God *all night*. At daybreak he called together all of his disciples and chose twelve of them to be apostles. Here are their names:
> Simon (whom he named Peter),
> Andrew (Peter's brother),
> James,
> John,
> Philip,
> Bartholomew,
> Matthew,
> Thomas,
> James (son of Alphaeus),
> Simon (who was called the zealot),
> Judas (son of James),

Jesus, I Need Some Quiet Time

Judas Iscariot (who later betrayed him).
(Luke 6:12-16)

When we are making important decisions in life, we too need to spend time with God seeking out His perfect will. And sometimes we just need to enjoy being with Him and our friend Jesus in the *quiet*.

صديقي

Enjoying the view from a hillside overlooking the Sea of Galilee with Lebanon, Syria and Jordan in the distance; I wonder if Jesus sat in this same spot enjoying the quiet and His Heavenly Father's presence (Tiberias, Israel) (May 2012)

Story: Peace and Quiet at the Sea of Galilee

Immediately after this, Jesus insisted that his disciples get back into the boat and cross to the other side of the [Sea of Galilee], while he sent the people home. After sending them home, he went up into the hills *by himself* to pray. Night fell while he was there *alone*. (Matthew 14:22-23)

Encountering Jesus

I LOVE HEADING out on an adventure. Getting away from the normal routine and exploring. Nothing planned. Just heading out to see what God has planned. And I enjoyed doing that one morning by the Sea of Galilee...a place where Jesus and His followers spent much time. And a place where Jesus would go up the hills *by himself* to pray.

<u>Journal Entry, Israel, May 16, 2012:</u>

"I was planning to relax at the hotel when we got back about 4:30pm. I got to the room, laid down on the bed...and then asked myself, 'How often do I get to spend time in Israel at the Sea of Galilee?' So...I got back up, ate a granola bar, grabbed a bottle of water and my phone, and headed up the mountain/hillside behind Tiberius. I figured I could get to the top in time for sunset...the Lord willing! I headed out towards the Jewish tombs and Jewish neighborhood that I was somewhat familiar with. The street here twists and turns as it wraps around and in between the small, old homes and sidewalks. I noticed as I walked through the neighborhood that the signs were all in Hebrew...no English translations. I felt like a stranger and had a better appreciation for what it is to be an outsider. I was more hesitant this time to say hi to anyone given the Jewish woman's reaction to me. I opted not to look at any of the women who were walking along the sidewalk on occasion. I did say hi to a man and he did not smile or respond. I got the sense as I walked through this rundown neighborhood replete with open dumpsters, foraging cats, barred windows and small Israeli flags that this was an immigrant neighborhood of Jews who migrated here from communist countries. The people looked to be and sounded like they were from the 'stan's'...Uzbekistan, Kazakhstan, etc...very weather-worn faces with few smiles. I imagine they have been through a lot in life. I got the sense they were not trusting of strangers and I did not blame them.

"I went down a couple of dead end backstreets and found some signs to 'Mt. Bernice' and followed them up past the tiny homes and dirty streets. I was blessed to find the dirt road up the hillside and followed it as it wound along. What a view of the Sea as I hugged the road and fields. The road led to a set of ruins on a point overlooking the Sea and Tiberius below. The ruins consisted of walls, doorways, some short, round and very smooth columns, a deep square-shaped hole and a semi-circle set of sitting areas like we saw in the synagogue yesterday except in a half-circle shape, all overlooking the Sea. I wonder what this was.

Jesus, I Need Some Quiet Time

"I headed up further and a cow replete with horns was staring at me. I wondered if he thought I was a shepherd and figured he did not. :) I opted to get off of the dirt path and tried to follow the narrow cow paths that had been beaten on the land over who knows how many years. I had shorts on and there were burrs and I had to cut straight up at various spots. Wow, what a view as I climbed higher with the Sea behind me. I pictured Jesus and the disciples climbing these hills, you can cover a lot of ground in a short time. Jesus must have been strong and good at traveling. I pictured Him stopping for breaks and a snack of bread.

"Surprisingly, very high up was a paved small road and some picnic areas and a bike trail...go figure. I followed them for about 10 minutes and climbed under a gate in order to get up to the summit. I was not able to get all the way up so I turned and headed back down as there were trees up here that blocked the open view of the Sea and Tiberius way below... The hotel looked like a lego from up here. I got to a barbed wire fence and wondered if it was electrified...so I quickly touched it as if I would only quickly be electrified if it was a live wire...! Fortunately for me and the cows it was not electrified so I slowly climbed through it as it tugged at my shorts in a couple of places.

"I emerged from the barbed-wire fence and walked through the gold knee-high grass for a couple of minutes and found myself at the most amazing overlook...a wow moment! I was at the edge of an overlook with a panoramic view of the Sea! A picture just could not capture the moment. I laid back and looked up at the blue sky with whiffs of white... What a moment. I reached my hands up to the blue and felt like my hands were touching it. I see why Jesus often went up to be alone with His Heavenly Father...so many distractions below to keep us from that intimate relationship with our Creator. I once again prayed for [my wife, daughter and son]. The sun disappeared behind the hillside behind me and I knew it was time to go.

"I headed down and got past the barbed wire for the last time, this time climbing over and thankful my shorts weren't left on it! The air was cooler now and I passed the friendly dog off to the left where he was apparently with his owners. This time, he glanced over at me and opted not to go back into town with me again...I figured he had had enough sight-seeing for one week.

"I arrived back at the hotel in time for an 8pm dinner. Mom and Dad had eaten and mom stayed with me while I ate, dad headed back to the room to prepare tomorrow's devotion for the Green Bus. Wow, was I hungry from the hike. Another special day in the Land that is Holy because of Jesus and only because of Jesus the Christ. Amen."

מֵרֵעַ

Watching the sunrise over the Sea of Galilee (Tiberias, Israel) (May 2012)

Story: Quiet Time under an Olive Tree in Jerusalem

Before daybreak the next morning, Jesus got up and went out to an *isolated place* to pray. (Mark 1:35)

*I*T'S IMPORTANT TO find quiet time in our fast-paced and noisy lives. If Jesus needed to find isolated places to relax and connect with His Heavenly Father, how much more should *we*.

Jesus, I Need Some Quiet Time

Journal Entry, Israel, May 19, 2012:

"After a powerful morning in Jerusalem, which was packed with pilgrims, tourists, Jews, Muslims, Christians, Hindus, honking cars and large buses slipping through narrow streets, we got off the beaten path for a bite for lunch. The place was surprisingly not crowded and the food was great. More Middle Eastern fare, I had the pita filled with chicken, vegetables, sauce, spices and, yes, french fries inside the pita. Yum! The Muslim call to prayer began from a tower about a block away, loud but eerily short, I pictured Muslims around the community getting down and praying, but did not see any doing that at the restaurant.

"We had an hour of free time after lunch to shop or walk around. I opted to walk in the surrounding neighborhood, which was affluent with gated condos and homes and several UN cars. I walked through the neighborhood and up past them to the grass and stone fields. Up I went to the top of the hill overlooking Jerusalem. What an amazing city. On top of the hill was a poor section of shanties and mobile home type structures. Also up there were ruins consisting of rock fences/short walls and olive trees. I was blessed to sit under an olive tree for the first time. It is so much cooler in the shade and I pictured Jesus sitting under an olive tree. The wind blew through the leaves and created a sound I have not heard before, very different than the wind/leaves I'm used to. Sitting under that tree in the quiet, I could see why Jesus oftentimes got away from the crowds to be with His Father. Jesus reminded me that prayer is both talking with and listening to God, I don't have to be on my knees or have my hands together before me…it's not complicated, it's being in relationship with Jesus. What a peaceful moment sitting up there under the shade of the olive tree looking out over Jerusalem."

ENCOUNTERING JESUS

The olive tree I rested under (Jerusalem, Israel) (May 2012)

Story: Relaxing with Jesus on the Mountainside of Lebanon

One day as he saw the crowds gathering, Jesus went up on the mountainside and *sat down*. His disciples gathered around him. (Matthew 5:1)

*O*N THE LAST full day that I was in Lebanon, I joined Pastor Muneer[77] and his wife, son and daughter on a fun journey along the coast of Lebanon and then up into the mountains. Lebanon is a beautiful country. *Breathtakingly beautiful.* They picked me up at the hotel in Beirut and we headed north to first tour the coastal town of Jounieh and then on to Byblos. It was nice to be a tourist for the morning visiting ancient Roman ruins, enjoying the Mediterranean coast, and walking around with their children laughing and shopping. We enjoyed a delicious open-air lunch before heading into the mountains that rise quickly up from the crystal blue waters of the Mediterranean.

I was in for an unexpected treat. They were taking me to visit the Pastor's in-laws at their home in the mountains overlooking the Mediterranean Sea. We drove up and up and wound along narrow mountain roads. What a beautiful countryside with the fresh sea air and such a cool breeze. Beautiful! We arrived at

---

[77] Name changed for privacy reasons. *Muneer* is an Arabic name and means "shining."

his in-laws' home, which has an amazing view out over the Mediterranean. I was warmly welcomed and, in typical Lebanese and Middle Eastern culture, made to feel like one of the family. That afternoon was a great gift after so many refugee camps and sad stories and checkpoints and drives through the dark nights of Iraq and drives so close to the war in Lebanon. There we were in a *peaceful* vista taking in the cool breeze, enjoying some delicious fruit and nuts, and smiling and sharing with each other. It was like visiting family that I have not seen for ten years. What an amazing gift from the Pastor, his wife and her parents.

They are growing over 50 different vegetables and fruits. We tasted many of them while drinking coffee and enjoying the cool breeze and chit-chat. His father in law showed me around the gardens and we ate fruit straight off of the trees. Delicious! The refugee camps and wars seemed so far from there but were so close. It had been a wonderful trip.

They showed me the small rooms/house on the mountain where they fled to during the war with Israel in 2006. It was Pastor Muneer's grandfather in law's house. Daniel (the Pastor's son) was only four years old then. Most people's dream in Lebanon is to have a place in the mountains, one of the reasons being that if/when bombs begin, they will have a place to escape to. It's a different mindset in a country that has been in three wars since 1975, the first of which lasted 15 years.

ENCOUNTERING JESUS

Enjoying some quiet and peaceful time with my new friend, Pastor Muneer's father, in his garden (Mountainside of Lebanon) (June 2015) (face blurred for privacy reasons)

Enjoying a peaceful afternoon at my new friend's garden overlooking the Mediterranean Sea below; such a contrast to the military zones and refugee camps (Mountainside of Lebanon) (June 2015)

24   Jesus, You're Bleeding

> He prayed more fervently, and he was in such agony of spirit that his sweat fell to the ground like *great drops of blood*. (Luke 22:44)

*M*Y SAVIOR BLED. My friend bled…*badly*. My friend hung on a cross bleeding and dying. And most of His friends *abandoned* Him. Betrayed Him. Gave up on Him. The soldiers cast lots (rolled dice) to see who would get to have Jesus's clothing. Emotional and physical pain that is impossible to imagine.

I know how much it concerns a mother when her young son gets cut badly. I can't imagine what it was like for Mary watching her son tortured and humiliated in public for all to see and for some…many…to *scorn*.

> So they said, "Rather than tearing it apart, let's throw dice for it." This fulfilled the Scripture that says, "They *divided my garments* among themselves and threw dice for my clothing." So that is what they did. Standing near the cross were Jesus' mother, and his mother's sister, Mary (the wife of Clopas), and Mary Magdalene. (John 19:24-25)

And then Jesus was nailed to the cross and died…for you, me and everyone else in the world:

> One of the soldiers, however, *pierced* his side with a spear, and immediately blood and water flowed out. (This report is from an eyewitness giving an accurate account. He speaks the truth so that you also may continue to believe). (John 19:34-35)

My friend Jesus lived a life of love and died a violent death. For me. *In place of me*.

מֵרַע

The Damascus Gate entryway into the Muslim Quarter of
the Old City of Jerusalem (Jerusalem, Israel) (May 2012)

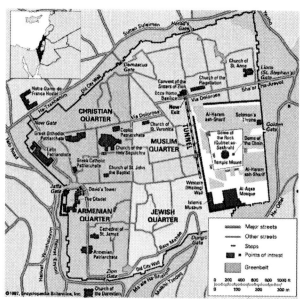

Map of Old (Walled) City of Jerusalem
(with the Damascus Gate and the Via Dolorosa noted)

Jesus, You're Bleeding

Story: Via Dolorosa in Jerusalem

But he was *pierced* for our transgressions, he was *crushed* for our iniquities; the punishment that brought us peace was on him, and by his *wounds* we are healed. (Isaiah 53:5 NIV)

ONE WAY TO step back in time almost 2,000 years ago...one way to connect *personally* with Jesus...is to walk the route that He walked through Jerusalem as He carried His cross to His execution. It's one of the times that I have felt *closest to Jesus*.

Journal Entry, Israel, May 20, 2012:

"1st and 2nd stations: The gate at the top of the stairs was closed where the marker is for the first station, which apparently leads into a courtyard of the Antonio Fortress, which is where Pilate ruled from when he condemned and tortured Jesus. However, both stations can be done together in the Church of the Flagellation and courtyard and chapel. The Antonio Fortress was a huge fort with four towers, looked like a city within a city back at the time of Jesus. It was named after Mark Anthony and rebuilt by Herod the Great, and was guarded by 10,000 Roman soldiers. Jesus is judged/condemned by Pontius Pilate in the open courtyard of it and flogged/scourged on a pillar, which involved being whipped with glass and metal shards on the end of the whips. Flogging/scourging could kill a person even before crucifixion. Jesus said goodbye to his mother and friends here. He was given a death sentence although He had done nothing wrong...

"6th station: Now climbing up a small side street as we head towards the place where Veronica lived and wiped the sweat and blood off of Jesus' face. What a courageous act of love to a condemned man, how easy it would be to step inside your home, close the window, and wait for this miserable scene to pass by...isn't life complicated enough without getting involved in other people's messes? How wonderful that Veronica blessed Jesus in this way and now blessed us as we reflected on what she did...

"8th station: Jesus consoles the women of Jerusalem...He's always caring for others, even during the imposition of His death sentence. He comforts us during His time of deepest sorrow. There is a small cross cut into the stone wall of a Greek monastery here."

Carrying the cross along the Via Dolorosa in the Old City of Jerusalem, a powerful reminder of the suffering of Jesus (Jerusalem, Israel) (April 2013)

Sign marking the route through Jerusalem of the Via Dolorosa (Israel) (May 2012)

25 I'm Tired, Jesus

Jesus was sleeping at the back of the boat with his head on a cushion. The disciples woke him up, shouting, "Teacher, don't you care that we're going to drown?" (Mark 4:38)

*I*F JESUS NEEDS rest, then we do too. The trips that I am so fortunate to take to the Middle East are challenging from a number of perspectives. One is an endurance perspective. Flights landing in the middle of the night. Car rides through dangerous places. So many checkpoints. Lack of sleep. So much sadness. So much trauma that the refugees have suffered. The refugee children's eyes sometimes have a "lost-hope" look in them, which *breaks my heart*. I've heard it said before that a person's eyes are windows to his soul. As I kneel down looking at a precious refugee child's eyes…I wonder what they have seen. The children are so incredibly precious.

As I go about these journeys with Jesus, I ask God along the way to *please strengthen me* for the journey…to please strengthen me physically and emotionally. Here's one of the prayers I typed in my journal in Lebanon along the way:

Lord, please strengthen me for the rest of this journey, long and amazing days, a lot to take in emotionally, have only slept about five hours per night for a week, thank God for prayers of friends…and for Middle Eastern espresso! :)

So, as I headed towards the end of the 2015 trip to Iraq and Lebanon, I was blessed to enjoy an amazing meal of Lebanese food with two Pastors and the teenage son of one of them…three new *friends* in a far-away land.

ENCOUNTERING JESUS

Sprite and Diet Coke Arabic style
(Northern Iraq) (June 2015)

Story: Refreshed by Jesus Somewhere in Lebanon

Jacob's well was there; and Jesus, tired from the long walk, *sat wearily beside the well* about noontime. (John 4:6)

THE FOOD IN Lebanon is *incredible*. Tabouli, meats, pickled vegetables, hummus, eggplant, fresh warm bread, Turkish coffee, some type of date syrup drinks, on and on…simply *delicious*! And wow, is Middle Eastern coffee a treat. So there I was, eating in a local café somewhere in Eastern Lebanon probably not more than 20 miles from the war. I was with three new friends who I did not know the week before. We had spent the day with refugee families as well as getting to meet the amazing people who are *choosing* to be there so close to the war to serve the refugees by running a school for the refugee children. They are inspiring people to spend time with.

As we enjoyed the feast, I smiled and told my new friends, "If I died right now, I'd die with a smile on my face." We all laughed and they were visibly pleased that I was enjoying the Lebanese food and hospitality. Hosts in the

I'm Tired, Jesus

Middle Eastern culture take great pleasure in pleasing their guests with wonderful local hospitality.

I told the Pastor's teenage son that since he eats like a king, I was going to start calling him King Daniel from now on...and he got a big kick out of that as he enjoyed some chicken kabob. I began calling his precious younger sister a Princess and she no doubt enjoyed that too. It's so fun when I'm so far away from home to spend time with the local and refugee children.

מֵרֵעַ

Pastor Kadin and me at the meal with new friends
(Central Lebanon) (June 2015) (face blurred for privacy reasons)

26 Jesus, Please Catch Me

Don't let your hearts be troubled. Trust in God, and *trust also in me*. (John 14:1)

HAVE YOU EVER done that test of trust where you stand facing away from someone who is standing behind you…and you slowly fall backwards *trusting* that the person is going to catch you? That's a scary moment as you begin to fall backwards wondering if the person is in fact going to catch you…wondering if you can *truly* trust that person. And what a great feeling when you fall into their arms instead of onto the ground.

It's just not the same when someone *tells you* that they would be there for you no matter where, when or what the circumstances…as opposed to someone *showing you* that is in fact the case. How can we know for sure that we can trust Jesus…that He really will be with us always no matter where, when or what the circumstances…unless we find ourselves in one of the moments and places in life where Jesus is *all we have?* And, in that moment and place, Jesus shows up…He catches us…and then we believe…then we *know*…*without a doubt*…that Jesus will indeed *always* be there to catch us when we are falling into fear…into danger…into loneliness…into despair.

Friends don't abandon each other…and Jesus our friend will *never abandon us*. As the Proverb tells us:

Never abandon a *friend*. (Proverbs 27:10a)

I am so thankful to have gotten to find out in places so far outside my comfort zone…places where I have felt terribly vulnerable and alone…that Jesus my friend will *always* be there to *catch me*.

Jesus, Please Catch Me

Story: Alone in Istanbul: Jesus is Always with Us

And be sure of this: *I am with you always*, even to the end of the age. (Matthew 28:20b)

ON THE JOURNEY to Iraq by way of Istanbul, I found myself in the Istanbul airport without access to wi-fi…without a way to contact my family…and I found *comfort* in knowing that Jesus was there *with me*.

Journal Entry, Istanbul, June 20, 2015:

"Sometimes in life you feel so small and so far away from home, like when sitting at the Istanbul airport without wi-fi and no way to let your family and friends know you arrived safely. I hope they are not worrying for not hearing from me. I thought for sure that an airport as big as Istanbul would have reliable wi-fi. I was wrong. Thank God that Jesus is always with us. Always."

"I board a flight to Iraq *in an hour*."

"Sometimes you feel so small and so far away from home."

ENCOUNTERING JESUS

A long way from home (Northern Iraq) (June 2015)

Story: The Gate to Iraq: "Feeling" Alone without Jesus

For God has said, "I will never fail you. *I will never abandon you.*" (Hebrews 13:5b)

*D*URING THESE MIDDLE Eastern trips, I experience moments where I feel as small and vulnerable as the tiniest flea...*completely vulnerable*...so far away from home and things familiar to me...so far away from family and friends. One of those moments during the trip to Iraq and Lebanon was at the departure gate in Turkey waiting to get on a night-flight to Iraq that would deliver me into that war-torn country in the dark of night.

JOURNAL ENTRY, ISTANBUL, JUNE 20, 2015:

"As I walked to gate 503 at the end of the international terminal to wait for the flight to Iraq, the eight or so Americans I saw near the entrance to the terminal became no Americans...except me. Many men dressed for the *Hajj* (pilgrimage to Mecca in Saudi Arabia) in all white robes passed me,

Jesus, Please Catch Me

apparently just having arrived from Saudi is my guess. There are veiled women here at the gate as well as men wearing white robes and white turbans, the first I have ever seen men like them in the Middle East, dressed like I envision the three wise men who visited Jesus shortly after his miraculous birth, they are dark skinned like the color of Ethiopians. I know Jesus is here with me but I continue to look around for an American, someone to talk with, someone I have something in common with. But I don't see any. I approached one man who looked American but he is not, not sure what European country he is from. Getting ready to fly into Iraq in the middle of the night. Wow I feel small and helpless. Thank God that Jesus never leaves me, I just wish I could see Him right now. I wonder what people think when they see me here. I stick out to say the least. CIA? Military? NGO? USAID? Other?

"The gate next to us is going to Khartoum (Sudan). I pray for the safety of everyone on that flight.

"A man says hello to me with a heavy accent. He looks to be 30 years old and wearing shorts and a t-shirt, he looks Eastern European, he's from Anbar province in Iraq, a war torn area. He lives in Erbil now where's it's safer. He asked me why I was going to Erbil. I told him to help the refugees. He said he thought I was US military. I guess most of the Americans he's met are that. I'm glad he met someone going to help the refugees. He was not sure how to respond when I told him that. We talked in Arabic a little. He wants to go to Canada in two years to study to be a doctor. I wonder if his dream will come true. Dreams are a great thing.

"A man asked me through motions and showing me the numbers '503' on a piece of paper if he was at the right gate. He does not speak English. I showed him my passport cover and he showed me his: Bangladesh.

"Now I see what the turbans are about. They are [on the flight] to Khartoum in Sudan. I wonder if they are tribal leaders. Probably are. One man looks just like the tribal leaders you see in newspaper pictures in places like Sudan and Afghanistan. Wow have they been through so much war and terrorism.

"I'm wearing the leather bracelet with a cross on it that I've enjoyed wearing lately that the kids and I got at a camp we go to each summer. I felt prompted by God before the trip to wear it. I wonder what people

ENCOUNTERING JESUS

think when they see it. I hope there are some Christians here but I just don't know if there are.

"I feel very small as I get ready to board a night flight to Iraq. The flight path from the connection city of Antalya, Turkey to Erbil looks to fly right over the Turkish/Syrian border where battles are taking place this week. *Lord, please bless the people on the ground there, especially the children. Amen*"

מֵרֵעַ

Boarding pass to Erbil...it's time to board the night flight
(Istanbul, Turkey) (June 2015) (photo altered for privacy reasons)

Story: Encouragement from Jesus

May God, who gives this patience and *encouragement*, help you live in complete harmony with each other, as is fitting for followers of Christ Jesus. (Romans 15:5)

I HAVE ALSO learned during the Middle East trips that Jesus...our *friend* Jesus...knows when we need encouragement...when we *badly* need it. And He has proved Himself to be a *faithful* and *encouraging* friend over and over and over.

Jesus, Please Catch Me

Journal Entry, Istanbul, June 20, 2015:

"The Lord knows when we need a boost of encouragement! Shortly after I typed the message about feeling so small and so far from home as I waited for the flight to Iraq, it was time to present our boarding passes and board the bus that would take us to the plane. I went over by a guy that looked American...and turns out he is Brian the lawyer from [America]! We hit it off. He's a nice guy and works for the US Atty's office and is in Erbil for two weeks helping a friend teach English. He and I know some of the same lawyers in [the city where he lives] and he lives in the [same] school district where I grew up and his kids will go to the same middle school I went to!

"He let me use his phone to text mom and [a close friend of mine] on the bus that drove us to the plane, what a blessing!

"Then we get on the fairly large plane...and I'm in 6C on the aisle and he's in 6D on the other side of the aisle! We both laughed about that and agreed that God knew we both needed some encouragement. Brian's flight to [the connection city in the U.S.] was delayed and he missed his overnight flight and is a day behind his original schedule. He's the only other American on this flight from what I can tell. He is married and they have young children too. *Thank You Lord, You know what we need at just the right time. Amen*"

Outside the Erbil International Airport at 1:45am...my new friend and I had arrived! (Erbil, Iraq) (June 2015)

Sunflowers in Iraq…they grow there too
(Northern Iraq) (June 2015)

27   Jesus, Let's Go For a Walk

One day as Jesus was walking along the shore of the Sea of Galilee, he saw two brothers—Simon, also called Peter, and Andrew—throwing a net into the water, for they fished for a living. Jesus called out to them, *"Come, follow me,* and I will show you how to fish for people!" (Matthew 4:18-19)

WALKING ON THE path in Israel through the valley where Jesus would have walked through with his friends. Wow.

I love going for walks in the Middle East. So much to explore…so many new experiences…so much excitement in seeing what *Jesus* has planned. Jesus seemed to be a guy who liked to go for walks…alone as well as with old friends…and with new friends. One morning I found myself going for a walk by the Sea of Galilee with a *surprising* new friend.

صــديقي

Walking along a path that Jesus would have commonly used walking to Jerusalem with the disciples (Israel) (May 2012)

Encountering Jesus

Story: Going for a Walk with a New Friend in Israel

Soon a Samaritan woman came to draw water, and Jesus said to her, "Please give me a drink."...The woman was *surprised*, for Jews refuse to have anything to do with Samaritans. She said to Jesus, "You are a Jew, and I am a Samaritan woman. Why are you asking me for a drink?" (John 4:7, 9)

JESUS DID A lot of walking with His friends in what is modern-day Israel and the West Bank. I went for a jog one morning in Tiberias, a town on the shore of the Sea of Galilee. And I was joined by a surprising new friend in an unexpected place.

Journal Entry, Israel, May 16, 2012:

"Started off the day going for a jog in Tiberias. The sun began to rise over the Sea of Galilee as I ran up the hillside that overlooked the city. What a sight to see my first sunrise here! There is a Jewish cemetery nearby. It was a pretty sight to see the sun's light shine over the tombstones written in Hebrew. Many looked new and towards the back of the cemetery up on the hillside were much older graves, some crumbling from who knows how long being exposed to the weather. An old set of stony walls was at the back end of the area...I wondered if it was an old house from centuries ago or a synagogue. It's my understanding that Jewish custom did not allow graves to be located in the city since dead bodies were considered unclean. I wondered if this location used to be out in the countryside. The sunlight literally sparkled like jewelry on the water...it was stunning.

"I ran higher up the hillside and a pretty big dog started barking and running back and forth looking agitated that I was there. He then started running towards me so I picked up a large rock ready to defend myself out on this country road. He stopped about 40 feet away and we sized each other up. I thought, if he charges me, I'd better not miss! I knelt down and put my hand out and he walked over still not sure...He got to me and I petted him and talked to him and he started wagging his tail...my first new friend of the day on the shores of Galilee. He ended up running alongside me for the rest of the run. When I got down to do pushups, he would

Jesus, Let's Go For a Walk

sometimes lick my head. We had a nice time and I told him I had a feeling he only understood Hebrew.

"We ran up the hill until the road ended at a gun range, not sure what that is there for. We ran back down and saw signs for the Tomb of Rachel. A Jewish woman was walking down the road and I said hi to her. She walked a few steps on and then started yelling in Hebrew and kicking the sandy dirt...! Wow, she was mad. She continued on down the hill and I could still hear her yelling (in I am assuming Hebrew). I was glad to have my friend the dog with me. I asked him what that was all about and then remembered that he probably only understood Hebrew. Experiencing her reaction to what was obviously a Gentile walking among a Jewish neighborhood gave me a richer understanding of how radical it was for Jesus as a Jew to announce to the Jewish people that salvation had come for the Jew and the Gentile. I can better understand how furious the Jews of that day would have been to hear a fellow Jew saying that. So far in Tiberias, I've been chewed out by two Jewish people and befriended by one Jewish dog. There's a message in there for me that I'm still trying to understand.

"Jesus was indeed a radical guy with an even more radical message. I think one of the messages for me is how good it felt to have the dog join me on my journey. No lecture, no judgment, just spending time together and giving me company. I need to learn to do that for people in my life. What a contrast to the Jewish woman yelling at me as she kicked the dirt in apparent disgust. *Thank You Lord for this lesson in life and forgive me for all the times I have reacted to others in my heart with anger and judgment, please help me be more like the friendly dog. Amen.*

"I arrived back in town after jogging back down the hillside...and the dog was still with me as I got back into town. I told him he really needed to go back as I did not think the hotel allowed dogs. He trotted off."

Life is full of adventures, surprises and new friends!

מֵרֵעַ

ENCOUNTERING JESUS

The view my new friend and I enjoyed together that morning along the Sea of Galilee (Tiberias, Israel) (May 2012)

Story: Walking Where Jesus Walked

One day as he saw the crowds gathering, Jesus went up *on the mountainside* [by the Sea of Galilee] and *sat down*. His disciples gathered around him, and he began to teach them. (Matthew 5:1-2)

I ENCOURAGE YOU to visit Israel...visit the West Bank...visit the places where Jesus walked, talked, taught, wept, died and *rose*. Please don't let fear or anxiety keep you from going there. It truly is the trip of a *lifetime*. It is hard to describe in words what it is like to be at a place where Jesus was at...to be looking at the sunrise over the Sea of Galilee picturing Jesus sitting there watching that *same sunrise* 2,000 years before. To be walking where *He walked*. To be seeing what *He saw*. Wow that is an *amazing* experience. And I am so thankful that my parents took me on a trip there with their church family. That was an *awesome* gift.

Jesus, Let's Go For a Walk

JOURNAL ENTRY, ISRAEL, MAY 16, 2012:

"We then drove to the Mount of Beatitudes, where Jesus spoke the Sermon on the Mount with authority to thousands of people on the hillside. This location is a natural amphitheater with a beautiful view of the Sea of Galilee below. This location is also referred to as 'the way of the sea' since it is a crossroads to places like Damascus, Syria and Lebanon. What a great location for Jesus to teach at. An octagonal church was built here in 1937 and each of the eight sides represents one of the Beatitudes. The grounds are beautiful and well landscaped. I went in the church and prayed near the altar. It was a special time of prayer. I heard so clearly from the Lord: *'Come walk with me, let's talk.'* Jesus found relationships to be so important, including having a personal relationship with Him. I can get so busy in life that I miss out on walking with Jesus.

"We then drove to the Church of the Multiplication, which marks the location of where Jesus fed 5,000 people with five loaves and two fish, and had 12 baskets of bread left over! There is a Benedictine Monastery Tabgha located here as well. [The Palestinian tour guide] pointed out a 500-year old olive tree in the courtyard and explained that the olive tree represents peace. I lit a candle for [my wife, daughter and son] and placed it on the table with other lit candles before a painting of Jesus. The heat off the candles felt good. What a pretty setting in the sanctuary with the glow of the candles. The church has a 5th century mosaic floor. Saw nuns in the various churches today from various countries.

"We went down to the seashore and it was a wonderful spot where the dark pebble beach met the water in a small cove about 50 yards across. To the left side and adjacent to the shore is an old church and to the right side of the cove were some large boulders. The water slowly lapped up on the pebbles. This was the place where Jesus called to the disciples from the shore to cast their net to the right side of the boat after they had not caught any fish that night and the net was pulled up full. Jesus was cooking some fish on this shore and probably spent a lot of time with the disciples here. There are three stones shaped like hearts that are about the size of a wheelbarrow wagon. They were placed in the ground here by early Christians to memorialize the three times that Jesus asked Peter if he loved Jesus, which followed Peter's denial of Christ three times. Amazing to look at monuments put there so many centuries ago. A lot of us took off our shoes and waded into the Sea. It felt so great, especially since Jesus had done the same thing before in the same cove. I waved my hands under the water and was amazed to be in this Sea."

The shore where it is believed that Jesus called to the disciples and cooked some fish for them (Tabgha, Israel) (May 2012)

Story: Walking on the Streets of Beirut: Jesus Walks With Us

Follow *me*. (Luke 5:27b NIV)

ONE OF THE things I love about following Jesus is that He will lead you to places you *never imagined* you would end up at. If you had told me four years ago that I would learn some Arabic and find myself going on a walk through Beirut "by myself," I would have told you that you were crazy...that that was ludicrous to even suggest. So there I was on my first morning in Beirut walking the streets...and *following Jesus*.

Jesus, Let's Go For a Walk

Journal Entry, Beirut, June 25, 2015:

"I went for a walk this morning in Beirut. What a contrast between the terribly poor Hezbollah neighborhood...that large section of the city looked apocalyptic at places with war hero banners hanging by the street showing large pictures of Hezbollah members who have died in Syria according to the taxi driver...and compare that to the Saint George's Yacht Club down at the Mediterranean waterfront. I walked down to the marina past abandoned dilapidated buildings, and security for some reason allowed me past the guard station into the marina. What a contrast to see massive yachts there. I walked along the boardwalk to the water and stepped over a rope type of fence and a Lebanese soldier with a machine gun sprung up from his chair...we were both surprised to see each other! I apologized and introduced myself to him in Arabic (*'Sabah Al khair, aasif, ana Abu William'*)('good morning, I'm sorry, I'm Abu William'). He spoke some English and I came to understand that important people are on the yachts, so he guards them and of course the yachts...some of the biggest yachts I've ever seen. There was also a security guard dressed in black and wearing tan army boots patrolling the boardwalk by the yacht club as someone went for an early morning swim in one of the beautiful pools there. I wished him good morning in Arabic.

"What a stark contrast to Hezbollah's section of Beirut. It struck me that I am a member of the wealthy part of America and, like the people at the yacht club, I tend to set up a bubble of a life that keeps the Hezbollah/poor neighborhoods on the other side of the bubble. It's not a guilt trip kind of thing, just more of an eye opening to my own life. I guess it's human nature to do that. What a contrast it will be to the yacht club and massive yachts to be in a refugee camp later this morning. Seems to be a theme of this trip that God wants me to see and think about. What is God trying to show me about my own life?

"I prayed while sitting by the boardwalk and asked God to guide the Pastor's and my path today and to bless the people of Lebanon, and I prayed for the people who are praying about this trip. I prayed about other people and things too."

View of the yacht club in Beirut from the spot where I prayed and met a Lebanese soldier (Lebanon) (June 2015)

28   Jesus, Let's Go for a Swim

After his baptism, as *Jesus came up out of the water*, the heavens were opened and he saw the Spirit of God descending like a dove and settling on him. And a voice from heaven said, "This is my dearly loved Son, who brings me great joy." (Matthew 3:16-17)

*J*ESUS WAS BAPTIZED. He *actually went under water* in a little river on this planet and *came back up*…at a place you can go visit today. And His hair was wet. So often I picture Jesus up in Heaven…so far away…and then there are times when I picture Him right here on this planet with humanity. I can see Him *smiling* as He rose up out of the water. I imagine the sun was shining hot like it does in the Middle East. I imagine that the cool water felt *refreshing* to Jesus. When you visit the place where Jesus was baptized…the narrow Jordan River that flows and winds itself through that hot desert region…and when you are then baptized in that same little river…the *humanity* of Jesus *becomes so real*. He was there in that place. He walked and talked there and had friends there.

מֵרֵעַ

Visiting the location where Jesus was baptized, this time on the Jordanian side of the Jordan River (Jordan) (March 2014)

Story: Visiting the Site Where Jesus Was Baptized

Then Jesus went from Galilee to the Jordan River to be *baptized* by John. (Matthew 3:13)

*H*OW DO YOU describe what it's like to visit the spot on the Jordan River where Jesus was *baptized*? I've been fortunate to visit it on the Israeli side of the Jordan River in 2012 and then on the Jordanian side in 2014. What an experience to stand there on the bank of the narrow river picturing Jesus standing there 2,000 years ago. He seems *so real* at a moment like that. The Jesus who came down from Heaven, walked the earth and whose skin was *touched* by the Jordan River water.

Journal Entry, West Bank, May 19, 2012:

"The next place we are visiting is the baptismal location in the Jordan River. Yesterday we bought white covers to wear for the baptism, which is required in keeping with tradition. I remember watching the candidates getting baptized at [a local U.S.] Catholic Church during the Easter vigil service. How exciting to be baptized in the same river where Jesus was baptized. So amazing to be following in his footsteps in so many places. *Lord, please help me follow in His footsteps where it truly matters...* Being kind to a stranger, loving all people, considering others more important than myself, dying to self, and worshipping the Lord through continual thanksgiving and praise and being in constant communion and prayer with the Lord. I remember His earlier words to me on the hillside overlooking the Sea of Galilee...*'come walk with me, let's talk.' Lord, I'm sorry for making my relationship with You so complicated when it can be so simple and beautiful. Thank You for being so full of mercy and grace. Amen.*

"We drove through an Israeli checkpoint and passed signs and barbed fencing warning of mine fields on both sides of the bus. The place where Jesus was baptized has mine fields around it. The dove of peace and the Holy Spirit descended on Him here and the talons of a war bird descended on the land here. This special place at the Jordan River brings together Christians from all areas of the world. One group was singing praise music in a language I did not recognize. Two Israeli soldiers with machine guns sit in the shade while people on the Israeli border here get baptized and experience the Jordan River and this amazingly special place. The river is about 20 feet across, much narrower than I had envisioned. It has many tall grasses growing up and over some of it. On the other side directly across from this spot is a similar deck area on the Jordan side of the river. There are two Jordanian soldiers on that side, one wearing a machine gun. A baptism ceremony was taking place over there for a baby as what looked to be an Orthodox priest sang and chanted in another language. I wondered how difficult it is being a Christian in Jordan. On that side of the river is a beautiful sand-colored church with two towers.

"Steps lead down to the water on both sides. People get fully emerged, sprinkled and just enjoy touching the water and scooping some of it up in bottles. Mom, dad and I got into the water together with Pastor H.[78] First mom was baptized, then dad, then me. What a special moment. Tears and joy and praise to the King of kings and Lord of lords! Pastor H was the last to be baptized in our group as he was doing the baptizing for us. Rick and I were in the water with him and the Lord put upon us the blessing to get to jointly baptize Pastor H. The Spirit was upon us, praise God! I got

---

[78] Name removed for privacy reasons.

some water from the Jordan in my mouth and decided to swallow it, another baptism from the inside out.

"I watched the baptism on the Jordanian side some more, it's quite an event with singing and chanting. Another contrast between peace and war...a naked baby set in the water of Jesus while a Jordanian soldier with a machine gun strapped to his back watched about 10 feet back.

"As we were leaving, I introduced myself to the Israeli soldiers, greeted them with the Arabic *'Salam Alechem'* and one of the soldiers returned *'Alechem Salam.'* I asked them if they have gotten baptized and they said no...I hope they do some day. I thanked them for being there and we headed out. It was a nice visit with them.

"It is blazing hot out here in the desert, such a contrast to the cool, salty water of the Jordan River. Driving out we pass the mine fields on both sides, an Israeli guard box, bunkers and a couple of pieces of metal in the sand. I wonder if they are parts of tanks or artillery. We passed the Jordanian army bunkers that are empty now, a sign reads, 'Military Zone No Entry.' The Mount of Temptation is on the right of us as well as a monastery dating back to the 5th century. There is a plantation of dates as well, lots of them. We tasted dates yesterday, they are delicious.

"Riding on the bus through the desert I get a sense of completeness. This is a pilgrimage and that word has been with me since a friend in [the U.S.] mentioned it a few weeks before this trip. I don't think we generally know what we are going to experience on a spiritual level during a trip like this. I am experiencing at this moment immense peace in Jesus. How do you describe what it is like to be baptized in the Jordan River? I can't describe it with words. It's a personal experience with Jesus...those words don't even touch a description of it. Instead of describing it, I just want to thank my Heavenly Father and praise Him!!!!!!!!!!!!!"

Jesus, Let's Go for a Swim

Looking from the Israeli side of the Jordan River to the Jordanian side at the location where Jesus was baptized (Jordan River, Israel) (June 2012)

Story: Swimming Laps at the Pool with Jesus

Remember those in prison, as if you were there yourself. *Remember* also those being mistreated, as if you felt *their pain* in *your own bodies*. (Hebrews 13:3)

MY LIFE IS different now that the world's refugee crisis has become *personal* to me. It's no longer just a news article. It's the *faces* of the children in the refugee camps. It's the *walks* through the desert regions that can be so hot and dry. It's the *taste* of a cold drink of water on a very hot Middle Eastern desert day. It's the *gracious hospitality* of a person who has so little, welcoming me into their tent or room with a smile and a tea. My life goes on here in America but now, so often, I picture the *smiling children* in the refugee camps and I struggle with that...with *missing them*...with wanting to help make their lives *better*. Many of those children have probably never swam in a pool of clear, cool water. And many of them probably never will, at least not on this side of eternity.

Encountering Jesus

Journal Entry, America, August 22, 2015:

"Swimming laps at a local pool on a Saturday morning, no one else in the pool, looking up at the clear blue sky as I swam the backstroke. No threat of missiles or bombs. A plane flies over with a white jet trail behind it and I don't have to worry about whether it's going to drop a barrel bomb[79] on us. The water is so clear and cool as the day warms up. I think about Jesus and the refugees, especially the refugee children's faces who were crying in photos taken of them as they tried to get by border guards in Macedonia in their struggle to survive and escape the war in Syria. I'm thankful for getting to go for a swim with Jesus. He's a great friend."

---

[79] A brutal weapon used in Syria that has killed many civilians. It's an unguided improvised bomb typically made from a large barrel-shaped metal container that has been filled with explosives as well as shrapnel, oil or chemicals. They are oftentimes dropped from a helicopter, are crudely made and kill indiscriminately. It is evident that the Syrian government forces have used them, although that is denied by Syrian President Bashar Assad.

Yazidi Iraqi refugees (Northern Iraq) (June 2015)

29   Jesus, I Like Children Too!

> But Jesus said, "Let the children come to me. Don't stop them! For the Kingdom of Heaven belongs to those who are like *these children*." (Matthew 19:14)

I ADORE MY family. We have been blessed with the gift of a precious daughter and son. They are a great *joy* to us. I love spending time with them exploring the world, laughing, hugging and just *being together*. I love watching them enjoy life. I love being there for them and encouraging them. Every child deserves that but so many children around the world have lost one parent...sometimes both parents...and have suffered *so greatly*. We owe it to them to take a risky step across an ocean, through checkpoints and despite our fears...to go *be with them* and *love them*. Jesus loves children and it must warm His heart to see people caring for and loving children who are *hurting*.

I often tell people that one of my favorite things to do *on this planet* is to be in a refugee camp laughing and smiling with the children there. I just know *that I know* that part of God's plan for my life is to enjoy some amazing moments with the refugee children. And so that's what I go and do. I oftentimes picture their faces...wondering how they are doing...wondering what their lives will be like...wondering if I will get to see them again. They are incredibly special times in those refugee camps playing with the children and enjoying *their smiles*. I especially love getting to know the children who are shy...who are a bit stand-offish...no doubt they have all been through so much...so much that children should not have to go through. I love when they get comfortable with me and, before we know it, they go from being stand-offish to getting close to me and laughing, giggling and smiling those beautiful smiles of theirs. I love those moments...they are so precious and such a *gift* from God.

I love that Jesus *loves* children...so much so that He chastised the disciples for trying to prevent the children from coming to Him:

> One day some parents brought their children to Jesus so he could lay his hands on them and pray for them. But the disciples scolded the parents for bothering him. But Jesus said, "Let the *children* come to me. *Don't* stop them! For the Kingdom of Heaven belongs to those who are like these children." (Matthew 19:13-14)

Jesus, I Like Children Too!

מֵרֵעַ

Precious Syrian refugee children (Zahle, Lebanon) (June 2015)

Story: Laughing with Refugee Children in Iraq

Then people brought *little children* to Jesus for him to place his hands on them and pray for them. (Matthew 19:13 NIV)

*A*S I SIT here at the computer typing, I picture the *faces* of the refugee children at the camp in Northern Iraq…and of the refugee children living in squalor in an urban area of Jordan…and those walking along the road next to their mother near Camp Zaatari in Northern Jordan near the war…and in the West Bank, who were so excited that a stranger from a far-off land bought them ice cream…and in Lebanon near the war who sang a song for us…and who jumped with a jolt at a refugee camp in Lebanon when a car backfired nearby. I cannot even begin to imagine how much God loves these precious children…and how badly *His heart breaks* for the suffering that they are going through. What an awesome gift that God has given me to get to go spend time with some of these children who are so *precious* to Him.

Journal Entry, Iraq, March 17, 2014:

"[The refugee children's] lives have been changed forever. Most walked to Iraq with family, showing up with almost nothing, crossing the river to escape the war. They live in a camp near here and were so excited to have two American visitors today. I laughed with them and showed them their pictures on my phone. Within 10 minutes I was surrounded by excited children. They wear winter coats in the containers they go to class in because it's so cold. Today was a special gift."

Smiling Syrian refugee children…bundled up for a cold day in their container-style classrooms with muddy floors (Northern Iraq) (March 2014)

Jesus, I Like Children Too!

Story: Gifts for Surprised Refugee Children in Iraq

Then Jesus *called* for the children. (Luke 18:16a)

NEEDLESS TO SAY, refugee children usually receive few if any gifts. Our kids are lavished with gifts on special occasions or "just because"…and I love giving our children gifts. It is a joy to watch a child's eyes light up and a smile emerge on their precious face as they receive a special gift…a *cherished* gift. God graciously allows me to go to refugee camps in the Middle East and give cherished gifts to precious children.

JOURNAL ENTRY, IRAQ, JUNE 21, 2015:

"When we got to the camp, some men were smelling small bunches of very aromatic plant leaves that they eat. In typical Middle Eastern hospitality, one of the refugee men gave me his bunch. I walked on with them (would be rude to refuse such a gift). I fell behind the others as I stopped to visit with some of the children. I gave one little girl (picture below) the bunch. She was surprised and excited at such a special gift from a stranger. As she took them, one *single small leaf* fell to the ground. She quickly picked it back up, she wanted every precious one of them. And I walked off trying not to cry.

"I had a wonderful time doing one of my favorite things: walking around a refugee camp or street by myself greeting people and making new friends. I did that today and before I knew it, I had bought candy for 30 of the children and was surrounded by children and adults excited to meet a stranger from a far off land. The kids were giggling and loved that my name in Arabic is Abu William. We spoke in some Arabic, Kurdish and English. I hope those memories last a lifetime for these children and replace some of their traumatic memories. They were precious. I would take their picture and then show it to them, they loved that."

Little Syrian refugee girl with her cherished gift...of leaves
(Northern Iraq) (June 2015)

Syrian refugee children (Northern Iraq) (June 2015)

30   Campfire With Jesus

Jesus took the loaves and gave thanks *to God. (John 6:11a)*

I ENJOY CAMPING. In fact, I've got a sticker on my Jeep that states, "Eat. Sleep. Camp. Repeat." I love being in the outdoors…in a forest…taking in the fresh, crisp air. Hearing the wind blow through the trees. Listening to the crackle of a campfire as we talk about the day's adventures. Admiring the glow of the coals in the campfire as they cast shadows around the campsite. Enjoying the stars *sparkling* in the clear night sky. Hiking through the woods following a well-worn path. Chatting with our son as we walk along the trail or just enjoy being together in the silence of the forest.

I wonder what it would be like to camp with Jesus. To sit around a campfire with Jesus, having spent the day fishing on the Sea of Galilee and now resting with a great friend as we reflect on the day's adventures. Wow what a campfire that would be to listen to *Jesus* say the blessing before we started eating the fish and bread. Listening to the water lapping on the shore nearby. Enjoying the company of a *faithful friend*…a brutally faithful, forgiving and loving friend…Jesus. I imagine looking at His hands as He prepares the food…maybe turning the fish over so they don't burn. And I imagine being *completely at peace* in His company…no hurry or need to go or desire to be somewhere else. Just satisfied to sit around the campfire with Jesus…my friend.

מֵרֵעַ

Encountering Jesus

Bonfire celebration during Persian new year of Newroz
(Northern Iraq) (March 2014)

Story: Kabobs Cooking over Hot Coals in Iraq

The others stayed with the boat and pulled the loaded net to the shore, for they were only about a hundred yards from shore. When they got there, they found *breakfast waiting for them*—fish cooking over a charcoal fire, and some bread. "Bring some of the fish you've just caught," Jesus said. (John 21:8-10)

O NE OF THE fun things about going to Northern Iraq in March is experiencing the annual holiday of Newroz. Families take several days off from work and normal life and head into the surrounding mountains for picnics. People cook kabobs on little portable grills. We enjoy the beauty of the mountains and the smell of the little cooking fires. Some women make bread and cook it…fresh bread…warm to the touch as you take your first bite. Chicken kabobs fresh off the grill. Sitting on a blanket enjoying the Middle Eastern feast and *fun*. Playing Kurdish-style checkers with the Kurdish men, some of whom are wearing pistols and one of whom is a war hero. *Laughing* as we play dominoes. No TVs or cell phones to distract us. Just fun times together with families and friends in the Middle East mountains near Turkey and Iran.

Moments like these in the Middle East help me better imagine what it was like for the disciples to spend time eating with Jesus and enjoying the outdoors together with Him. Some things have changed a lot in the Middle East since Jesus was living there…and some things haven't changed much at all.

Enjoying a picnic on the mountains
(Northern Iraq) (March 2014)

Encountering Jesus

Playing Kurdish-style checkers with an Iraqi Kurd during a picnic on the mountains…life is full of surprises (Northern Iraq) (March 2014)

Story: Gifts of Food and Drinks in the West Bank

When you enter a town and are welcomed, eat what is *offered* to you. (Luke 10:8 NIV)

*M*IDDLE EASTERN HOSPITALITY is hard to describe. How do you describe what it's like as a stranger to be welcomed into someone's home or refugee tent and given smiles, hugs, kisses on the cheek, and delicious tea. Since I have experienced the *welcoming* Middle Eastern hospitality throughout Iraq, Jordan, Israel, the West Bank and Lebanon, I have been able to better imagine what it was like for Jesus to be *welcomed* into Mary and Martha's home in that same area of the world (Luke 10:38-42). I have also been able to better imagine what it was like when Jesus prepared breakfast on the shore of the Sea of Galilee *for his friends* (John 21:11-13). One of the places I have enjoyed *gracious* hospitality is in Jericho, where I have spent the most time in the West Bank.

Journal Entry, West Bank, April 23, 2013:

"*Sabah al khair from Ariha* (good morning from Jericho). My new friend Nadir is a trained chef, we went into central Jericho this morning to buy food to make breakfast. We rode the local bus, full of people going to work...and one American :) I have not seen another American here yet in the local community, only at the tourist spot nearby. I heard the word '*mishmish*' spoken at the grocery this morning which made me smile, Nadir was asking about the apricots :) The store owner gave me a small courtesy coffee and a banana and greeted me by telling me the name *Allah* is in the *Qur'an* 99 times. He was a nice man. His name is Abu Muhammad. *Ma a'salaama* from *Ariha*...

"Old woman in one of the refugee settlements (the one I jogged in last year and met the Palestinian police). Amazingly kind woman, fed us and gave us cola to drink as she and her two daughters sat on the floor. She kissed me on both cheeks when I arrived, and loved seeing her picture on my camera. I vote her in the top 10 toughest (and kindest) women of Jericho. Treated me like family. Interpreter told her that I said that my mama in America would be glad to know she fed me :) She has very little and gave us much, typical of Arab hospitality to visitors. She told us how much she likes the Christians...She is an impressive woman/survivor."

Sunset after another amazing day with new friends in a West Bank refugee camp (Jericho, West Bank) (April 2013)

31   Jesus the Medal of Honor Winner

We know what real love is because Jesus *gave up his life for us*. So we also ought *to give up our lives* for our brothers and sisters. (1 John 3:16)

THE MEDAL OF Honor is the United States' highest award for bravery in military service and has been awarded since 1863. The Medal of Honor recognizes the *willingness* of someone to sacrifice *everything* for their fellow soldiers.

On April 24, 2004, in the town of Karabilah, Iraq, a young Marine soldier named Corporal Jason Dunham was attacked by an insurgent as he approached an Iraqi vehicle that was departing from an ambushed United States convoy. Corporal Dunham wrestled the insurgent to the ground. During the struggle, he saw that the insurgent had released a grenade. He immediately alerted his fellow Marines to the threat and, without hesitation, "covered the grenade with his helmet and body, bearing the brunt of the explosion and shielding his fellow Marines from the blast. In an ultimate and selfless act of bravery in which he was mortally wounded, he saved the lives of at least two fellow Marines."[80] Corporal Dunham *gave his life* so that others *could live*.

Imagine being one of the soldiers who was saved as a result of what Corporal Dunham did. And imagine getting to spend time with Corporal Dunham *after* he died…getting to thank him in person…getting to know him better. Imagine the *friendship* and *level of trust* you would have with someone who had *given his life for you*. Just imagine.

Jesus gave His life *for you*…for me…for all of us. He would have given His life for you if you were the *only* person on this planet. And we can have a *friendship* with Him…a real relationship. But *He's waiting for you*…for me…to desire that friendship and to seek out that friendship. Just imagine what a friendship like that could be like. *Just imagine.*

מֵרֵעַ

---

[80] Date of Issue: January 11, 2007; www.history.army.mil; Medal of Honor Recipients, Iraq War.

Paintball advertisement at ski resort in Iraq mountains...showing a soldier shooting next to a burned-out Humvee (Northern Iraq) (June 2015)

Story: Mothers Abandoning Babies in Nairobi

> But when she could no longer hide him, she got a basket made of papyrus reeds and waterproofed it with tar and pitch. She put the *baby* in the basket and laid it among the reeds along the bank of the Nile River. (Exodus 2:3)

THE FIRST TIME I set foot on African soil was in 2004. I had received the gift of salvation in my car four months earlier. I was just getting to know Jesus. And God was clearly nudging me to go to Africa...so *I went.*

Africa was a new place to me. All I really knew about Africa was what I had seen in movies and on TV and what I had read in books. The land of safaris, tribes and the Nile River. Pyramids in the north. Great white sharks off the southern coast. I was ready for *adventure*...ready to experience Africa.

The group that had asked me to go to Kenya was a Christian group and was doing what was called a "vision trip," which meant that we would visit different places around the capital city of Nairobi. One place was an orphanage for children. There were so many children there. And they were so *precious*...so excited to have visitors from a foreign land. Another place was the Fountain of Life Ministry where I met Pastor James Mbai and Mama Florence. Yet another place was a school out in the middle of *nowhere*...way out in the prairie land. It looked *abandoned*...broken windows, no sign of life...*dead*. But then, after we got out of our cars and started to walk towards the school, little heads of curious children began popping up and looking through the windows of broken glass. It turned out the place was *full* of children. They too were excited to have visitors from a distant land.

We learned that the children walk *miles* each way to school...thankful to have the opportunity to get an education. And we learned that there was *no food* at the school...the kids would eat something in the morning before walking the long walk to school...and then they would not eat again until that night after walking the long walk back home. It was a lot to take in on that trip...so many emotions swirling around in me...my heart *breaking* yet also *excited* to help bring smiles to the children's faces.

At one orphanage we visited, a sweet little girl no more than six years old quietly walked up to me and gave me a handwritten note. I could see that it took courage for her to do that, as her friend stood next to her silently watching this courageous act. I leaned down, looked at her, smiled and thanked her for the note. It wasn't until we were back in the van that I opened it. As I read it, I began crying. In the handwriting of a small, precious child, it read:

"Thank you for visiting us. If we told you our story, you would cry."

My heart was broken. Shattered. Weeping...*for her*. No telling what she had been through. What she had seen. What had been done to her. A dear, precious child. I can still picture her running up to me, quickly handing me the note, and standing there looking up at me.

As the "vision trip" continued on, we visited a hospital in Nairobi, or what you could call a hospital. It was dirty and rundown. Shocking to someone like me who at that point had only been in very clean hospitals in America. This one was *very* different.

We walked in the front entrance and passed eight or so mothers who were holding their babies in their arms as they sat in chairs against the hallway wall waiting to see a doctor. I smiled and nodded to them as we walked by, saying "*jambo*" in Swahili for "hello." The hospital guide who was giving us the tour led us down the hallway and then stopped at some glass windows. Through the windows was a small room full of newborn babies in little baby holders. There were many babies...over a dozen. I love seeing newborn babies, so I *smiled* at the sight of new life in a city with so much death...a city where many were dying in the slums from AIDS and bacteria-laden drinking water. The woman explained that this was the newborn baby room...for *abandoned* babies. The smile immediately dropped from my face as my brain raced to comprehend what she just said. What was that I just heard? *Abandoned* babies? How *awful* I thought...how could a *parent* do that...how *selfish* to care so little for a new life as to just *discard* it.

I spoke up and asked how these babies get to the hospital. And I was surprised at the answer: "Their mothers come here to give birth. And then, during the night, the mothers *sneak out* of the hospital." I was experiencing so many emotions as she calmly explained this, some of which was anger...how could a mother do that? Care enough to carry the child to the time of birth...care enough to go to the hospital to give birth...but yet *sneak out* in the middle of the night? I asked why a mother would do such a thing. The response: "Because they know that the best chance their child has to *survive* is to be taken in and raised by a children's home or some other group...and not in the slums."[81] I was speechless. The mothers I was so angry at were actually *heroes*. What an extreme example of someone putting the interests of someone else *ahead of* their own interests. The mother who loves her child so much that she is willing to give up *ever seeing the child again*...so that the child could survive and grow up with a better life...maybe even a life outside of the *deathly grip* of the slums.

Since I heard about those heroic mothers that day in that Nairobi hospital, I have since pictured a mother sneaking out of the hospital in the middle of the night...tip-toeing silently through the hallway...past the newborn baby room...stopping to look once more through the glass at her precious baby...tears running down her face and dropping quietly onto the hospital floor...and then she finally knows she must go on...and she turns away from her sleeping baby's peaceful face for *the last time*...and walks down the hallway and out of the hospital into the night...walking, crying and desperately wanting to turn around...but knowing that her newborn's best shot at survival is for her to *just keep walking away*.

Jesus tells us that, "There is no greater love than to *lay down one's life* for one's friends" (John 15:13). It is humbling how these mothers laid down their lives for their children as they walked out that hospital door. And Jesus loves you so much that He willingly laid down His life for *you*. That's amazing love.

---

[81] I learned later in the trip that parents in the slums oftentimes don't name their newborn babies for as long as a year in order to first wait to find out if the baby survives the harsh slum conditions. That way, the death of the baby will hopefully not be as personal as it would be if the baby had a name. *Many* babies don't survive that long.

Jesus the Medal of Honor Winner

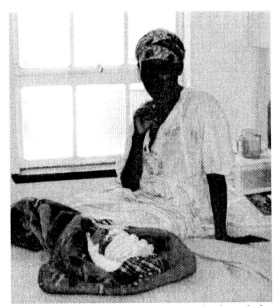

Mother with new baby at maternity hospital
(Nairobi, Kenya) (July 2004)

32   Jesus the Boss

Work willingly at whatever you do, as though you were *working for the Lord* rather than for people. Remember that the Lord will give you an inheritance as your reward, and that the Master you are serving is Christ. (Colossians 3:23-24)

I HAVE A boss at the place I work. He's been my boss for all five years that I've worked there. He's a great boss. However, my *ultimate* boss is Jesus. When I show up at work, I want to please my earthly boss. But even more importantly, I want to please my Heavenly Boss. However significant or insignificant a task is that I am working on at the office, I have an extra incentive to do it well when I remember that I am ultimately doing it *for the Lord*. I look forward to payday at work...we get paid twice a month. But wow should we get even more excited about the payday waiting for us from the Lord...the inheritance of *eternal life*. Granted, we don't *earn* our eternal inheritance...it's a *free gift* of God (Ephesians 2:8). But it sure helps our attitude at work or at home as a homemaker or as a volunteer coach or in anything else we are doing...to remember that we are doing it *for Jesus*, not people. That converts humdrum work, taking out the trash, helping a child with school work, or whatever else we're doing into an act of *worship*.

Doorway on a church portraying different scenes from the life...and death...of Jesus (Nazareth, Israel) (June 2012)

Story: Worshipping God at the Office

So whatever you eat or drink or whatever you do, do it *all* for the glory of God. (1 Corinthians 10:31 NIV)

I OWNED A business for several years, which was started three and a half years after I met Jesus. It was a small office and there were several other people who worked there. It was a fun season of life. We enjoyed working together as well as praying together for the business...for the clients...for our families. We did a Bible study together about living out our faith at work. The business even had a Christian-based mission statement that we hung up in the office for everyone who visited there to see:

Mission Statement

Our mission is to glorify God by serving others with integrity, respect and gratitude. As part of this mission, we acknowledge that all good things come from the Lord, that we are stewards of all that He has provided us, and that it is a privilege and blessing to serve Him by serving others.

As a small business, we had immense latitude to pray with clients, talk about Jesus, and even have "extreme casual Friday," where everyone could wear jeans or shorts. In fact, some of the employees would walk around the office barefoot.

Our intentions as Christians were good ones, but looking back, I can see how some people could have easily looked at me (and probably did!) as an *obnoxious* Christian business owner...obnoxiously living out my faith at work. I'm laughing out loud as I type this! God is amazingly *gracious* with us..."warts and all."

There's a lot to be said for "living out your faith" and "shar[ing] the Gospel at all times, and if *necessary*, us[ing] words."[82] When Jesus changes your heart and gives you new life...eternal life...and peace, joy and love...it's hard *not* to be fired up about that. But we've also got to meet people where they are and not try to impress people with our faith or anything else. I love the New Living Translation in Philippians:

> Don't be *selfish*; don't try to *impress others*. Be *humble*, thinking of others as *better than yourselves*. Don't look out only for your own interests, but *take an interest in others*, too. You must have the same attitude that Christ Jesus had. Though he was God, he did not think of equality with God as something to cling to. Instead, he gave up his divine privileges; he took the *humble position of a slave* and was born as a human being. When he appeared in human form, he humbled himself in obedience to God and *died a criminal's death on a cross*. (Philippians 2:3-8)

Wow can we put on our Christian "cheerleading outfit" and try to impress others...at church, at home, at work...anywhere and everywhere. This is not about condemnation...thank God that "there is now no condemnation for those who are in Christ Jesus" (Romans 8:1). This is about being *real* and *honest* with ourselves. Why are we doing the Christian-type things that we are doing? To impress ourselves? To impress God? To impress others? Are we focused on where other people are in *their* faith journey? Or are we the bull storming into the

---

[82] Quote generally attributed to Francis of Assisi, an Italian religious leader in the 12th to 13th centuries who founded the Franciscans.

crystal shop as everyone runs for cover? I'm laughing again as I type this and shaking my head slowly back and forth. You've got to be able to *laugh at yourself*. Thank God for God's mercy and for laughter!

At the office, there was an older, African-American man who stopped by regularly to clean everything. His name was James. He would dust off the furniture, vacuum the carpet, clean the kitchen, wipe the windows, sweep the floors…and scrub the toilets. He was a gentle and kind spirit. I always enjoyed talking with him…and just being *around* him. *He never said a negative thing about anything or anyone.* He was always willing to pause what he was doing to *listen* to someone. He was *thankful* for what we paid him. He was *respectful* to everyone. And he did his job with *joy*. I came to learn that he loved Jesus and had been following Jesus for a long time…for decades. And he was a leader in the local church that he attended. I'm smiling as I type this. He was a *great gift* to all of us and no doubt prayed for us and the office. Probably more than I did.

Looking back, it is so clear to me that James did his job for the *glory of God*. James vacuumed those floors for the *glory of God*. And James scrubbed those toilets for the *glory of God*. I know that because of his loving and kind spirit. I never felt judged by James. He never said a curt word towards me or anyone else. I think that's because he was having so much fun enjoying giving God glory.

מֵרֵעַ

A statue of my new boss Jesus (125-foot tall statue) (Rio de Janeiro, Brazil) (November 2004)

33 Going to Church in Iraq With Jesus

And he is the head of the body, the *church*. (Colossians 1:18a)

*I*ALWAYS ENJOY attending a Christian worship service in the Middle East. I am inspired by the people following Jesus in an area of the world where it is so difficult to follow Him. I admire their *courage*. It's amazing to attend a worship service in Arabic…all of us there worshipping the King in different languages. I am reminded that God's Church is throughout the world. And people are worshipping Him in many languages in places that don't look like churches in America. Wow are the people *fired up* there for *Jesus*.

Early morning walk in Northern Iraq (June 2015)

Story: Info about Northern Iraq

> This time Jonah obeyed the LORD's command and went to *Nineveh* [in modern-day Northern Iraq], a city so large that it took three days to see it all. (Jonah 3:3)

NORTHERN IRAQ IS a beautiful area of the world. I have enjoyed spending time there and making many *new friends*...both Muslims and Christians. Shia Muslims are the majority in Iraq. Since Saddam Hussein (a Sunni Muslim) was toppled, the Shia rose to power in a democratic-style government. The Shia apparently have been oppressing the minority Sunni (payback time in a tribal society) in response to Saddam's brutal reign during which he oppressed the Shia majority. Saddam also oppressed the Kurdish people in the Northern area of Iraq, who are not Arabs. He had many of them killed by torture, war and the use of chemical weapons.[83] *Entire* Kurdish villages were *wiped out*. The leader of Syria (Assad) is a Shia Muslim and is apparently doing the same to the Sunni Muslims there.

This is a dangerous breeding ground for ISIS, which is Sunni, as Sunnis in Iraq resent how Shia leadership has been treating them. Iran is a Shia majority country, hence their help in fighting Sunni ISIS. They back Assad as well as the new Shia-led Iraqi government. Saudi Arabia has a Sunni majority as does Turkey, so it is believed in the area where I visited that they are secretly (or not so secretly) backing ISIS. Iran (Shia) and Turkey (Sunni) have been fighting the Kurdish rebel group (the PKK[84]) for decades, so Turkey and Iran presumably oppose the US providing weapons to the Kurdish Peshmerga (the Northern Iraq Kurdish military force). But the Kurdish Peshmerga is the only ground force in that region that has continually won battles against ISIS. They are a hardened fighting people but do not have a nation of their own. In fact, they are the largest people group in the world without their own nation.[85] They commonly call Northern Iraq "Kurdistan" and even have their own flag like the Palestinians do.[86]

---

[83] http://news.bbc.co.uk/2/shared/spl/hi/middle_east/02/iraq_events/html/chemical_warfare.stm
[84] Kurdistan Workers' Party or PKK (Kurdish: Partiya Karkerên Kurdistan).
[85] www.thestar.com/news/world/2015/07/25/kurds-worlds-largest-minority-group-without-home-state.html
[86] www.bbc.com/news/world-middle-east-28147263

Going to Church in Iraq With Jesus

The Iraqi government and the Kurds are in a gridlock of diplomacy. The Iraqi government in Baghdad regularly withholds salaries to government workers in the Kurdish North to show them who's boss. Ironically, Turkey and Iran are important trading partners with the Kurds in Northern Iraq, so their relationships with the Kurds are *"sweet and sour"* as one man put it to me there. It's a complicated web of politics and centuries-old tribal, feuding societies.

صــديقي

A shepherd and his sheep rest along the mountain road between Soran and Erbil (Northern Iraq) (June 2015)

Story: Soran: City of Refugees

> [God] defends the cause of the fatherless and the widow, and loves the *foreigner* residing among you, giving them food and clothing. (Deuteronomy 10:18 NIV)

SORAN IS IN the Kurdish area of Northern Iraq. It is a *city of refugees*. It previously had about 20,000 people and was cut off from the world due to the mountain range and gorges between Soran and Erbil (where I flew in to Iraq), until a road was cut through the mountains from Erbil to Soran about 80 years ago. Refugees over the years have flooded to Soran from Iran (18 miles to the East), Turkey (24 miles to the North), and from within Iraq itself. There is a Freedom Martyrs Quarter there that consists of 300 small homes given to

Kurdish families that have lost fathers in war...it's a *fatherless community*. The Refuge community center is located in that neighborhood, which Christians built over the past five or so years. The community center was built at the direction of the American family I stayed with there in 2014, who are part of a non-profit called World Orphans. The host family I stayed with in June 2015 is also part of World Orphans.[87] Soran now has about 80,000 people as a result of the Kurdish refugees who fled Saddam Hussein and Iran. As such, Soran is in essence *75% refugee now*. You could call it a *city of refugees*. How awesome that these Christian families here are serving them as well as the new refugees that continue to arrive from Mosul, Iraq and other areas.

Soran is a 45-mile drive northeast from Erbil towards the Iraq mountainous borders with Iran and Turkey. It's a daunting road that winds through narrow mountain passes and along river gorges. In 2015, I landed at 1:45 a.m. local Iraq time on a Sunday morning. I had never landed in Iraq in the middle of the night. A gracious friend of the families there drove from Soran to pick me up and drove me back that night along the dark mountain roads. We arrived in Soran at 3:45 a.m. The drive through the mountains and river gorges to Soran will get your prayer life *more active*...it did for me! Most parts of the road are not painted with *any* stripes and there are very few street lights. Thanks be to God that we had a safe drive as we passed through so many security checkpoints that I lost count.

The host family has a small garden outside of their house, which is a stark contrast to the desert-dry and hot surroundings. While my new friend watered the garden one morning, I learned from him that there is water rationing in Soran. Water is sent to the community in pipes every two days. A pump at each house (which *better* be working) sends the water up to the tanks on the rooftop. Then the water shuts off and that's the water you have for two days.

I was a long way from home. And made some wonderful new Kurdish, Iraqi, European and American friends.

מֵרֵעַ

---

[87] www.worldorphans.org/

Going to Church in Iraq With Jesus

Label on a UN refugee tent at the Refuge community center (Northern Iraq) (June 2015)

Story: Worship Service in Iraq: No Church Building

All the nations you have made will come and worship before you, Lord; they will bring *glory* to your name. (Psalm 86:9 NIV)

IT'S A NEW experience for most Americans...it sure was for me...to be in a city of 80,000 people and the only public crosses were the cross-shaped *telephone poles*. No church buildings. No Bible stores. Just mosques. The borders with Iran and Turkey close by. And a harrowing drive to get there through the mountainous river gorge. Add all that up and you feel very far away from home and from the Church.

During my first visit to that area of Iraq in 2014, I went for a walk and ended up across the street from one of the mosques in town.[88] Some of those cross-shaped telephone poles stand directly across the street from the mosque. What an image it was to see the mosque on one side with Arabic writing on part of its wall, the cross-shaped telephone poles on the other side, and the bright Iraqi sun shining down between them.

---

[88] In fact, I ended up *inside* that mosque and attended the Friday *jum'a* service. That story is detailed in *Vacation in Iraq*.

During the second visit to Iraq in 2015, I was back in that same town. I still didn't see any crosses other than those same cross-shaped telephone poles. I still didn't see any church buildings. But this time I got to attend a Christian worship service...the type you have in that kind of a place. No crosses. No church buildings. But *intimate worship* with Jesus and a small group of new friends.

The family I was staying with is an Australian man and his American wife, along with their three young children. They are wonderful people and have a *passion* to serve the people of Iraq, including the refugees. He plays the guitar and is great at it. The Sunday morning I was there, he and I and the three others who were staying with their family headed to the local community center. The three others consisted of two women originally from Poland and Italy, who are now missionaries based in England, and an American student who was serving in Iraq for part of the summer. A unique group! The center is called the Refuge and was built as a service to the local community and includes a soccer field. The second floor of the community center is a large room about the size of a gym. It's open like a gym...no interior walls...just one big cavernous room.

The five of us walked up the outside stairway to the second floor and entered the large gym-sized room. It was quiet. The hot Iraqi day was working its way up past 100 degrees. My friend had his guitar. So there we were...in a building in Iraq near Iran and Turkey. And we *worshipped*. My friend played some praise songs and we all joined in. How awesome it was to be attending church in Iraq. How amazing it was to worship the King in Iraq. No fancy church building. No crosses. *Just Jesus*. It was wonderful. We finished singing some songs and began praying for Iraq...for the people...for the refugees...and for the terrorists. And it was a taste of Heaven. I was so privileged to be there with those four others lifting up the people of Iraq...lifting up that war-torn nation...not with worldly weapons but with *prayer*.

Worship service with new friends...Iraq style
(Northern Iraq) (June 2015)

The cross-shaped telephone poles across from the mosque
(Northern Iraq) (June 2015)

34 Jesus the Prince of Peace

For to us a child is born, to us a son is given, and the government will be on his shoulders. And he will be called Wonderful Counselor, Mighty God, Everlasting Father, *Prince of Peace*. (Isaiah 9:6 NIV)

*W*E ALL WANT peace, but there is only *one place* to find it. And that's with *Jesus*.

I am leaving you with a gift—peace of *mind and heart*. And the peace I give is a gift *the world cannot give*. So don't be troubled or afraid. (John 14:27)

And that's why Jesus is called the Prince of Peace. When we ask Jesus into our heart, we receive the Holy Spirit.[89] And one of the fruits of the Spirit that we receive is peace (Galatians 5:22-23).

Iraq is a country of *contrasts*. My experience has been that much of the Middle East is a powerful contrast. One of the contrasts is between war and peace. I sat one night in a backyard in Iraq with new friends. It was quite a contrast of war and peace. Please pray for the Middle East to have peace through Jesus.

---

[89] Ephesians 1:14, 2 Corinthians 1:22.

Jesus the Prince of Peace

Camp Baserma near the dirt airstrip where US soldiers arrived at the start of the 2003 Iraq war (Northern Iraq) (June 2015)

Story: Day of Contrasts in Iraq

A week later his disciples were in the house again, and Thomas was with them. Though the doors were locked, Jesus came and *stood among them* and said, "*Peace* be with you!" (John 20:26 NIV)

*I*N VAST DESERTS of sand, an oasis is a place with water and the cool shade of a tree. In vast deserts of war, an oasis is a place with *peace*. As I travel in the Middle East through war-torn lands, it is a joy to find an *oasis of peace* along the way.

JOURNAL ENTRY, IRAQ, JUNE 22, 2015:

"We are back late this evening from a backyard family gathering at a local Muslim family's home (pretty much everyone in this city is a Muslim). The day of contrasts continued this evening. The U.S. State Department issued an updated security alert for Iraq, which I received by email right before we left at 8:30pm. Things get started late here since its Ramadan and Muslims are not eating or drinking from sunrise to sunset.

"We went to the friend's house as invited guests and in contrast to the State Dept warnings about kidnappings and attacks, they have a serene Iraqi backyard...it's like being in a backyard in Florida...well almost. A fountain, lots of grass, trees and a white picket fence that runs along the inside of the cement perimeter wall/barrier. It's a small yard by American standards...very small...but amazingly large by Iraqi standards. We were treated very well in the spirit of Middle Eastern culture and the stars were out in the clear sky. The kids were running around playing as the adults drank hot tea and ate sweets.

"Then in a contrast to the peacefulness, the grandfather of the big family arrived and he was using a cane and his hand and arm were disfigured. He had a fun personality and we learned he had survived a bombing by Saddam Hussein, fortunate to have lived through it. I wondered if a missile would cross the peaceful and starlit night sky or a bomb would go off in the city as we sat there drinking tea and watching the children play and giggle. Neither happened. It was a wonderful evening with new friends. I'm starting to believe that Iraq is quite a country of contrasts. War in one area, family gatherings in another. The empty ski resort towering over the refugee camps down in the valley. People dying in explosions and tent fires and babies being born in refugee camps. I guess life in general is full of contrasts...they just seem more pronounced in Iraq.

"...It was a great day with new friends."

מֵרֵעַ

Jesus the Prince of Peace

Relaxing in a new friend's backyard complete with a white picket fence and a cement barrier wall behind it (Northern Iraq) (June 2015)

Story: Hungry for Peace in Beirut: Jesus is the Only Source

And let the peace that *comes from Christ* rule in your hearts. (Colossians 3:15a)

P EACE…SO MANY people pursue peace but just can't seem to find it. So many hearts are *restless*. So many ask, "Where is the peace?" "When will there be peace?" "How can there be peace in the Middle East?" "Why am I not at peace?" "If just so-and-so would happen, then I'd be at peace." "How can I have peace amidst so much conflict?...amidst so many wars?" God's Word is clear that the *only* source of genuine, honest-to-goodness peace is *Jesus*. Period. And the peace of Christ surpasses all understanding…it's so amazing…it's so *unexplainable*.

> Don't worry about anything; instead, pray about everything. Tell God what you need, and *thank him* for all he has done. *Then* you will experience God's peace, which exceeds anything we can understand. His peace will guard your hearts and minds as you live in Christ Jesus. (Philippians 4:6-7)

And the peace of Christ does not just show up. We have to *live in* Christ Jesus...live our lives following Him...live our lives obeying God's Word...live our lives not worrying but instead praying about *everything*...live our lives *thanking* God for all He has done...*then* the peace of Christ arrives. And wow is it an incredible gift. No matter what a person's circumstances in life, a person can have the peace of Christ.

One night at the hotel in Beirut, I was in the lobby saying hi to some of the people who work there. It was a small hotel and there was a little bar that was really nothing more than a counter and some shelves. They were making some type of Lebanese drink and asked me if I wanted to taste it. I accepted their hospitality and enjoyed visiting with them. As we talked about Lebanon, the man who runs the hotel where I stayed said that the one thing Lebanon does not have is *peace*. It was sad to hear him say that...he said it with the demeanor of someone who doesn't think peace will *ever* come to Lebanon.

I told him how much I love Lebanon. He then asked me what I had done that day in Lebanon. When I told him and the other men in the lobby that I had been in the town of Zahle, they were *shocked*, probably because Zahle is *so close to the war*...just about 10 or so miles from it and the Syrian border. I was enjoying God's *peace* during the trip and had enjoyed it during the visit to Zahle. In Zahle, I was fortunate to spend a lot of time inside tents with some of the refugee families, smiling and laughing with some of the children, and meeting some amazing people who are there serving the refugees. I imagine I appeared to the men in the lobby that evening to not only be at peace but also *joyful* about being there. Being at *peace* in Zahle so close to the *war*. Them not being in peace in Beirut farther away from the war.

I hope and pray that they will encounter the peace of Christ and enjoy the peace that can be experienced right now...right at this moment during the wars, conflicts, headlines and sadness. The peace of Christ truly is the peace that surpasses all understanding...and I'm so thankful that I have received it.

Jesus the Prince of Peace

The refugee camp in Zahle with the Syrian border in the background...a peaceful place near a brutal war (Zahle, Lebanon) (June 2015) (faces blurred for privacy reasons)

Standing in a refugee camp where the precious children jumped when a car backfired nearby (Zahle, Lebanon) (June 2015)

35   Friendship With the World Instead of With Jesus

> You adulterers! Don't you realize that *friendship with the world* makes you an *enemy of God?* I say it again: If you want to be a friend of the world, you make yourself an enemy of God. (James 4:4)

OUCH. THAT'S WHAT I call a tough, direct-to-the-point, kind of Word. This book is about having a *friendship* with Jesus. So the last thing I want to do is become His *enemy*. But I feel like I do love the world. It's a beautiful place with so much to explore and enjoy. It's God's creation. Or is it?

This Scripture reminds me of some of the things Jesus said that were no doubt *hard to hear* by the people standing by Him…I know they're hard for me to *read* almost 2,000 years later. Things like:

> If you want to be my disciple, you must *hate everyone else by comparison*—your father and mother, wife and children, brothers and sisters—yes, *even your own life.* Otherwise, you cannot be my disciple. (Luke 14:26)

> Another disciple said to him, "Lord, first let me go and bury my father." But Jesus told him, "Follow me, and *let the dead bury their own dead."* (Matthew 8:21-22 NIV)

What point was Jesus trying to get across to His listeners…to us? That we should hate our families? That we should refuse to go to funerals for our loved ones because it's more important to go to a Bible study? No, of course not. God is *love* (1 John 4:8)…so Jesus is *love*…they are One in the Same. God tells us in fact that, if we don't provide for our relatives and especially for our own household…our spouse, our children…we have *"denied the faith"* (1 Timothy 5:8). He tells us to *love our neighbors* (Matthew 22:39)…to *look out for the interests of others* (Philippians 2:4)…to be willing to *give up our lives for others* (John 15:13)…to have *faith* and *hope* and *love* (1 Corinthians 13:13). Jesus will never contradict Himself…after all, He's the Son of the Living God.

So what then does it mean to have "friendship with the world"? He is trying to make the same point in *each* of these teachings…about friendship with the world…about our love for our families…about wanting to look out for the needs of our families. His point is that our *relationship* with Him…our *friendship*

Friendship With the World Instead of With Jesus

with Him...our *love* for Him...should be so *intimate*, so *real*, so *deep* and so *passionate* that all other relationships and desires *pale in comparison*. Just typing that and focusing on that takes my breath away. Causes my heart to skip a beat. Makes me take a *hard look* at how important...or *unimportant*...Jesus really is to me.

And here I am typing this...the guy who was recently counting his closest friends on his fingers...and it didn't even *cross my mind* to include Jesus. Thankfully, that was the beginning of this journey with Jesus...my friend Jesus...a journey and a relationship that is not yet finished. I'd like to think that the next time I count those friends on my fingers...Jesus will be the *first one*. Regardless, I love knowing that my friend Jesus loves me in a way I cannot begin to understand. He cares for me...He never gives up on me...and He even *died for me*.

You know, it's a funny thing with Jesus...being *friends* with Jesus...that the deeper your relationship gets with *Him*, the deeper your relationships get with *others*. Being friends with Jesus has some very unexpected results. Pursuing Jesus impacts our lives in ways we *cannot imagine*. Loving Jesus enriches the love we have for others, for our precious families, for our friends...and even for our enemies.

صــــديقي

Standing by the road that winds its way through the Southern Lebanese desert...Jesus has taken me to places I never imagined I would go (June 2015)

Lokman and me in the middle with two other new friends; friends are a great gift (Camp Baserma, Northern Iraq) (March 2014)

Epilogue

Love your *neighbor* as yourself. (Mark 12:31a)

So, AM I brave? Am I courageous for going back to the Middle East time after time? *No.* I'm just doing what God has told me to do and, by His grace, He gives us what we need for the task at hand. As Corrie ten Boom explained:

> Whatever bravery or skill I had ever shown were gifts of God—sheer loans from Him of the talent needed to do a job. (*The Hiding Place*, p.243)

As Jesus calls you to go…as you get banged up in life…I encourage you to get to know Jesus and go where He calls you to go…no matter what. Amy Carmichael wrote a poem that sums up following Jesus:

> We follow a scarred Captain,
> Should we not have scars?
> Under His faultless orders
> We follow to the wars.
> Lest we forget, Lord, when we meet,
> Show us Thy hands and feet.

As we go where Jesus calls us to go, and do what He calls us to do, we need to be careful not to take any of the credit for it…God should get *all* the credit and glory. Brother Yun's wife, Deling, explained in *The Heavenly Man* what her husband says about this…they are hard words for me to read but I know they are right and true:

> I know my husband's heart. His heart and his faith are solid…I respect him for his love and commitment to God…Yun often tells me, "We are absolutely nothing. We have nothing to be proud about. We have no abilities and nothing to offer God. The fact that he chooses to use us is only due to his grace. It has *nothing to do with us*. If God should choose to raise up others for his purpose and never use us again we would have *nothing to complain about*." (p.345)

God has been *amazingly gracious* to me. Jesus has shown Himself to be a *wonderfully faithful friend*. I'm so thankful for the journeys I have gotten to go on in the Middle East. So thankful for the friends I've made along the way…especially my new friend Jesus.

Thank you for joining me on my journey to Beirut…a journey with you and with Jesus.

My prayer for you is:

Jesus loves you deeply and sacrificially and gave His life for you. Jesus is always with you. He eagerly waits for you to give your heart to Him. Do not be afraid of terrorists or any other enemies in your lives, because the LORD your God is always with you. God will never leave you or turn His back on you. His loving eyes are on you always and He will show you which way to go. May you always trust Him because He knows what is best. God has a great plan for your life…a plan of hope and an eternal future with Him. No matter what you go through, God will bring good out of it for you as long as you love Him. May the LORD bless you and keep you. May His smile always be on you, may He be gracious to you always. May the LORD give you His favor and give you His amazing peace. Amen[90]

Brian Becker a/k/a Abu William
October 2015

---

[90] Prayer based on God's *promises* in John 3:16, 1 John 3:16, Matthew 28:20, Revelation 3:20, Deuteronomy 31:6, Psalm 32:8, Proverbs 3:5-6, Jeremiah 29:11, Romans 8:28 and Numbers 6:24-26.

Epilogue

Out for a walk in Northern Iraq…just me and my dear friend Jesus
(June 2015)

A   Resources

Plans fail for lack of counsel, but with many advisers they *succeed*. (Proverbs 15:22)

The Bible (should always be first)
The Story of Christ and His Disciples (books of Luke and Acts, Arabic-English translation), by International Sharif Bible Society (free download at www.sharifbible.com/English.html)
The Quran (English translation by Professor (Dr.) Syed Vickar Ahamed)
Encountering the World of Islam course (www.encounteringislam.org)
Muslims, Christians and Jesus by Carl Madearis
e-Sword (www.e-sword.net) (free computer download/app)
Hudson Taylor by J. Hudson Taylor
The Hiding Place by Corrie ten Boom with Elizabeth and John Sherrill
Tramp for the Lord by Corrie ten Boom with Jamie Buckingham
Gold Cord by Amy Carmichael
The Heavenly Man by Brother Yun with Paul Hattaway
The Signature of Jesus by Brennan Manning
God's Smuggler by Brother Andrew with John and Elizabeth Sherrill
God's Call by Brother Andrew with Verne Becker
Gladys Aylward by Catherine Swift
Isobel Kuhn by Lois Hoadley Dick
Mary Slessor by Basil Miller
Jesus Freaks by D.C. Talk and The Voice of the Martyrs
24 Hours That Changed the World by Adam Hamilton
Redeeming Love by Francine Rivers
Ashes for Beauty by Joyce Meyers
Not a Fan by Kyle Idleman
Radical: Taking Back Your Faith from the American Dream by David Platt
Strong's Exhaustive Concordance of the Bible by Dr. James Strong
The Arabic Alphabet by Nicholas Awde and Putros Samano
Rosetta Stone: Arabic I, II and III
The Voice of the Martyrs (www.persecution.com)

B Ways to Help Refugees

He ensures that orphans and widows receive justice. He shows love to the foreigners living among you and gives them food and clothing. [19] So you, too, must *show love to foreigners*, for you yourselves were once foreigners in the land of Egypt. (Deuteronomy 10:18-19)

You can learn about more ways to help refugees by contacting:

Manara International at projects@manarainternational.org or via Hope Builders at www.hope-builders.org, Hope Builders, P.O. Box 5465, Charlottesville, Virginia 22905

World Orphans at http://www.worldorphans.org/iraq-emergency-fund/ or at 1-888-ORPHANS, P.O. Box 1840 Castle Rock, Colorado 80104

The Foundation for Relief and Reconciliation in the Middle East at http://frrme.org/

Open Doors at https://www.opendoorsusa.org/ or 888-5-BIBLE-5, P.O. Box 27001, Santa Ana, California 92799

World Wide New Testament Baptist Missions, P.O. Box 725, King's Mountain, NC 28086, Attn: Lebanon Refugee Aid

מֵרֵעַ

Ways to Help Refugees

Syrian refugee girls at a camp in Northern Iraq (March 2014)

Syrian refugee children singing a song and making a joyful noise (Zahle, Lebanon) (June 2015)

C   Photo of drowned boy sparks outcry

Let the little children come to me, and do not hinder them, for the kingdom of God *belongs to such as these*. (Mark 10:14b NIV)

How God's heart must break over the suffering of so many precious people…so many young children. I can't fathom the suffering that this father has gone through for his family…and the suffering our Heavenly Father has gone through too. Below is one of the news articles that came out after a small refugee child *washed up on Turkey's shore.*[91]

BBC News: Migrant crisis: Photo of drowned boy sparks outcry

3 September 2015

From the section Europe

BBC's Fergal Keane reports on the death of **two young boys, found drowned on a Turkish beach**

At least 12 Syrians trying to reach Greece have drowned off Turkey after the boats they were travelling in sank.

An image of one of the victims - **a young boy lying face down on the beach** - has sparked an international outcry over the human cost of the crisis.

The picture, released by a Turkish news agency, is trending worldwide on Twitter under the #KiyiyaVuranInsanlik ("humanity washed ashore") hashtag.

Thousands of migrants have died this year trying to reach Europe by sea.

Warning: This article contains a distressing image

---

[91] http://www.bbc.com/news/world-europe-34133210

Photo of drowned boy sparks outcry

The Turkish coastguard said the migrants had set off from Turkey's Bodrum peninsula for the Greek island of Kos in the early hours of Wednesday morning, but the two boats they were in sank shortly afterwards.

Twelve bodies, including five children, were recovered. Of 23 people on board the two boats, only nine people are thought to have survived - some made it to shore with life jackets.

The beach where the bodies were found has become suddenly notorious, but on any day there you will find the debris - deflated dinghy parts, the abandoned belongings of those attempting the crossing - of the desperate

The image of the young boy, shown wearing a red T-shirt and lying face-down on the beach near Bodrum, was published shortly after **the bodies washed up on shore** at about 06:00 local time.

Turkish news agency Dogan said he and the rest of the group were **Syrians from the besieged town of Kobane who had fled** to Turkey last year to escape advancing militants from the Islamic State (IS) group.

Turkish media describe **relatives breaking down as they identified the bodies.**

The pictured boy is reported to be three-year-old Aylan, who drowned along with his five-year-old brother Galip and their mother, Rihan. Their father, Abdullah Kurdi, survived.

Syrian boy's father tells of drowning

He and his family reportedly sought asylum in Canada before attempting the journey - but their refugee application was turned down.

Teema Kurdi, Abdullah's sister who lives in Vancouver, told Canada's National Post newspaper that she had been trying to help them leave the Middle East.

Abdullah is reported to have been kidnapped and tortured during the siege of Kobane by Islamic State or another jihadist group.

Photo of drowned boy sparks outcry

"I was trying to sponsor them [...] but we couldn't get them out, and that is why they went in the boat," she said.

The family is believed to have no other option because Syrian Kurdish refugees in Turkey find it almost impossible to get an exit visa unless they have a passport, which few do.

A local fisherman who discovered the bodies on the shore said: "I came to the sea and I was scared. **My heart is broken.**"

According to the BBC's Fergal Keane, the beach where the bodies were found has become suddenly notorious, but on any day there you will find the debris - deflated dinghy parts, abandoned belongings - of the desperate.

'Tragic reminder'

The BBC has chosen to publish only one **photograph of Aylan, in which he is being carried by a Turkish police officer** and is unidentifiable.

However, several news organisations have published more graphic images of the boy.

A **paramilitary police officer carries the lifeless body of a migrant** near the Turkish resort of Bodrum

The boy's lifeless body was captured in a series of images released by a Turkish news agency

UK newspaper The Independent said it had decided to use the images on its website because "among the often glib words about the 'ongoing migrant crisis', **it is all too easy to forget the reality of the desperate situation facing many refugees**".

Despite the reaction to the image online, there has been little reaction from European leaders.

The dead boy's father desperately tried to save his family, his aunt Teema Kurdi told Canadian journalist Terry Glavin.

Photo of drowned boy sparks outcry

"He made it, but his wife didn't and there's a terrible story he told about swimming from one to the other," Mr Glavin said in an interview with BBC Radio 5 live.

Abdullah found both of his sons and his wife dead - although initially he was not able to recognise her because her body had been so badly damaged by the rocks.

Justin Forsyth, chief executive of the charity Save the Children, said the "tragic image" was *a reminder of "the dangers children and families are taking in search of a better life"*.

"This child's plight should concentrate minds and force the EU to come together and agree to *a plan to tackle the refugee crisis*," he added.

Some 350,000 migrants have made the perilous journey to reach Europe's shores since January this year, according to figures released by the International Organization for Migration (IOM) on Tuesday.

The IOM said *more than 2,600 migrants had drowned trying to cross the Mediterranean in the same period.*

Earlier this week, the Turkish government said its coastguard had rescued over 42,000 migrants in the Aegean Sea in the first five months of 2015 and more than 2,160 in the last week alone.

Photo of drowned boy sparks outcry

Young Syrian refugee boy
(Zahle, Lebanon) (June 2015)

Photo of drowned boy sparks outcry

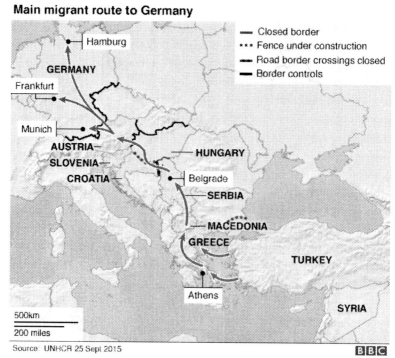

Map showing the treacherous migrant route to Germany...to hope...to anything better than a war zone (Source: UNHCR, Sept 25, 2015)

D   Drowned boy's father speaks of heartbreak

The LORD is *close* to the brokenhearted; he rescues those whose spirits are crushed. (Psalm 34:18)

*H*ERE ARE SOME of the words spoken by this suffering father…words I can imagine our Heavenly Father speaking as well.[92]

BBC News: Migrant crisis: Drowned boy's father speaks of heartbreak

3 September 2015

From the section Europe

Abdullah Kurdi: **"My children were the most beautiful children in the world"**

The father of a **three-year-old Syrian boy found drowned on a beach in Turkey** has told the BBC of the harrowing circumstances of his death.

Alan Kurdi's father Abdullah said that shortly after their boat left Turkey for the Greek island of Kos it was hit by waves and the captain swam off.

"I tried to catch my children and wife but there was no hope. One by one they died," Mr Kurdi said.

The family were among thousands fleeing Syria and seeking a new life abroad.

Images of Alan's body being recovered from a beach near Bodrum caused an outpouring of sympathy for the plight of those fleeing Syria's civil war and criticism of European governments for not doing enough to answer the crisis.

Thousands of migrants have died this year trying to reach Europe by sea.

---

[92] http://www.bbc.com/news/world-europe-34143445

Drowned boy's father speaks of heartbreak

"I tried to steer the boat but another **high wave pushed the boat over.** That is when it happened," Mr Kurdi said.

"My children were the most beautiful children in the world. **Is there anybody in the world for whom their child is not the most precious thing?**" Mr Kurdi said.

"My kids were amazing. They woke me every day to play with me. What is more beautiful than this? **Everything is gone.**"

"I would love to **sit next to the grave of my family now** and relieve the pain I feel," he said.

Undated image taken from internet of Alan and Ghalib Kurdi
Alan (left) and his brother Ghalib are believed to be from the besieged Syrian town of Kobane

The story of Alan Kurdi's family

Alan, his five-year-old brother Ghalib and mother Rehanna were among 12 Syrians who died after two boats capsized soon after setting off for Kos.

Turkish police have arrested four suspected traffickers over the deaths. The four men are all Syrian nationals aged between 30 and 41, according to the Turkish Dogan news agency.

Alan and the rest of the group his family was travelling with are believed to have been **Syrians from the besieged town of Kobane who had fled to Turkey last year to escape advancing militants** from the Islamic State (IS) group.

A Turkish hospital official told AFP news agency that the bodies of the family would be flown to Istanbul and then to Suruc on the Turkish border before reaching Kobane.

Abdullah's sister in Vancouver, Teema Kurdi, said she had wanted to bring him and his family to Canada but had first tried to sponsor another brother - an application that had failed.

Drowned boy's father speaks of heartbreak

Canada's department of citizenship and immigration confirmed that there was no record of an application for Abdullah Kurdi and his family.

صـــديقي

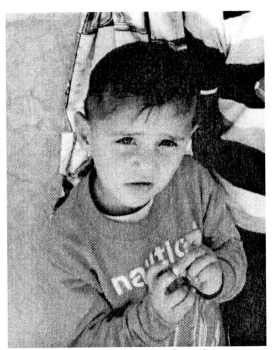

Young Yazidi Iraqi refugee boy
(Northern Iraq) (June 2015)

E   Lebanon pivotal to Iran's reach across Middle East

But the godly will flourish like palm trees and grow *strong* like the cedars of Lebanon. (Psalm 92:12)

*H*ERE IS AN informative article about Lebanon and the Bekka Valley where I visited. The place where I visited with some amazing people who *choose* to be there helping the refugees. They are about 10 miles from Baalbek.[93]

BBC News: Lebanon pivotal to Iran's reach across Middle East

By Kevin Connolly
BBC Middle East correspondent, Beirut

26 June 2015

From the section Middle East

Lebanese singer Assi Hallani performs during the opening of the Baalbek international festival in July 2014

The Baalbek festival takes place against a **backdrop of turmoil and war just across the border**

On the road to Baalbek, in the hot afternoons of Ramadan, the Bekaa Valley shimmers in the midsummer sun.

The soaring columns of the ruined temples of Baalbek are one of the glories of the ancient world - but there are few tourists around these days to admire them.

Lebanon's own civil war petered out 25 years ago, leaving tensions smouldering below the surface of daily life. Syria's is raging uncontrollably just a few kilometres up the road.

---

[93] http://www.bbc.co.uk/news/world-middle-east-33281739

Lebanon pivotal to Iran's reach across Middle East

The town is cradled by snow-capped mountains and surrounded by emerald fields under sapphire skies - but the bewitching quality of the landscape isn't enough to attract visitors in the numbers that Baalbek's economy needs.

Tourists are understandably risk-averse, and the proximity to Syria is enough to deter all but the bravest.

So, not for the first time, Baalbek is hoping that its cultural festival will bring the visitors flooding back. It has worked before.

In the dreary years after the Second World War, the Baalbek festival - held against the spectacular backdrop of the ruined temples - was a sign that better and brighter days lay ahead.

Now, after it was suspended in recent years because of the fighting in Syria, the festival is to open again this summer.

Pragmatic course

It is a fact of political life in this part of the Bekaa Valley that ***a decision of this magnitude requires the consent of Hezbollah - the powerful Lebanese militia founded and funded by Iran.***

Its local dominance indeed may also be a factor in keeping visitors away.

Hezbollah, of course, is heavily committed to the fighting in Syria where it is the most disciplined and effective element in the coalition struggling to keep Bashar al-Assad in power.

Sharmine Narwani: "Nuclear deal or not things will change, understandings have been established"

But even as it is engaged in a vicious civil war with strong sectarian overtones on the Syrian side of the border, it has demonstrated in Lebanon a pragmatic ability to coexist with rival communities in the context of a demographic patchwork which is rather similar to Syria's.

No-one should be under illusions about the nature of that coexistence, of course - **most Lebanese assume, for example, that Hezbollah was behind the car bomb that killed the powerful Sunni politician Rafik Hariri in February 2005.**

But optimists believe it shows that Hezbollah's sponsor Iran is prepared - to some extent at least - to be flexible and pragmatic about the way it exercises influence in the Middle East.

Hassan Hamad from the Baalbek Municipality told me: "The moderate social policy that Hezbollah follows here helps to keep Lebanon safe from terrorism and from the Syrian war.

"They recognise that Lebanon is Lebanon - it isn't Iran and it isn't Europe."

New 'Cold War'

Now, this all matters because an old order is disintegrating in the Middle East - the order imposed by France and Great Britain on the ruins of the Turkish Empire which collapsed here at the end of the First World War.

The US-led Western Alliance is still a player in the battle for influence now raging but **the real struggle is between Shia Islam under Iranian leadership and a grouping of Sunni powers led by Saudi Arabia.**

Iranian border guard looks through binoculars (file photo)

Shia Iran and regional Sunni powers view each other with deep suspicion

In Yemen, Iraq and Syria, their proxies fight each other - you could draw a modern comparison with the Cold War between the United States and the Soviet Union or perhaps more accurately with the division of Europe in Catholic and Protestant camps in the 16th and 17th Centuries.

To some extent, Iran's modern leaders are reviving an ancient Persian appetite for influence in the Arab world. In Beirut, political commentator Charmine Narwani told me that West does not work hard enough to understand the changing Middle East from Iran's point of view.

Lebanon pivotal to Iran's reach across Middle East

She says there is resentment in Tehran that the country is always portrayed as a destabilising force with dangerous nuclear ambitions, and points out that Iran is in the frontline of a battle with Sunni extremism which is hostile to the West as well as to Shia Islam.

"Iran is probably Ground Zero - a centre for the fightback against Islamic State and al-Qaeda and Sunni extremists in the region," she said.

"The only boots on the ground fighting this fight in earnest are backed, funded and supported by Iran."

That analysis may underplay the role that the Kurds are playing in fighting Islamic State in Iraq but it does help to explain why everyone in the Middle East is talking about Iran.

State-with-a-state

The US-led Western powers are currently seeking a political deal with Iran in which the lifting of crippling economic sanctions could be traded for some sort of verifiable cap on Iranian nuclear ambitions.

But even as those long negotiations approach what will probably prove to be a protracted end-game, the underlying attitude towards Iran remains one of suspicion.

That is partly, of course, because Iran is a revisionist power which feels it has the right to export revolution.

But it is partly because of the way in which *Hezbollah - so pragmatic in Lebanon - has emerged as the cutting edge of Iranian power on a wider stage.*

In that role, it has been blamed by the West for bomb attacks against Jewish and Israeli targets as far afield as Bulgaria and Argentina.

Girl waves Hezbollah flag at a rally in Nabatiyeh (24/05/15)

Hezbollah, which began as a force against Israel, has grown into a major social, political and military movement

And within Lebanon, Hezbollah may offer a glimpse of how Iran sees the future of the Middle East.

What was created as a vehicle to fight Israeli forces of occupation in Lebanon in the 1980s **has grown into a powerful state-within-a-state.**

Equipped and funded by Iran, it comfortably outguns the Lebanese Army and has perhaps 25,000 fighters under arms.

The movement has social and political responsibilities, too, in its own areas like southern Lebanon but Iran does not seem to aspire to a Hezbollah takeover of the whole country - partly, at least, because it does not need to.

Nothing can happen in Lebanon unless Hezbollah agrees to it and for now it enjoys many of the advantages of being a state - like possession of a powerful army - without the problems that would come from responsibility for Sunni, Christian or Druze regions.

Strategic vision

It is possible that Iran may hope to create other similar non-state Shia entities elsewhere in the Middle East, especially if old multi-confessional nation-states like Syria and Iraq turn out to have reached the limit of their viability.

It does help to explain why Hezbollah is so important to Iran.

I have heard it argued that Iran's involvement is not really about using Hezbollah to maintain President Assad in power - it is more about keeping Mr Assad in office to maintain the land-bridge through which it supplies Hezbollah in southern Lebanon.

Funeral in Tehran of Iranian Revolutionary Guard member killed in Syria (25/06/15)

Iran is heavily involved in supporting Syria's regime in the war, seeing Damascus as a critical gateway to Lebanon

Lebanon pivotal to Iran's reach across Middle East

At a turbulent time in the Middle East, when it feels like influence is up for grabs, Iran has a strategic vision and it brings to it a sense of purpose and energy which other regional players appear to struggle to match.

So when Baalbek holds its festival this summer, it may feel as it has felt before, like a sign of better days to come in the Middle East.

But make no mistake - **this is a time of profound upheaval based on deep rivalries between regional powers like Iran and the Gulf monarchies.**

And the changes that will flow from that upheaval are far from over.

מֵרֵעַ

Two nuns enjoying the breeze off of the Mediterranean Sea
(Byblos, Lebanon) (June 2015) (faces blurred for privacy reasons)

F　Luke 15:11-32 in Arabic

God is *love*. (1 John 4:8b)

ARABIC IS A beautiful language. And the story of the Prodigal Son in Luke 15:11-32 is a *beautiful* story about God's unconditional, redemptive and faithful love for each of us…*no matter what.*

Luke 15:11-32:

مَثَلُ الابنِ الضّالّ

11 ثُمّ قالَ يَسوعُ: «كانَ لِرَجُلٍ ابنانِ 12 فقالَ أصغَرُهُما لِأبيهِ: يا أبي، أعطِني نَصيبي مِن أملاكِكَ. فَقَسَّمَ الأبُ ثَروَتَهُ بَينَ ابنَيهِ. 13 ولَمْ تَمضِ أيّامٌ كَثيرَةٌ حتّى جَمَعَ الابنُ الأصغَرُ ما يَخُصُّهُ كُلَّ ما وسافَرَ إلى بَلَدٍ بَعيدٍ. وهُناكَ بَدَّدَ كُلَّ مالِهِ في حَياةٍ مُستَهتِرَةٍ. 14 وبَعدَ أنْ صَرَفَ كُلَّ ما معَهُ، أصابَتْ ذلِكَ البَلَدَ مَجاعَةٌ شَديدَةٌ فابتَدأَ يَحتاجُ. 15 فَذهَبَ وعَمِلَ لَدى واحِدٍ مِنْ أهلِ ذلِكَ البَلَدِ، فأرسَلَهُ إلى حُقولِهِ لِيَرعى الخَنازيرَ. 16 وكانَ يَتَمَنّى لَوْ أنَّهُ يَستَطيعُ أنْ يُشبِعَ نَفسَهُ مِنْ نَباتِ الخَروبِ الّذي كانَتِ الخَنازيرُ تَأكُلُ منهُ، لكِنَّ أحَداً لَمْ يُعطِهِ شَيئاً.

17 فَعادَ إلى رُشدِهِ وقالَ: كَمْ مِنْ أجيرٍ عِندَ أبي يَشبَعُ ويَفضُلُ عَنهُ الطَّعامُ، أمّا أنا فَأَتَضَوَّرُ جوعاً هُنا! 18 سَأقومُ وأذهَبُ إلى أبي وأقولُ لهُ: يا أبي، لَقَدْ أخطَأتُ إلى اللهِ وإلَيكَ، 19 ولَمْ أعُدْ جَديراً بأنْ أُدعى ابناً لَكَ فاجعَلني كواحِدٍ مِنَ العامِلينَ. 20 ثُمَّ قامَ وذَهَبَ إلى أبيهِ.

عَودَةُ الابنِ الضّالّ

وبَينَما كانَ ما يَزالُ بَعيداً، رآهُ أبوهُ، فامتَلأ حَناناً، ورَكَضَ إلَيهِ وضَمَّهُ وقَبَّلَهُ بِذِراعَيهِ. 21 فقالَ الابنُ: يا أبي، أخطَأتُ إلى اللهِ وإلَيكَ ولَمْ أعُدْ جَديراً بأنْ أُدعى ابناً لَكَ. 22 غَيرَ أنَّ الأبَ قالَ لِعَبيدِهِ: هَيّا! أحضِروا أفضَلَ ثَوبٍ وألبِسوهُ إيّاهُ، وضَعوا خاتَماً في يَدِهِ وحِذاءً في قَدَمَيهِ. 23 وأحضِروا العِجلَ المُسَمَّنَ واذبَحوهُ ودَعونا

Luke 15:11-32 in Arabic

فَوَجَدتُهُ ضالاً وَكانَ الحَياةِ، إلَى فَعادَ مَيِّتاً كانَ هَذا ابنِي لِأنَّ 24 وَنَحتَفِلْ نَأكُلْ
فَبَدَأوا يَبتَهِجونَ وَيَحتَفِلُونَ.

الابنُ الأكبَرُ

25 أمّا الابنُ الأكبَرُ فَكانَ فِي الحَقلِ. وَعِندَما جاءَ وَاقتَرَبَ مِنَ البَيتِ سَمِعَ
صَوتَ مُوسِيقَى وَرَقصٍ. 26 فَدَعَى واحِداً مِنَ الخُدّامِ وَسَألَهُ عَمّا يَجرِي. 27 فَقالَ لَهُ
الخادِمُ: ‹رَجِعَ أخُوكَ فَذَبَحَ أبُوكَ العِجلَ المُسَمَّنَ لِأنَّهُ عادَ سَلِيماً مُعافَى.›
28 فَغَضِبَ الابنُ الأكبَرُ وَلَمْ يَقبَلْ أنْ يَدخُلَ فَخَرَجَ أبُوهُ يَطلُبُ إلَيهِ الدُّخُولَ.
29 فَقالَ لِأبِيهِ: ‹لَقَدْ عَمِلتُ بِجِدٍّ عِندَكَ كُلَّ هَذِهِ السَّنَواتِ وَلَمْ أعصِ لَكَ أمراً
قَطُّ. وَمَعْ ذَلِكَ لَمْ تُعطِنِي حَتَّى جَدياً لِكَي أحتَفِلَ مَعَ أصدِقائِي! 30 وَعِندَما جاءَ ابنُكَ هَذا، الَّذِي بَدَّدَ
أموالَكَ، عَلَى السّاقِطاتِ، ذَبَحتَ لَهُ العِجلَ المُسَمَّنَ مِنْ أجلِهِ!›
31 فَقالَ لَهُ الأبُ: ‹يا بُنَيَّ، أنتَ دائِماً مَعِي، وَكُلُّ ما أملِكُهُ هُوَ لَكَ. 32 لَكِنْ كانَ
لا بُدَّ أنْ نَحتَفِلَ وَنَفرَحَ لِأنَّ أخاكَ هَذا كانَ مَيِّتاً فَعادَ إلَى الحَياةِ وَكانَ ضالاً
فَوُجِدَ.›94

The former prodigal son…loved and forgiven
(Byblos, Lebanon) (June 2015)

---

94 Arabic Bible: Easy-to-Read Version, Copyright © 2009 World Bible Translation Center. All rights reserved.